Strange Laughter:
Early Penny Bloods and Humour

~

Celine Frohn

Crookesmoor
Sheffield

Strange Laughter: Early Penny Bloods and Humour is a reproduction of a thesis of the same title, submitted for the degree of Doctor of Philosophy at the University of Sheffield in September 2022, and was successfully defended in December 2022.

Published by Crookesmoor, Sheffield, United Kingdom

© 2023 Crookesmoor

ISBN 978-1-9163669-9-2

A catalogue record for this book can be obtained from the British Library.

All rights reserved. No part of this publication may be reproduced by any means without the prior written permission of the publisher, except in the case of brief quotations embodied in critical articles and reviews.

Acknowledgements

Without the generous financial support of the Elisabeth Brandenburg Memorial Fund, Muller Fonds, Fundatie van Renswoude, Stichting Niemeijer Fonds, and the Dutch Culture Fund, I would not have been able to complete the research that underpins this thesis. Thank you.

I would also like to thank my supervisors, Andrew Smith and John Miller for their invaluable insights over the years.

Finally, thank you to everyone who let me talk about penny fiction and humour to them throughout this process. From conference attendees to taxi drivers, loved ones and family – every time I explained my research to you, my arguments crystallised just a tiny bit further.

Contents

Introduction	1
INTRODUCTION	1
CONTEXT AND TERMINOLOGY	5
THE QUESTION OF GENRE	11
HUMOUR THEORY	17
STRUCTURE OF THESIS	24
Chapter One: *The String of Pearls* **by James Malcolm Rymer**	29
INTRODUCTION	29
THE ALIENATED WORKER AND SOCIETAL CANNIBALISM	35
FOOD AND THE CARNIVALESQUE	40
THE MELODRAMATIC	59
ROMANCE AND DOMESTIC ROMANCE	64
CONCLUSION	84
Chapter Two: *Valentine Vaux* **by Thomas Peckett Prest**	87
INTRODUCTION	87
VENTRILOQUISM AND HISTORY	89
FROM *VOX* TO *VAUX*	101
THE POLITICS OF HUMOUR AND VIOLENCE IN *VALENTINE VAUX*	113
VOICE, SOUND AND THE CROWD	128
CONCLUSION	139
Chapter Three: *Jack Rann* **by James Lindridge**	141
INTRODUCTION	141
KNIGHTS OF THE ROAD	144
JOHN RANN, HIGHWAY ROBBER	155
DISGUISE, HUMOUR, AND CLASS	168
THE SHADOW OF TYBURN	179
CONCLUSION	189

Chapter Four: *Paul Jones* by Pierce Egan the Younger   **191**
INTRODUCTION   191
PRIVATEERS, BUCCANEERS, AND OTHER PIRATES   195
A SAILOR'S SPEECH   204
DOMESTIC MATTERS AND THE NATION   213
LAUGHTER, RACE, AND EMPIRE   227
CONCLUSION   238

Conclusion   **241**

Bibliography   **247**

Introduction

INTRODUCTION

Although it has been the pleasure of certain critics to declaim against cheap literature, the number of readers increases every day. This fact, of course, spurs on the writers of such compositions to greater vigour and animation in a cause that, to say the least of it, has popularity on its side.[1]

Despite the enduring popularity of nineteenth-century literature, very few people have heard of the authors whose works are featured in this thesis: James Malcolm Rymer, Thomas Peckett Prest, James Lindridge, and Pierce Egan the Younger. Yet the works of these authors were widely read during the early Victorian era; they were among the popular authors of cheaply produced texts that were published as serials between 1837 and 1850, now called the penny blood. These texts carry negative connotations even now, or in Ian Haywood's words, 'an aura of disrepute', despite their popularity during the nineteenth century.[2] Nineteenth-century critics considered penny literature 'politically and morally debased.'[3] As one journalist writes in a damning section titled 'Demoralizing

---

[1] Thomas Peckett Prest, *Luke Somerton; or, The English Renegade* (London: Edward Lloyd, 1845), p. iii. Although the manuscript does not bear Prest's name, Léger-St-Jean at *Price One Penny* attributes *Luke Somerton* to him: Marie Léger-St-Jean, 'Luke Somerton', in *Price One Penny* <http://www.priceonepenny.info/database/show_title.php?work_id=126> [accessed 26 September 2022].
[2] Ian Haywood, *The Revolution in Popular Literature. Print, Politics and the People, 1790-1860* (Cambridge: Cambridge University Press, 2004), p. 162.
[3] Haywood, *Revolution*, p. 162.

Publications' in *The People's Newspaper* in 1847, 'such periodicals as are published by Lloyds' – one of the most well-known of penny blood publishers – are 'a most polluted source of evil', or a 'heap of abomination and trash falsely denominated "cheap literature"'.[4] The author of the article feared that readers of penny fiction were encouraged 'to sympathise with rogues and villains', and rather than an appropriately moral response, 'admiration too frequently takes the place of terror and disgust.'[5] As many of the later commentators on penny fiction, the author of the article feared emulation of the crimes depicted in penny fiction. They particularly point out the violent content of penny fiction, from the 'progressive strides iniquity makes towards some grand climax of blood and guilt', to the 'favourite theme' of penny fiction authors, murder: 'for they look on man as a hound that requires blood to whet his mental appetite.'[6] The author quips that the Newgate Calendar, a serial that showcased the crimes of various criminals, should be subtitled 'Vice Exemplified and Crime made Easy'.[7]

Penny fiction's reputation of violence has persisted into the twenty-first century. For several decades, it was Louis James' *Fiction for the Working Man* (1974) that provided the most extensive study of the production and textual elements of penny fiction, tracing the development of penny fiction from the late 1830s to 1850. For James, the 1836 plagiarisms of Charles Dickens' works attributed to Thomas Peckett Prest signal the start of the penny serial, while he also identifies Gothic stories and the historical novel as literary influences. It is the Gothic and violent aspects of penny fiction that subsequent scholars have primarily focused on; as Jarlath Killeen asserts, penny bloods are sensationalist fiction with plots that 'were merely vehicles to get the reader from one scene of gore, violence and torture to the next', an assessment that echoes the *People's Newspapers* appraisal, made almost two centuries earlier, of how a

---

[4] 'Demoralizing Publications', *The People's Newsletter*, 20 June 1847, p. 5.
[5] 'Demoralizing Publications', p. 5.
[6] 'Demoralizing Publications', p. 5.
[7] 'Demoralizing Publications', p. 5.

reader 'is led from deeds of blood and violence to scenes voluptuous excitement'.[8]

Current academic interest in the penny blood mainly stems from the field of Gothic studies. In Anthony Mandal's contribution to *The Cambridge History of the Gothic* (2020), the penny blood is positioned as the successor of the Gothic chapbook as part of a larger phenomenon of the 'street Gothic', which also includes the penny dreadful in the latter half of the nineteenth century.[9] In another recent study, *Violent Victorians* (2012), Rosalind Crone includes penny fiction in her study of the 'very violent content of a range of prominent genres of entertainment' between roughly 1802 and 1870, reading them as part of a 'culture of violence' present in England in the nineteenth century.[10] The forthcoming edited collection *Penny Dreadfuls and the Gothic* (2023) aims to explicitly analyse the penny blood as part of the history of the Gothic, including Gothic readings of Reynolds' *Wagner, the Wehr-Wolf* (1847) and Rymer's *Newgate: A Romance* (1847).[11] These studies have been fruitful, providing necessary context to the cultural significance of penny fiction in the 1840s. Other studies have explored the material realities of the penny publishing business, such as *Edward Lloyd and His World* (2019), an edited collection focusing on the successful penny fiction publisher Edward Lloyd and popular penny authors, including

---

[8] Jarlath Killeen, 'Victorian Gothic Pulp Fiction', in *The Victorian Gothic. An Edinburgh Companion*, ed. by Andrew Smith and William Hughes (Edinburgh: Edinburgh University Press, 2012), pp. 43-56, p. 50. 'Demoralizing Publications', p. 5.
[9] Anthony Mandal, 'Gothic Fiction, from Shilling Shockers to Penny Bloods', in *The Cambridge History of the Gothic*, ed. by Dale Townshend and Angela Wright (Cambridge: University of Cambridge Press, 2020), pp. 139-161, p. 140.
[10] Rosalind Crone, *Violent Victorians. Popular entertainment in nineteenth-century London* (Manchester: Manchester University Press, 2012), p. 7, 9.
[11] *Penny Dreadfuls and the Gothic: Investigations of Pernicious Tales of Terror*, ed. By Nicole C. Dittmer and Sophie Raine (Cardiff: University of Wales Press, 2023 [forthcoming]).

ner, and George W.M. Reynolds.[12] Anna Gasparini ie history of medicine, specifically the 1832 Anatomy Act, dily anxieties are expressed in penny fiction.[13] Rob Breton sses Rymer and Reynolds in his recent monograph *The litics of Victorian Popular Fiction* (2021), with the aim to uncover how penny fiction used radical content. Extensive bibliographical work has been completed by Helen R. Smith, and the searchable database of penny fiction compiled by Marie Léger-St-Jean, *Price One Penny*, is an invaluable resource.

At the same time, penny blood studies are in many ways still in their infancy. The sheer volume of the texts published by Edward Lloyd and his contemporaries complicates comprehensive studies, and while the Gothic legacy is relatively well-explored, the other generic influences on the penny blood deserve more consideration. Penny fiction is not merely violent or full of terror: it is also irreverent, playful, and comic. These tones occasionally stand in contrast to other modes present (such as Gothic or melodrama), while at other times they blend the humorous with the violent in complex ways. This thesis aims to add to the growing field of penny blood studies, as well as the broader field of popular fiction studies in the nineteenth century, by investigating an aspect of the penny blood as yet unexplored: the humour that is present in these texts. Amongst other questions, this thesis asks, how do we interpret the emotional state of 'comic amusement' associated with comedy and laughter in these supposedly gory and thrilling texts?[14] These instances of laughter are vital in understanding the pleasures Victorians might have experienced reading these texts.

In the remainder of this introductory chapter I will touch on three aspects that shape the subject of this thesis. First, I will briefly outline the material and historical conditions that shaped the early

---

[12] *Edward Lloyd and His World. Popular Fiction, Politics and the Press in Victorian Britain*, ed. By Sarah Louise Lill and Rohan McWilliam (New York: Routledge, 2019).
[13] See Anna Gasparini, *Nineteenth Century Popular Fiction, Medicine and Anatomy. The Victorian Penny Blood and the 1832 Anatomy Act* (Basingstoke: Palgrave Macmillan, 2019).
[14] For the emotional state of comic amusement, see Noël Carroll, *Humour: A Very Short Introduction* (Oxford: Oxford University Press, 2014), pp. 4-5.

Victorian penny press. This section touches on print history, as well as the culture of leisure at the time. It also provides some disambiguation of the terminology surrounding penny bloods. In the second section, I will turn to the subject of genre, as this topic lies at the heart of the project of this thesis. Where humour provides a specific lens through which to investigate the politics of the texts discussed in this thesis, the question of genre always functions in the background: should we consider penny bloods a genre in their own right, and what would this entail? Throughout the thesis, we encounter various genres and modes that are part of the historical resonances of the texts discussed, and the preliminary discussion on genre provides a necessary framework for these discussions. In the third section, then, I will discuss humour theory. Humour studies is a broad and interdisciplinary field in its own right, and in this section I will outline the approach to humour this thesis takes, based on both contemporary as well as historical discussions of the role of humour in society. Finally, this chapter provides a brief introduction to the four penny bloods that are analysed in this thesis, providing an outline of the thesis structure.

CONTEXT AND TERMINOLOGY

The entertainments available to the working people of England underwent large changes from the eighteenth to the nineteenth century under the influence not only of increasing industrialisation and urbanisation, but also technological developments and changes in legislation. In the nineteenth century it became cheaper to produce print publications, due to improvements to printing technology such as the Fourdrinier machine, which made rolls of paper rather than separate sheets. This significantly sped up the paper production process, and consequently allowed for lower paper prices. While early nineteenth-century chapbooks might have cost between fourpence and sixpence, in the 1830s and 1840s the market was flooded with weekly publications sold for only a penny.[15] At this price point, these penny magazines, which contained serialised fiction, short stories, news, and articles on various topics, became affordable for the working classes of the newly urban readerships. The production of textual entertainment (newspapers, magazines, books) was largely concentrated in London, and Fleet Street was considered the epicentre of literary production.[16] Here both 'taste and culture high or low' were drawn up, and it is where Edward Lloyd was based from the 1843 onwards at Salisbury Square, just off Fleet Street.[17] As Ian Haywood writes about both Lloyd as well as George W.M. Reynolds, 'Their careers exist on the borderline between respectability and scandal, popular enlightenment and "trash", journalistic innovation and populist regression.'[18] The earliest texts considered to be part of the penny bloods are published in 1836, when Edward Lloyd started publishing Prest's plagiarised weekly imitation of Dickens' *The Pickwick Papers* (1836-1837), as well as a serialised collection of highwayman exploits, *Lives of the Most Notorious Highwaymen* (1836-1837) in penny instalments.[19] The penny fiction publishing landscape that evolved in the subsequent years can be described as frantic as well as chaotic. Not only did many publishers try to find profit in the growing market, due to the rapid speed in publication and low wages, penny authors were forced to write very quickly, sometimes writing multiple serials simultaneously. Some penny authors, including Prest and Rymer, whose works are discussed in later chapters, were immensely prolific and wrote dozens of titles

---

[15] Helen R. Smith, 'Introduction' in: *Penny Dreadfuls and Boys' Adventures. The Barry Ono Collection of Victorian Popular Literature in the British Library* by Elizabeth James and Helen R. Smith (London: The British Library, 1998), pp. vii-xx, p. xi.
[16] Jerry White, *London in the 19th Century. A Human Awful Wonder of God* (London: Vintage Books, 2008), p. 226.
[17] White, *London*, p. 226. Sarah Louise Lill and Rohan McWilliam, 'Introduction. Edward Lloyd, Eminent Victorian' in *Edward Lloys and His World. Popular Fiction, Politics and the Press in Victorian Britain* ed. by Sarah Louise Lill and Rohan McWilliam (New York: Routledge, 2019), p. 9.
[18] Haywood, *Revolution*, p. 162.
[19] Smith, 'Introduction', p. xi.

amours' of the main character are said to have been omitted 'as the work was destined for the main part to fall in youthful hands'.[24] Considering the low price, easy availability, and custom of reading stories out loud in communal spaces, it seems likely that the audience for mid-century penny fiction was heterogeneous in gender and age. This stands in contrast with the penny dreadfuls of the second half of the century; as John Springhall has argued, the dreadfuls were marketed directly to a youthful audience.[25]

As penny fiction was printed on cheap, fragile paper that was often reused, relatively few copies have survived into the twenty-first century. The most extensive collection of penny bloods and penny dreadfuls is the Barry Ono collection, held by the British Library. An invaluable source for penny fiction scholars, it contains close to seven hundred penny fiction volumes, and an extensive collection of related texts, including individual penny magazine issues. Many of the manuscripts in the collection have been digitised and can be accessed through Gale.[26] All of the texts studied in this thesis are part of the Barry Ono collection – though *The String of Pearls* is a special case. While the extended 1850 version of *The String of Pearls* is available through the British Library, this thesis uses the original 1846-1847 serialised version as its source, reprinted by Wordsworth Editions in 2005.[27] Selecting only a handful of texts from this expansive corpus is challenging, as the majority of the texts have only been catalogued in databases such as Price One Penny but not examined in detail. My aims are therefore not to conclusively define the generic boundaries of the penny blood, but to explore the various tones and tropes present within a handful of penny bloods in-depth. The texts are chosen not to represent the genre as a whole, but to represent the diversity of stories and tones

---

[24] James Lindridge, *Jack Rann. Alias Sixteen-String Jack* (London: G. Purkess, 1840), p. 1.
[25] John Springhall, '"A Life Story for the People"? Edwin J. Brett and the London "Low-Life" Penny Dreadfuls of the 1860s', *Victorian Studies*, 33:2 (1990), 223-246, pp. 226-227.
[26] For more information about Barry Ono (born Frederick Valentine Harrison), see Smith, 'Introduction', pp. vii-xx.
[27] More information about the sources used can be found in their respective chapters.

within a handful of years. For writers who could sustain this pace of publication, writing penny fiction could be quite lucrative; in his memoirs, Thomas Frost discusses writing for Lloyd, among others:

> That was a happy time! I was "running" – as our American cousins say – four stories at the same time, three in numbers, and one in a periodical [...] Yet, by methodical and steady working, I found leisure to cultivate my little garden, to indulge my love of long rambles in the woods and fields [...][20]

Edward Jacobs sees this print culture, together with the 'penny gaffs', a form of cheap theatre, as part of the same urban street culture.[21] This interpretation is supported by the repeated creative borrowing and adaptation that is apparent between penny fiction, criminal broadsheets, and penny theatre – all of these forms influence one another, as will be explored in further chapters where some of these webs of influence will be traced.

While the exact readership of penny fiction is disputed, Haywood claims that Lloyd's penny fiction was popular across genders and drew both lower and middle-class readers.[22] Crone argues for this relatively broad readership as well, pointing out that *The String of Pearls* was published in the *People's Periodical and Family Library*, where it was '[s]urrounded by other instalments of romantic fiction and short advisory articles on marriage and family matters,' making it 'clear that Lloyd intended it to be read by working- and lower-middle-class men, women and children.'[23] That this might be true for penny fiction in a broader sense is supported by the preface to *Jack Rann*, published by George Purkess, where the 'private

---

[20] Thomas Frost, *Reminiscences of a Country Journalist* (London: Ward and Downey, 1886), p. 84.
[21] Edward Jacobs, 'Blood in the Street: London Street Culture, "Industrial Literacy," and the Emergence of Mass Culture in Victorian London', *Nineteenth-Century Contexts*, 18 (1995), 321-347, p. 321.
[22] Haywood, *Revolution*, p. 162, 168.
[23] Crone, *Violent Victorians*, p. 1.

within the genre. To this end, the four chosen texts are all attributed to different authors, are published by two different publishers (Lloyd and Purkess), and all feature vastly different plots and tropes. They will be introduced in more detail below.

It is worth noting that, while useful, the term penny blood is an anachronistic one; Lloyd certainly did not advertise his penny fiction as 'penny bloods' nor as 'penny dreadfuls'. Instead, these texts are accompanied by generic markers such as 'romance', 'domestic romance', or 'nautical romance' (on one occasion, even the creative 'nautico domestic romance').[28] I was unable to find any primary source material that uses the two-word label 'penny blood' in the period of relevance (up to roughly 1850). It is therefore unlikely that this exact wording was in common usage during the 1840s. I agree with Springhall that it is useful to separate the texts published by Lloyd from the juvenile fiction of the 1850s, and he argues to use 'penny blood' for the former, and 'penny dreadful' for the latter.[29] Yet I think there is a certain flaw in using 'penny blood' as a signifier for the wide variety of texts published by Lloyd and other penny fiction publishers in the late 1830s and 1840s. 'Penny blood' is closely associated with violence and Gothic elements – and it remains to be seen whether a possible violent content represents the core of the genre. In essence, over the last fifty years since the publication of James's *Fiction for the Working Man*, few scholars have heeded his assessment of the centring of the Gothic in penny fiction:

> The term 'Gothic' has been used indiscriminately to describe early Victorian penny-issue fiction ever since Montague Summers published his *Gothic Bibliography* in 1940, and the practice is encouraged today by booksellers who find this raises the price of these novels on the American market. If by 'Gothic' we really mean the tale of terror, [...] the fashionable usage is misleading. In this

---

[28] Thomas Peckett Prest, *The Smuggler King; or, The Foundling of the Wreck* (London: Edward Lloyd, 1844).
[29] Springhall, '"A Story for the People"?', p. 227.

popular fiction the genres of the domestic romance, the fashion novel, and stories of criminal life are more common.[30]

If anything, it is essential to trace the engagement with Gothic tropes and themes in the penny blood, where they are sometimes used to Gothic effect (such as in *The String of Pearls*), but also where Gothic readings are negated or precluded, such as the public hanging of Jack Rann, discussed in the third chapter. The Gothic is but one mode or generic heritage that can be found in the collage of the penny blood. Categorising these texts definitively as 'penny bloods' runs the risk of inscribing a certain scholarly bias into the foundation of the emerging field of what might be called penny blood studies. It leads to generic confusion, as it raises the question whether all penny bloods are Gothic, as penny bloods are currently mostly studied from within a Gothic framework. As will be shown in this thesis, the penny blood supports a wide variety of topics and modes, and too narrow a focus on either violent or Gothic content could lead to the exclusion of important texts and subsequent impoverishment of the field of study. We need to be careful not to reduce the significance of the penny blood to a footnote within the long history of the Gothic. At the same time, 'penny fiction' has the disadvantage of being rather indistinct – how does one disambiguate between penny fiction from Lloyd and penny fiction from the latter half of the century? An argument could be made to move from 'penny blood' to 'domestic romance', the generic marker that was used contemporarily for these texts. While this thesis follows current scholarship in the terminology of 'penny blood', I also want to raise the question whether we should simply inherit this term from previous scholarship, despite its anachronism. I will reflect more on this topic in the conclusion of this thesis.

---

[30] Louis James, *Fiction for the Working Man. 1830-1850* (Harmondsworth: Penguin, 1974), p. 83.

THE QUESTION OF GENRE

Penny bloods are seen as a group of texts identified by their mode of production during a certain historical moment, with certain material characteristics (serials printed on cheap paper, often but not necessarily accompanied by an illustrated front page) and a certain monetary value (sold for a penny or less). At the same time, penny bloods are considered to be a *genre* of texts on a conceptual and textual level. In other words, penny bloods are assumed to reveal certain characteristics in their story structure, story content, or tone, that are shared across the group of texts. The critic from the *People's Newspaper* quoted previously, for example, implicitly groups together the 'periodicals as are published by Lloyd', suggesting a kinship between these texts. They state that they contain plots that 'follow [rogues and villains] step by step through the paths that lead to ruin.'[31] Upon closer inspection, however, this abstraction of the penny blood does not hold up to scrutiny: of the four texts studied in this thesis, only one features an outright sympathetic criminal (*Jack Rann*). As we will see in the second chapter, while *Valentine Vaux* features a trickster character who can be considered quite a nuisance, his relationship to law and authority is one where his actions uphold these concepts rather than undermining them. While the model posited by the author of the article in the *People's Newspaper* is therefore unsuitable for the penny blood of a whole, it does raise the question of genre: more specifically, whether penny bloods can rightly be seen as a *genre* of texts. Is there a generic coherence between these texts, in all of their diversity of themes and tropes, ranging (in this thesis) from ventriloquist pranksters to highwaymen tales?

The Western tradition of sorting texts into certain groups can be traced back to Plato's *Republic*, in which Socrates divides the works of poets and storytellers into three categories: 'pure narration', 'narrative that is effected through imitation', or a mixed form that includes both.[32] These categories rely on *how* a story is told

---

[31] 'Demoralizing Publications', p. 5.
[32] John Frow, *Genre* (London: Routledge, 2006), p. 55.

(particularly, how the speech of characters is represented), rather than its contents. In the following centuries, John Frow argues, theorists have either been occupied with various taxonomies of genres 'without concern for the grounds on which they are differentiated', or with constructing a 'systemic account of genre' based on Plato's three representational modes.[33] Toward the end of the eighteenth century, genre theory developed to assess the historical aspect of genre – the idea that genres are tied to a certain time period, and that they may change over time.[34] Within literary theory, various schools of thought have considered genre over the last couple of centuries, including Formalist, structuralist, and modernist critics.[35] Meanwhile, those working within the field of applied genre studies seek to find efficient ways to instruct others to create communications in a specific genre (think for example of teaching academic English to undergraduates).[36] Genre theory attempts to bridge the inherent tension that exists between the uniqueness of every text on one hand, versus the interconnectedness and commonalities between multiple texts on the other. Genres are seen as contributing to the 'social structuring of meaning', providing a certain context to any communication (consider for example how the same sentence would carry a different meaning when communicated as a newspaper headline versus a stand-up comedy show).[37] What similarities constitute a family relationship between texts (other metaphors include 'species', 'prototypes', 'discourses'), depends on the approach and specialism of the scholar.[38] Some of the similarities might lie in the realm of audience,

---

[33] Frow, *Genre*, p. 58.
[34] David Duff, 'Introduction', in *Modern Genre Theory* (London: Routledge, 2014), pp. 1-24, p. 4.
[35] Duff, 'Introduction', pp. 3-7.
[36] John M. Swales, 'Worlds of Genre - Metaphors of Genre' in *Genre in a Changing World* ed. by Charles Bazerman, Adair Bonini and Débora Figueiredo (West Lafayette: Parlor Press, 2009), pp. 3-16, p. 15.
[37] Frow, *Genre*, p. 1.
[38] Swales, 'World of Genre', p. 6.

rhetorical situations, modes of thinking, forms, or the social action a text accomplishes.[39]

French philosopher Jacques Derrida provides a critical reading of the concept of genre in the paper 'The Law of Genre', originally presented as a conference paper in 1979 and translated into English in 1980.[40] Derrida's body of work is preoccupied with the idea that 'no single beginning or origin is ever available as such.'[41] For Derrida, there is no pure beginning to any gesture or word – an idea which also extends to how he thought of genre. When Leslie Hill writes of his scholarship as including the idea that 'repetition and otherness are inseparable', this duality also lies at the heart of his thought on genre.[42] Derrida draws attention to several characteristics of genre. In 'The Law of Genre', written in a style in which the language of the paper itself reflects on its topic, Derrida notes that genre is occupied with delineation. He writes that '[a]s soon as the word "genre" is sounded, as soon as it is heard, as soon as one attempts to conceive it, a limit is drawn. And when a limit is established, norms and interdictions are not far behind.'[43] In order to sort texts (or any kind of communication) into genres, lines have to be drawn: for text A to be classified as genre B rather than genre C, there needs to be a difference between B and C. However, the issue arises that this limit is permeable, or as Derrida writes, 'neither separable or inseparable.'[44] Generic categorisation is necessarily of a different order from the genre it describes – it is a 'label' ascribed to a text, which is outside of the text, yet still is intrinsically connected to the text. The work we create when discussing genre, in itself, creates a genre of texts (which are of a different genre than the texts

---

[39] Carolyn R. Miller, 'Genre as Social Action' *Quarterly Journal of Speech* 70 (1984), 151-167, p. 151.
[40] Jacques Derrida, 'The Law of Genre', trans. by Avital Ronell, *Critical Inquiry*, 7:1 (1980), 55-81.
[41] Leslie Hill, *The Cambridge Introduction to Derrida* (Cambridge: Cambridge University Press, 2007), p. 16.
[42] Hill, *Derrida*, p. 17.
[43] Derrida, 'Law of Genre', p. 56.
[44] Derrida, 'Law of Genre', p. 56.

it supposes to refer to). As Leslie Hill notes in her discussion of Derrida's work:

> For just as a label is found only on the outside of a tin and not inside it, so the title, heading, or other descriptor that identifies, advertises, and regulates a genre cannot itself logically already be part of the genre it names.[45]

Reading Derrida, it is clear that this thesis sits within the tension of the dichotomy of any attempt at genre description – while this thesis is about the genre of the penny blood, it is in itself not part of that genre, yet is intimately connected to it due to its subject matter. Secondly, there is a paradox inherent in the act of trying to delineate genres: not only is the delineation itself not part of the genre whose boundaries it tries to describe, it is permeable. In my view, it is not only permeable in the sense that a book can move from one genre to another, but also that a book can be part of several genres along various dimensions, defying hierarchy in a conventional sense (consider for example how a book can be a coming-of-age story, a romance, and magic realism, without either of these categorisations deserving the distinction of constituting the 'primary' genre).

Following Frow's description of texts as 'performances of genre rather than reproductions of a class to which they belong' draws attention to the fact that genre is never static.[46] Over time literary genres overlap, encapsulate aspects of each other, separate, come together again, and/or fade. While this thesis argues that penny bloods should not be subsumed within the history of the Gothic, it also acknowledges that the penny blood does engage with the Gothic, and inherits some of its preoccupations – while at the same time not being defined by the Gothic. The Gothic is but one of many inheritances found within the penny blood, and it is this specific way of mixing various forms within itself that is the core principle of the penny blood. In the case of the penny blood, they were overwhelmingly advertised as 'romances', implying a specific

---

[45] Hill, *Derrida*, p. 64.
[46] Frow, *Genre*, p. 3.

generic positioning as a marketing tactic, implying both a kinship between penny bloods themselves as well as the idea of them being part of a longer lineage. This thesis takes a descriptive approach, keeping in mind the difficulties that are inherent in any attempt at generic categorisation. This descriptive approach is rooted in history, starting from the assumption that the historical context in which texts are written, produced, and published are an integral aspect to understanding the familial pattern between texts, which is what we consider genre. In the case of penny bloods, the mode of production and material and economic parameters narrow the definition of the genre to a relatively brief window, roughly between 1837 and 1850. After this time, the material conditions changed, inevitably also changing the publication of penny fiction. In this thesis, this extended decade is seen as part of the same generic field, allowing for the exploration of the genre as a whole.[47] One of the theoretical issues ascribed to any attempt to describe a genre is the sheer diversity and changeability of genres – there is an essential tension between what might be called the 'family pattern' that can be recognised across various texts in the same genre and the individuality of every specific text. However, as Maria Antónia Coutinho and Florencia Miranda point out, genres *work*. They write that, 'despite diversity and mutability, speakers and writers, when they speak or write (and when they listen or read) do not have difficulty in identifying and using genres that they have experience with and which are part of their contemporary social world.'[48] While genres are difficult, if not impossible to pin down definitively, genre is a frame of reference that is widely shared socially – now as well as in the past. What a descriptive genre approach aims to do, then, is not to formulate a template or a set of rules that all texts within a

---

[47] It might be worthwhile for further research to take a more granular approach, and question whether the genre markers change or develop throughout the 1840s.
[48] Maria Antónia Coutinho and Florencia Miranda, 'To Describe Genres: Problems and Strategies' in *Genre in a Changing World*, ed. by Charles Bazerman, Adair Bonini and Débora Figueiredo (West Lafayette: Parlor Press, 2009), pp. 35-56, p. 36.

certain genre would have to adhere to, but to discover what expectations are created by the texts within the social context of their consumption, keeping in mind that any genre changes over time.

As Paul Prior points out, genre studies as a field is moving from a 'focus on genres as isolated phenomena' to 'how specific types of texts are formed within, infused by, and constitutive of *systems* of genres' (emphasis mine).[49] Throughout this thesis, it becomes clear that penny bloods use, reuse, and repurpose other texts within themselves – if anything, the penny blood is an amalgam of cultural influences, sometimes literally including snippets from theatre scripts (*Jack Rann*), plagiarising plots from other successful authors (*Valentine Vaux*), or using a short story as inspiration (*The String of Pearls*). The penny blood's engagement with genre, and the various genres of texts it mixes, collages, or integrates, is often incomplete or contradictory. When dramatic text is inserted into the penny blood, a reframing occurs: moving from a text that is intended to be performed on a stage now functions to be consumed in purely textual form without the dramatic component. At the same time, the excerpt retains some of its former functions, what I would call genericity: its preoccupations and tropes as expressed within the group of texts it would usually be consumed in conjunction with. This thesis is preoccupied less with tracing the textual origins of these various 'cannibalised' texts: instead, it reads the various types of texts that are found together in the penny blood, considering what the sum *meaning* is of these various, and often incongruous, parts. The lens through which this meaning is approached is humour – not only because humour is often on the surface of the penny blood, but also because of its particular challenge to the central tenet of violence that is currently seen as the core of the penny blood. Humour has the potential to unsettle straightforward readings of violence, complicating acts of physical and emotional violence. The various genres that constitute the penny blood bring their own emotional registers, sometimes leading to jarring

---

[49] Paul Prior, 'From Speech Genres to Mediated Multimodal Genre Systems: Bakhtin, Voloshinov, and the Question of Writing' in *Genre in a Changing World* ed. by Charles Bazerman, Adair Bonini and Débora Figueiredo (West Lafayette: Parlor Press, 2009), pp. 17-34, p. 17.

differences in the ways humour (or lack thereof) is integrated into the penny blood. In the following, I will briefly situate the way humour and laughter is conceptualised in this thesis within the broader field of humour studies.

HUMOUR THEORY

The aim of this thesis is to uncover who is included and who is excluded in laughter; who laughs at whom or what; and what this means in terms of power relations between people within the text. What are the relationships between the characters, and how does the humour relate to other tropes or themes present in the text? In turn, the close readings show how laughter can express a broad range of politics and sentiments. Analysing these aspects of the texts provide a foundation for defining the generic commonalities between the texts. There are various definitions of 'humour', and its related words that include laughter, wit, comedy, and comic. As Amy Carrell writes, 'For some, humor is its physical manifestation, laughter; for others, humor is the comic, the funny, or the ludicrous. For still others, humor is synonymous with wit or comedy.'[50] Humour studies, including studies of comedy and laughter, span broad theoretical fields, including but not limited to linguistics, psychology, anthropology, sociology, and literature. Due to advances in neuroscience it is now possible to investigate what centres in the brain are active when a person laughs, while linguistics focus on what linguistic scripts are recognised as humorous. In this thesis, I consider humour as the intent of the author of the text to induce in its reader a form of comic amusement. Additionally, it looks at how laughter functions *within* the text as characters laugh at each other or comic situations. In this section I will briefly engage with the extensive field of scholarly writing on humour that underpins this approach.

---

[50] Amy Carrell, 'Historical views of humor', in *The Primer of Humor Research* ed. By Victor Raskin (Berlin: Mouton de Gruyter, 2008), pp. 303-332, p. 306.

Humour studies are broad and varied, studying every aspect of the phenomenon of humour and laughter, yet customarily humour theories are divided into three general categories: superiority theory, release or relief theory, and incongruity theory.[51] These theories focus on the cognitive, social, and psychoanalytical aspects of humour, respectively.[52] Cristina Larkin-Galiñanes argues that these three theories can often overlap and need to be viewed as 'essentially complementary', as a way of comprehensively studying humour.[53] Not only would I argue that these three strands are complementary, I would add that although overviews of the history of humour theory have follow this same three-fold pattern since the 1950s,[54] none of the historical sources these overview accounts are based on support the reading that the theories are separate theories in their own right. Many of the historical texts discussed in the following have been attributed to multiple of the three 'theories'. Historically, at least, these three 'theories' would be more aptly be considered approaches rather than full-fledged theories in their own right. To avoid confusion, however, I will persist with the aforementioned terminology, while in the following pointing out some of the overlaps that are found in the historical sources, which in turn support the holistic approach to humour of this thesis.[55] Rather than choosing a single approach, I will take their various concerns and preoccupations into account in the analyses of the following chapters. At the same time, certain questions relating to humour were more salient to scholars in certain time periods, and a

---

[51] Cristina Larkin-Galiñanes, 'An overview of Humor Theory', in *The Routledge Handbook of Language and Humor*, ed. By Salvatore Attardo (New York: Routledge, 2017), pp. 4-16, pp. 4-5. Sheila Lintott, 'Superiority in Humor Theory', *The Journal of Aesthetics and Art Criticism* 74:4 (2016), 347-358, p. 347.
[52] Carrell, 'Historical views', p. 310.
[53] Larkin-Galiñanes, 'An overview of Humor Theory', p. 5.
[54] Joshua Shaw, 'Philosophy of Humor', *Philosophy Compass*, 5:2 (2010), 112-126, p. 113.
[55] For contemporary readings of the three-fold theory model, see Larkin-Galiñanes, 'An overview of Humor Theory', as well as Carrell, 'Historical views'.

brief chronological overview is useful to contextualise the works of theorists of humour that this thesis refers to.

Superiority theory is considered the dominant model of humour in European philosophy and literary criticism from classical Greek Antiquity to the end of the nineteenth-century, and was concerned with questions of which persons were the subject of laughter, and what implications this laughter might have in an ethical sense for the person who laughs.[56] At its core, superiority theory 'is concerned with the affective response that often accompanies comic amusement, which it maintains is an enjoyable feeling of superiority to the object of amusement.'[57] Plato, one of the earliest philosophers who contributed to what is now called superiority theory, was concerned about the derisive laughter he identified, which he considered an irrational emotion and therefore unbecoming of a virtuous person. Laughter's reputation retained its potentially disruptive and uncontrollable potential in the (relatively scarce) writings on humour in the following centuries. As Jorge Figueroa-Dorrego writes, 'for Christian thinkers laughter was too associated with the body, and the strict regulation of the body was a central issue in their ascetic approach to life on earth.'[58] In the seventeenth century, René Descartes too references the dangers of malicious laughter, but at the same time expands the concept to include the possibility of corrective laughter, where it can be used to 'reproving vices by making them appear ridiculous,' an idea that later inspired Henri Bergson.[59] In *Leviathan* (1651), Thomas Hobbes states that 'those *Grimaces* called LAUGHTER' are caused either 'by some sudden act of their own, that pleaseth them; or by the apprehension of some deformed thing in another, by comparison whereof they suddenly applaud themselves.'[60] In the eighteenth and nineteenth

---

[56] Larkin-Galiñanes, 'Overview of Humor Theory', p. 4.
[57] Lintott, 'Superiority', p. 347.
[58] Jorge Figueroa-Dorrego and Cristina Larkin-Galiñanes, *A Source Book of Literary and Philosophical Writings about Humour and Laughter* (London: Sage, 2005), p. 50.
[59] Figueroa-Dorrego & Larkin-Galiñanes, *Source Book*, p. 292.
[60] Thomas Hobbes, *Leviathan*, ed. by G.A.J. Rogers and Karl Schuhmann, Vol. I (London: Continuum, 2005), p. 48.

centuries, an appreciation developed of constrained forms of laughter, evidenced in discussions of the more socially acceptable 'wit', while superiority theory persisted.[61] William Hazlitt claimed in 1818 that '[w]e laugh to show our satisfaction with ourselves, or our contempt for those about us, or to conceal our envy or our ignorance.'[62] French philosopher Henri-Louis Bergson expands the concept of laughter in 1900 into one of a means of social control – the laughter of the group at an individual works as a social corrective, incentivising people to follow social norms. It should be noted that these philosophers did not necessarily consider superiority as *essential* to laughter, by which I mean that superiority is the necessary emotional mechanism through which laughter and humour is always created. As Sheila Lintott argues, philosophers like Plato and Hobbes were interested in a certain type of laughter, 'an important and common species of laughter', rather than attempting to typify the human experience of laughter overall.[63]

I will return to Bergson in a moment. The second approach, called either relief theory or release theory, posits that laughter provides physical relief from pent-up tension, leading the body to a more relaxed state. In the 1860s, philosopher and biologist Herbert Spencer turns to physiology to explain the physical expression of amusement into laughter. He argues that any feeling 'passing a certain pitch habitually vents itself in bodily action', and laughter causes 'an overflow of nerve-force undirected by any motive'.[64] In *Jokes and Their Relation to the Unconscious* (1905), Sigmund Freud formulated a theory of laughter that combines the idea of scornful laughter with his views on human nature. As dreams express unconscious desires, equally jokes allow unpleasant or unacceptable feelings like aggression to transform into the more

---

[61] Larkin-Galiñanes, 'Overview of Humor Theory', p. 7-8.
[62] William Hazlitt, *Lectures on the English Comic Writers*, ed. by William Hazlitt [the son] (London: John Templeman, 1841), p. 10.
[63] Lintott, 'Superiority', p. 355.
[64] Herbert Spencer, *Essays: Scientific, Political, & Speculative*, Vol. II (London: Williams and Norgate, 1891), p. 458.

pleasant feeling of laughter.⁶⁵ He analysed how different kinds of jokes 'release tensions generated by the mind's efforts to inhibit impulses toward nonsense, childish playfulness, and displays of aggression and sexuality.'⁶⁶ This idea that certain situations create rising tension or energy that find their release in laughter has been particularly of interest for researchers interested in the physical processes that accompany humorous amusement in addition to Freudian psychoanalysts.

The third approach, incongruity theory, considers the perception of an incongruity as the core mechanism of the comic. The history of identifying incongruity as a source of laughter has an equally long history as superiority theory: Aristotle was interested in what rhetorical devices could lead to comic amusement, noting that surprise or subverting expectations was important for an orator to successfully cause laughter in his audience.⁶⁷ This line of reasoning was developed by Cicero, who also explicitly connected laughter to incongruity.⁶⁸ Incongruity theory was expanded by philosophers like Immanuel Kant and Arthur Schopenhauer, and in the second half of the twentieth century became the dominant theory within psychological and linguistic investigations on humour and joke scripts.⁶⁹ In *Humour* (2019), Terry Eagleton considers incongruity theory 'the most plausible account of why we laugh.'⁷⁰ Although incongruity theory has been a fruitful way of conceptualising why jokes or situations are funny, Tomáš Kulka has pointed out that it is not the incongruous itself that defines whether or not a joke is funny – as many situations can be incongruous but are not considered humorous – but the resolution of incongruity which causes the amusement. He writes: 'The incongruous is thus the pre-requisite of

---

[65] Maria Christoff and Barry Dauphin, 'Freud's Theory of Humor', in *Encyclopedia of Personality and Individual Differences*, ed. by Virgil Zeigler-Hill and Todd K. Shackelford (New York: Springer, 2017), p. 2.
[66] Shaw, 'Philosophy of Humor', p. 117.
[67] Larkin-Galiñanes, 'Overview of Humor Theory', p. 12, Lintott, 'Superiority', p. 352.
[68] Larkin-Galiñanes, 'Overview of Humor Theory', p. 12.
[69] Carrell, 'Historical Views', p. 308, 311.
[70] Terry Eagleton, *Humour* (New Haven: Yale University Press), p. 67.

the pleasureable (whether humorous or aesthetic), but it is its resolution which effects it.'[71]

Dividing the history of humour theory into these three strands runs the risk of overstating the separation between the three. Immanuel Kant's writings have been argued to have been part of the incongruity theory, while others suggest that he too refers to concerns related to release theory.[72] While Herbert Spencer is more interested in the physiological aspects of the release of tension in the nervous system, his investigation starts from the question: 'How comes a sense of the incongruous to be followed by these peculiar bodily actions?'[73] To Spencer, the perception of incongruity and its subsequent release are clearly related concerns. Bergson's work, too, should not be subsumed by superiority theory, as Bergson is also concerned with what exactly it is that makes people laugh at deviant behaviour.[74] He posits the idea that it is the 'mechanical inelasticity', which stands in contrast to the 'wide-awake adaptability and the living pliableness of a human being' that causes laughter – in essence, he is typifying how a specific type of the incongruous functions as a deviation from the social script.[75] Freud's writing, too, can be interpreted both as part of the origin of release theory, as well as containing elements of superiority theory, when he discusses how repressed feelings of aggression towards another person become the source of certain jokes. Considering the overlaps of the superiority, release, and incongruity theories in the works of these authors, which are key texts in the development of the three

---

[71] Tomáš Kulka, 'The Incongruity of Incongruity Theories of Humor', *Organon*, 14:3 (2007), 320-333, p. 333.
[72] Shaw, 'Philosophy of Humor', p. 118.
[73] Spencer, *Essays*, p. 452.
[74] See also Shaw, 'Philosophy of Humor', p. 118.
[75] Henri Bergson, *Laughter. An Essay on the Meaning of the Comic*, trans. by Cloudesly Brereton and Fred Rothwell (London: Macmillan and Co., 1911), p. 10. This dichotomy between the mechanical or inflexible and the human or elastic is part of Bergson's broader metaphysics where he considers human evolution to be controlled by a certain life force (*elán vital*) rather than random mutations. For a discussion on the place of *Laughter* within Bergson's work, see Bernard G. Prusak, 'Le rire à nouveau: Rereading Bergson', *The Journal of Aesthetics and Art Criticism*, 64:4 (2004), 377-388.

aforementioned theories, I do not consider them to be truly theoretically distinct, at least historically.

Finally, a brief note on the carnivalesque, a separate theory which is generally not discussed within the framework of the three theoretical approaches to humour. The concept of the carnivalesque, which will also be touched on in various chapters, I argue is a reversal of superiority theory. In *Rabelais and His World* (1964), Russian philosopher and literary critic Mikhael Bakhtin sets out to analyse folk culture, and particularly the carnival, a festival during which hierarchies are suspended. This project has broader implications though, as 'the carnival principle corresponds to and is indeed a part of the novelistic principle itself.'[76] Where laughter is seen as a social corrective – essentially, a form of control – in superiority theory, within the Bakhtinian carnival laughter is a liberating force. The carnivalesque can redraw power relationships beyond the conventional hierarchy, creating new social bonds between laughers (which might be temporary). The carnivalesque has been a useful concept for assessing humour and the comic in literature, including within the Gothic, as recently demonstrated by Avril Horner and Sue Zlosnik in *Gothic and the Comic Turn* (2005) and Timothy Jones in *The Gothic and the Carnivalesque in American Culture* (2015). The carnivalesque is a specific subcategory of laughter – it should not be seen as a conceptualization of all humour. In this thesis, the carnivalesque is therefore seen as complementary to, and not conflicting with, other approaches to humour, and will be used to analyse certain instances of laughter where law and hierarchy are (temporarily) suspended within the text.[77]

In philosophy and literature, humour is often studied as a means to an end rather than for its own sake (and this thesis is no exception).[78] While various approaches have been formulated, both

---

[76] Hélène Iswolsky, 'Foreword', in Mikhail Bakhtin, *Rabelais and His World*, trans. by Hélène Iswolsky, (Bloomington: Indiana University Press, 1964), p. x.
[77] For a general discussion on the carnivalesque in Victorian culture, see Mark M. Hennelly, Jr, 'Victorian Carnivalesque', *Victorian Literature and Culture*, 30:1 (2002) 365-381.
[78] Lintott, 'Superiority', p. 356.

within the three approaches outlined above as well as outside of them, there is no one definitive comprehensive theory of humour and laughter – and considering the variability and complexity of the phenomenon, it is unlikely that there will be one in the future. This thesis therefore does not restrict itself to one theory in this evolving field, instead using various theories of and approaches to laughter, both from the nineteenth century as well as more recent reflections on the phenomenon. The aim is to shed a light not on the psychological or physiological mechanisms of laughter, but the cultural resonances of the jokes and humorous situations presented in the penny blood. This study is less concerned with what humour *is*, but more with how humour works and creates meaning in these texts. Bergson started his work on humour with the question, 'what does laughter mean?' – in this thesis, the question is narrowed to 'what does laughter mean *within the penny blood*'.[79] This approach allows for a flexible understanding of laughter. The insights of superiority theory are relevant to analysing how laughter can create imbalances of power between people; when someone laughs *at* someone rather than *with*, superiority theory gives us more insight into the social repercussions of such laughter. To this end I read some of the scenes in the following concurrently with for example Bergson, drawing out resonances between his ideas on laughter as a social corrective and the laughter present in some of the following texts. Equally, the concept of incongruity can raise questions like, why are these two elements presented in the text posited as incongruous, and what cultural assumptions do they refer to? Ultimately, how these insights bring us closer to understanding the place of these texts within early Victorian society.

STRUCTURE OF THESIS

An issue that arises when studying penny bloods is the amount of unexplored material. The majority of these texts within the Barry Ono collection have not received recent scholarly attention. Criticism has mainly focused on the three most well-known penny

---

[79] Bergson, *Laughter*, p. 1.

authors, Prest, Rymer, and Reynolds. This thesis aims to strike a balance between engaging with existing scholarship on two of these authors, namely Prest and Rymer, as well as including two lesser-known (and less prolific) authors, James Lindridge and Pierce Egan the Younger. By including *The String of Pearls* by Rymer, possibly one of the most studied penny bloods along with *Varney the Vampire* (1845-1847) and *The Mysteries of London* (1844-1845), I demonstrate how focussing on laughter provides a complementary reading to the existing scholarship that is invaluable to understanding the text as a whole. The other texts, then, provide a necessary exploration of the various thematic preoccupations of the penny blood, moving from the Gothic cannibalist humour of *The String of Pearls* to the ventriloquist-induced farcical clobbering in *Valentine Vaux*, and from the daring highwayman adventures of *Jack Rann*, to the nautical and domestic drama of *Paul Jones*. This thesis shows the breadth of stories published under the penny blood (or domestic romance) umbrella. It will provide an exploration of the diversity of texts while drawing attention to their commonalities at the same time. Attention, too, was paid to the publishers involved in the production and sale of the texts: while Edward Lloyd is rightly seen as a key figure in the popularisation of penny bloods, I aimed to not limit the thesis to Lloyd's products, and also included two from George Purkess, a fellow London publisher who occasionally collaborated with Lloyd.

This thesis does not include a text by Reynolds, despite his importance to the penny publication landscape both through his own writing (particularly his serial *The Mysteries of London* from 1844), as well as his role as the publisher of *Reynold's Miscellany*, which published both his own writing as well as that of others, like Rymer. Unlike the authors discussed below, Reynolds actively engaged in politics, particularly Chartism.[80] Overall, the connection between Chartism and the early mid-century penny press has been

---

[80] For more information of how Reynold's politics influenced his fiction, see Jamie Morgan, 'Portrayals of Protest: G.W.M. Reynolds and the Industrious Classes' (doctoral thesis, University of Sheffield, 2017).

explored elsewhere.[81] This thesis seeks out the politics that are present in texts where no circumstantial information is available – and where the politics are obscured, or unclear.[82] As superiority theory demonstrates, humour is intricately connected to power – to social control and hierarchy. This thesis explores how laughter reveals preconceptions regarding social structures such as class and race. It demonstrates that the penny blood as a whole is not unambiguously aligned with any one set of values, showing the contradictory and conflicted politics that underlie these texts.

The first chapter therefore examines *The String of Pearls* by Rymer, the story of the notorious murderous barber Sweeney Todd and his accomplice Mrs Lovett, who bakes Todd's victims into pies for human consumption. It explores the current scholarship on the text, which largely takes a Marxist perspective and the bodily anxieties that are expressed by the plot. This chapter then introduces the carnivalesque into its reading of *The String of Pearls*, complicating the Marxist reading by focusing on the humorous elements, including cannibalist jokes. It draws on the carnivalesque as well as contemporary approaches to the humorous Gothic by Timothy Jones in *The Gothic and the Carnivalesque in American Culture*, and April Horner and Sue Zlosnik in *Gothic and the Comic Turn*. The chapter then moves to explore the other genres present: melodrama and romance, both of which provide counterpoints to the humorous elements. I read these elements together to argue that the comedy and laughter in *The String of Pearls* are not merely a distraction, but are part of the emotional register of the text, expanding our current understanding of the text.

The second chapter focuses on *Valentine Vaux* by Prest, a plagiarised version of Henry Cockton's *Valentine Vox* (1839-1840). The chapter compares and contrasts these two texts, showing how Prest adapted the original to a different audience. Both Cockton's and Prest's Valentines are ventriloquists, able to project their voices to other people or spaces. The chapter explores how ventriloquism

---

[81] See Haywood, *Revolution*, and Rob Breton, *The Penny Politics of Victorian Popular Fiction* (Manchester: Manchester University Press, 2021).
[82] Interestingly, Barry Ono considered Reynolds's writing as too high-brow for them to be categorised as 'true' bloods. See Smith, 'Introduction', p. x.

has been used in fiction, including Charles Brockden Brown's *Wieland* (1798), seeking to understand how this has been adapted for the penny blood. Valentine's ventriloquial pranks are staged for an appreciative audience: most of his pranks are enacted in public spaces, leading to laughter, confusion, and chaos. Despite the destabilising effect of Valentine's voice, I argue that he ultimately supports conventional authority and the law through his relationship with the constabulary and magistrate. The chapter therefore concludes that *Valentine Vaux* reinstates rather than subverts hierarchy through its humour.

The third chapter features Lindridge's *Jack Rann, alias Sixteen-String Jack*, a fictional story (very) loosely based on the figure of the real highwayman of the same name. The chapter positions *Jack Rann* within the larger tradition of the highwayman story, showing how it draws from this rich history of storytelling. Disguise is an important part of the text, complicating class politics, it uses humour to displace and confuse the class identity of the main character. While the text contains various humorous adventures and an elaborate prank sequence, the story sees Jack convicted and ultimately hanged at a sombre occasion. Yet this serious ending does not present a straightforward closure of the unsettling in-betweenness that Jack embodies, instead being part of a continuous renewal within the highwayman storytelling tradition.

The final chapter concerns Egan's *Paul Jones*, a fictionalised story loosely based on the life of John Paul Jones, a Scotsman by birth who commanded an American ship during the Revolutionary War. *Paul Jones* is one of the many nautical texts that can be found within the penny blood corpus, yet it also demonstrates a tension within itself, struggling to reconcile the domestic plot with its nautical elements. The text equally struggles with the inheritance of empire and slavery: it condemns slavery, and shows how a black character leads an episode of communal corrective laughter, while at another point violence enacted upon the black character's body is the source of the laughter for the white characters. The chapter concludes by considering this ambivalence and ambiguity that characterises the politics of *Paul Jones*, expressing an inheritance of older nautical texts that no longer quite suit the narrative of the penny blood.

Through analysing these four stories, this thesis demonstrates how decentering the primacy of violence as the core principle of the penny blood allows for a broader understanding of the genre as a whole. Specifically, tracing the humorous elements moves the analysis of the penny blood beyond being subsumed within the history of other genres, such as the Gothic, revealing the patchwork of tones and textual inheritances that constitute the group of texts that we currently label as penny blood. At the same time, it demonstrates how these various elements align and conflict, expressing the contradictory politics of the genre.

Chapter One

The String of Pearls by James Malcolm Rymer

INTRODUCTION

In 1974, Louis James lamented that nineteenth-century working class literature published between 1830 and 1850 in penny magazines was woefully underexplored.[1] While the majority of penny serializations published during this period remain unexamined, James Malcolm Rymer's *The String of Pearls* (1846-7) is one of the few that has received scholarly attention. The enduring legacy of the story plays a significant part in the scholarly interest. The tale of Sweeney Todd, the barber whose customers do not leave his shop alive, has been told and retold since the nineteenth century. The origin of this character was the serial titled *The String of Pearls*, published in *The People's Periodical* from 11 November 1846 until 18 March 1847.[2] The original story ran for seventeen issues, but was later expanded and republished by Edward Lloyd in 1850. This collected edition, in comparison to the original serial which counted slightly less than three-hundred pages if put together, contained more than seven-hundred pages. The title was expanded as well:

---

[1] James, *Fiction*, p. xv.
[2] A reproduction of the front page of the first issue can be found in Robert L. Mack, *The Wonderful and Surprising History of Sweeney Todd* (London: Continuum, 2007), p. 90. An original is held by the British Library.

while the periodical serialization was simply called *The String of Pearls. A romance*, the 1850 novel was called *The String of Pearls; or, the barber of Fleet Street. A domestic romance*.[3] Dramatic adaptations began even before the completion of the original serialization, illustrating the story's popularity. It was dramatised by George Dibdin Pitt in March of 1847 to be performed in the Britannia Theatre, titled *The String of Pearls or the Fiend of Fleet Street*.[4] A significant later adaptation is Stephen Sondheim and Hugh Wheeler's *Sweeney Todd: The Demon Barber of Fleet Street*, a Broadway musical first produced in 1979. Director Tim Burton adapted the story for the screen, retaining some of the musical influences from the Broadway production, in 2007. Although the adaptations vary in content and plot, they are united by what is seen as the essence of the Sweeney Todd legend: the murderous barber killing people and his entrepreneurial accomplice disposing of the bodies by baking them into pies sold to unsuspecting customers. As Robert L. Mack, the author of *The Wonderful and Surprising History of Sweeney Todd* writes, it is the 'themes of avarice, ambition, love, desire, appetite, vanity, atonement, retribution, justice and cannibalism in all its many forms' that draws creators to adapt the story for audiences across time.[5] The tenacious constancy of the cannibalism plot can be seen as one in a 'long tradition of narratives dating into antiquity that play on what some might argue are "primitive" anxieties related to the consumption of human flesh.'[6] While the taboo of eating human flesh might be cross-cultural and cross-temporal, its specific expression in narratives reflects on its cultural and historical context. As Peggy Reeves Sanday writes: 'Cannibalism is [...] primarily a medium for nongustatory messages – messages having

---

[3] Rebecca Nesvet, 'Blood Relations: Sweeney Todd and the Rymers of London', *Notes and Queries*, 64:1 (2017), 112-116, p. 112.
[4] For the play's script, see George Dibdin Pitt, *Sweeney Todd, The Barber of Fleet Street; or, The String or Pearls. A Legendary Drama in Two Acts* (London: John Dicks, 1883).
[5] Mack, *History*, p. xvii.
[6] Brian Patrick Riley, '"It's Man Devouring Man, My Dear": Adapting Sweeney Todd for the Screen', *Literature/Film Quarterly*, 38:3 (2010), 205-216, p. 207.

to do with the maintenance, regeneration, and, in some cases, the foundation of the cultural order.'[7] In other words, the cannibalism exhibited in a text such as *The String of Pearls* can express ideas on class and power. However, as we shall see below, a too narrow view of the cannibalism plot leads to reductive readings of the original work, which was more complex than critics have allowed for.

So far Marxist readings of the cannibalist imagery have dominated scholarship on the text. In this current chapter, however, the cannibalism and other violent elements are reconsidered in the context of the story's humoristic tone, which leads to a re-evaluation of the political implications of the text. However, this reading is complicated by the fact that the text is not merely comical: melodramatic and romantic modes intersperse the comic, together completing the tonal register of the text. After discussing existing literature, these three modes will be discussed in turn. Before moving on to the contents of *The String of Pearls*, two further aspects of its publication are of note: its contested authorship, and the story's predecessors.

As the serial was published, no mention of the identity of the author was made. This was not uncommon for a penny serialization, which were often published under a pseudonym or without an attributed authorship at all. Over the years critics have assumed that it was either written by Prest or Rymer, two prolific writers who worked together closely with Edward Lloyd, based on advertisements in other penny fiction titles. Authorship of penny serials is generally unclear, and throughout the years misinformation has been repeated in haphazard bibliographical surveys.[8] Nor are works necessarily entirely written by a single author: there is, for example, some evidence that sections of *The*

---

[7] Peggy Reeves Sanday, *Divine Hunger: Cannibalism as a Cultural System* (Cambridge: Cambridge University Press, 1986), p. 3.
[8] Helen Smith, *New Light on Sweeney Todd, Thomas Peckett Prest, James Malcolm Rymer and Elizabeth Caroline Grey* (London: Jarndyce, 2002), p. 1. Smith mentions how someone, possibly J.P. Quaine, invented titles which made their way into Montague Summers's work.

String of Pearls might be written by a second author.[9] By comparing advertisements in Lloyd's various publications, Helen Smith has persuasively argued that it is indeed Rymer who wrote (the majority of) the story, an assertion corroborated by Dick Collins, the editor of a 2005 edition of the book.[10] The story's origins are likely a piece titled 'A Terrific Story of the Rue-de-la-Harpe, Paris' from 1825 in the magazine *The Tell-Tale*.[11] This story features the bare bones of the cannibalistic plot central to *The String of Pearls*. It was also recently brought to light that J.M. Rymer's father might be the Romantic novelist and poet Malcolm Rymer, usually stylised as M. Rymer.[12] *The String of Pearls* resembles M. Rymer's novel *The Spaniard* (1806) in the way that it also featured a barber, albeit in a slightly different role. Where *The Spaniard*'s barber Pedrosa represents a barber-*cum*-surgeon, pulling teeth and performing other minor medical procedures as was part of the barber's role before the nineteenth century, Sweeney Todd is ostensibly merely a hairdresser. Both main characters enact violence on their customers: Pedrosa out of duty, Sweeney Todd out of greed and cruelty. Both stories capitalise on the association of barbers with blood and danger, while illustrating a historical development, as a barber became a profession increasingly separate from that of a surgeon in the nineteenth century.

The story of *The String of Pearls* opens with a man and a dog walking across a square. The man, on a mission to give a young girl a string of pearls sent to her by her lover, enters a barbershop. He never comes out. As mentioned above, this premise is a direct adaptation from the *Tell-Tale* story, 'A Terrific Story of the Rue-de-la-Harpe, Paris' (henceforth referred to as 'Rue Harpe'). In 'Rue Harpe', two men and a dog enter the barber shop, and when the second man returns from a short errand in the neighbourhood, the

---

[9] James Malcolm Rymer, *Sweeney Todd. The String of Pearls*, ed. by Dick Collins (Ware: Wordsworth Editions, 2010), p. xviii.
[10] Smith, *New Light*. pp. 11-12, and Dick Collins, 'Introduction to the Revised Edition', in Rymer, *Sweeney Todd*, pp. vi-viii.
[11] James, *Fiction*, p. 190. Collins, 'Introduction', p. xix.
[12] Nesvet, 'Blood Relations', p. 112.

first man has disappeared, while the dog remains. In both versions, the dog's insistence on staying at the barbershop where their owner has been murdered presents a threat to the barber's murderous secret. In 'Rue Harpe', a story of a few pages, the story is resolved quickly by the dog revealing a secret passage in the barber's cellar. This is shown to be leading to the patisserie next door:

> The pastry-cook, whose shop was so remarkable for savory patties that they were sent for to the "*Rue de la* Harpe," from the most distant parts of Paris, was the partner of this peruquier,[13] and those who were murdered by the razor of the one, were concealed by the knife of the other, *in those identical patties*; by which, independently of his partnership in those frequent robberies, he made a fortune.[14]

The cannibalist twist is a true surprise within the context of this short tale: no hint is given to foreshadow this development until it is revealed in full in the last sentences. This stands in sharp contrast with *The String of Pearls*, where, as we shall see in the following, the cannibalism is repeatedly hinted at. In 'Rue Harpe', the cannibalism mainly serves to make an already violent story more gruesome. *The String of Pearls* borrows heavily from 'Rue Harpe', from the opening scene featuring a dog, to the murder victims being transported through underground passages. Rymer sets the story in London rather than Paris, and invents several new storylines that revolve around this central cannibalist mystery. Another interesting expansion is that of the role of the barber figure: in 'Rue Harpe' the barber is given only one line, and is otherwise a marginal figure. Rymer's Sweeney Todd on the other hand is an active, extensively-described character with strong agency within the plot, and a key figure in the narrative.

---

[13] *Perruquier* means wig maker in French. It refers to the barber.
[14] 'The Murderous Barber; Or, Terrific Story of the Rue de la Harpe at Paris', in *The Wonders of the Universe; or Curiosities of Nature and Art.* (Exeter: J. & B. Williams, 1836), pp. 1-3, p. 3.

The String of Pearls is written from multiple points of view and features surprisingly intricate plotting. Penny bloods are generally considered to be an inferior and simple literature.[15] Jarlath Killeen, for example, asserts that '[t]hey were written in staccato style, with short sentences and single-sentence paragraphs, and were extraordinarily repetitious.'[16] *The String of Pearls* makes efficient use of different points of view to tell its story, and its writing is of better quality than Killeen allows. It also stays relatively clear from the repetition that is a characteristic of penny fiction, though in the expanded 1850 version repetition becomes rife. The plot revolves around two mysteries, one sentimental, one horrifying: what is the fate of Johanna's lover, Mark Ingestrie? And in what villainous plot are Sweeney Todd and Mrs Lovett embroiled? Near the end of the book these two mysteries intersect, as Todd and Lovett are revealed to have imprisoned Ingestrie in the pie factory underneath Mrs Lovett's shop. Another notable plot involves Tobias, Todd's young apprentice, whom the reader fears might never escape his employer alive. Throughout the story Todd is threatening, all-powerful, and elusive. While later adaptations such as Sondheim's in 1979 have given Todd a backstory based on revenge which explains his murderous behaviour (or at least rationalises it), the evil of *The String of Pearls*'s Todd is not allowed such mitigating circumstances. Like his predecessor in 'Rue Harpe', he operates purely from selfish reasons stemming from greed, even killing his accomplice Mrs Lovett when she no longer serves his plan. As the character of Todd is essential to understanding *The String of Pearls*, closer attention to it will be given later on, especially in the context of the monstrous. In the following, I will first discuss the current scholarship on *The String of Pearls*. Then the analysis complicates the conventional reading of the story's cannibalism by discussing it in light of the carnivalesque. Subsequently, attention is given to the other genres

---

[15] Jonathan Rose for example has written in the context of penny dreadfuls that 'some books are like chewing gum, consumed in mass quantities but leaving no taste behind.' Jonathan Rose, *The Intellectual Life of the British Working Classes* (New Haven 2002), p. 370.
[16] Killeen, 'Pulp Fiction', p. 46.

and modes that are present in the text, namely that of melodrama and romance.

THE ALIENATED WORKER AND SOCIETAL CANNIBALISM

Many existing studies on *The String of Pearls* take a Marxist perspective. A core text in this regard is Sarah Powell's 'Black Markets and Cadaverous Pies: The Corpse, Urban Trade and Industrial Consumption in the Penny Blood' (2004). In this article, Powell uses two case studies of penny bloods to illustrate what historical anxieties concerning bodies underlie the genre. Reading *The String of Pearls* and Reynolds' *The Mysteries of London*, she argues that 'the penny blood exhibits a persistent preoccupation with the displaced corpse and with its black market commodification.'[17] In other words, in penny bloods corpses do not stay buried, and it is the bodies themselves that have commercial value. Popular penny bloods like *The Mysteries of London* and Prest's *The Old House of West Street* (1846) feature body-snatching, where corpses are either dug up or freshly created for the purpose of dissection. More specifically, Powell adds, the penny bloods 'constitute an articulation of the threat posed by city commercialism to the sanctity and survival of the working-class individual.'[18] As the readership of penny bloods were overwhelmingly individuals from the working class, she argues that it is the body of the working-class reader that is at stake. Powell argues that the 1832 Anatomy act created a deep-seated fear in working-class populations. This law disproportionally effected working-class citizens, as it allowed unclaimed bodies from workhouses and prisons to be used by anatomists. She expands on other corporeal anxieties plaguing the mid-century city inhabitants: animals were still slaughtered in inner-city slaughterhouses, their

---

[17] Sarah Powell, 'Black Markets and Cadaverous Pies: The Corpse, Urban Trade and Industrial Consumption in the Penny Blood', in *Victorian Crime, Madness and Sensation*, ed. by A. Maunder & G. Moore (Hampshire: Ashgate, 2004), pp. 45-58. p. 45.
[18] Powell, 'Black Markets', p. 45.

remains often exposed to the elements; faeces and decomposing bodies in cemeteries polluted water supplies; and, perhaps most importantly, working-class individuals gave their lives to create consumer products.

A cartoon that succinctly illustrates this anxiety was published in 1846 by George Cruickshank in *Our Own Times*.[19] A villainous man in a black suit with a broad smile and angry eyes (who, as Powell has noted, bears a physical similarity to Todd) operates a machine that grinds up the bodies of women, discarding their bodies when little bags of 'profit' are extracted from them. On the other side of a curtain, shoppers are appreciating the wares, one person exclaiming, 'I cannot imagine how they can possibly've made for the price!!'. The imagery is clear: in order to make cheap products, workers are exploited, being forced into a 'tremendous sacrifice', as the text underneath the image reads. This cartoon can be read as a form of symbolic cannibalism, where the consumption of goods requires the death of the workers. In *The String of Pearls*, conversely, people are literally being fed to machines which turn them into pies, which are to be sold 'beyond the curtain' – in this case, they are moved from the place of production in the basement, to the shopping space above. Like the shoppers in Cruickshank's cartoon who exclaim over the product could possibly be made, Mrs Lovett's customers do not realise the source of the meat they are eating. An analysis like Powell's gains strength from the fact that Mrs Lovett's pies are mass-produced by industrial machinery, while a lone worker operates them, 'enslaved and alienated within'.[20] As Powell writes, 'the popularity of the tale of Sweeney Todd testifies to the existence of a mid-century working-class perception that in a newly industrialized urban economy there existed not only a literal but a metaphoric relationship between the consumption of goods and a cannibalistic feeding upon one's fellow urbanites.'[21] Literary scholar Andrew King argues in a similar vein when he writes that

---

[19] For a reproduction of this print, see Powell, 'Black Markets', p. 55.
[20] Powell, 'Black Markets', p. 51.
[21] Powell, 'Black Markets', p. 50.

The String of Pearls is a 'warning about the dangers of capitalism in a city where people are reduced to commodities and alienated from the production processes of what they consume.'[22] In his recent work on penny fiction, Rob Breton too states that 'relation of production [...] dominate not just the main plotline, but the minor ones as well,' arguing that the story taps into working-class resentment.[23]

What Powell's analysis does not take into account is the very class-specificity of both the production as well as the consumption of the human pies. The humans turned into meat are not of the working class, as one might expect in a narrative mirroring Cruickshank's cartoon. Todd prefers his victims to be rich, as this provides more wealth when he steals their belongings, although he has no scruples killing lower classes if it suits him. Nor is Ingestrie, who is forced into a situation of alienated labour, easy to pin down from a class perspective. Though Ingestrie's guardian, his uncle, has destined for him to follow his footsteps into the law profession, Ingestrie goes off to 'seek his fortune' by sailing to India.[24] He moves from lower middle-class respectability to being a common sailor, then the owner of a fortune (the pearls), to an incarcerated factory worker. While this temporariness of his status as worker does not cancel out the criticism of working conditions the text expresses, this aspect should be taken into account. Finally, the cannibalistic tendencies of the law-clerks who greedily eat the pies cannot easily be explained by capitalist consumerism. It is not the exploited lower classes that are overwhelmingly eaten by the clerks, but their betters and their peers.

Marxist readings of *The String of Pearls* like Powell's are concerned with Ingestrie's imprisonment in the pie factory. The majority of the story, however, focuses on another character whose

---

[22] Andrew King, '"Literature of the Kitchen": Cheap Serial Fiction of the 1840s and 1850s', in *A Companion to Sensation Fiction*, ed. by Pamela K. Gilbert (Chichester: Wiley-Blackwell, 2011), pp. 38-53, p. 44.
[23] Breton, *Penny Politics*, p. 100.
[24] Rymer, *Sweeney Todd*, p. 13.

imprisonment is more metaphorical: Tobias, the apprentice of Sweeney Todd. He is just as powerless and shackled into labour as Ingestrie. Their parallel fates complicate a reading in which *The String of Pearls* is a straight-forward critique of mass-production and industrialisation. Nor is the titular string of pearls, a significant source of capital with colonial connections,[25] accounted for in any of the Marxist critiques. The pearls change hands repeatedly, being handed over, stolen, bartered, and regained. In Dick Collins' introduction to the Wordsworth edition of the story, he argues that the pearls are an addition made to the story by Rymer's wife, apparently basing this on the fact that she was a woman and must therefore yearn for jewellery. The pearls would then be the expression of a wish for wealth of a young middle-class couple which made its way into the narrative. There is no evidence to support this claim. King adds another element to his interpretation of *The String of Pearls*, by pointing out that the story is also explicitly a 'romance'. According to him, it is love that ultimately breaks down the exploitative system, signalling a victory of the sentimental. King complicates a straightforward Marxist narrative by touching on an aspect of penny fiction that works to destabilise social hierarchies, including the exploitation-related plot in *The String of Pearls*: gender ambiguity. It is Johanna who actively searches for her lost lover, while Ingestrie takes on the role of the Gothic heroine in captivity.[26] In this chapter I will expand King's assertion that the romance is essential in understanding *The String of Pearls* by arguing that the humorous, the romantic, and the melodramatic all need to be accounted for.

Apart from Marxist readings of class and their connection to cannibalism, there is another common thread in studies on Sweeney Todd: the penny blood's connection to modernity, relating industrialisation to selfhood and identity. A trace of this can be seen in Powell's description of the cacophony and dirtiness of mid-century London. Mack, the author of *The Wonderful and Surprising*

---

[25] For a short overview, see Nesvet, 'Blood Relations', p. 116.
[26] King, 'Literature of the Kitchen', p. 44.

History of Sweeney Todd, connects the cannibalistic imagery with the growth of the metropolis. He writes that the 'explosive growth of London and its rapacity' and the 'anxieties that characterize the threat of anonymity and disappearance within the brooding metropolitan environment [...] were an extraordinarily forceful part of the urban zeitgeist in the early 1840s.'[27] The modern experience is also the focus of Killeen's discussion of penny bloods. The violence that permeated Victorian society, from butchering animals in the street to the public spectacle of corporeal punishment, causes a trauma that lead to a 'collective loss of subjectivity', according to Killeen.[28] It is this trauma that penny bloods work through, as they are characterised by plots that 'were merely vehicles to get the reader from one scene of gore, violence and torture to the next.'[29] For Killeen the plots revolve around 'moments of intense violence.'[30] Again, this reading of the penny blood overlooks its romantic and melodramatic elements, relegating them to merely padding for what he perceives as the core characteristic of the penny blood – the violence that permeates its plots. If someone were to pick up *The String of Pearls* after reading Killeen's article, one might be disappointed by the lack of gore. While the cannibalist plot is suggestive and gruesome, the actual murdering of men by Sweeney Todd happens off-page, only referred to after the fact. The majority of on-page violence is farcical by nature, and does not lead to any lasting damage to any of the characters. If *The String of Pearls* indeed reacts to or expresses a collective loss of subjectivity, that is not achieved by the graphic pulling apart and indiscriminate killing of humans, expressing a world in which anyone could fall prey to this fate. Though continuously threatened, the main characters are safe from destruction by the hands of Todd.

---

[27] Mack, *History*, p. 150.
[28] Killeen, 'Pulp Fiction', p. 51.
[29] Killeen, 'Pulp Fiction', p. 50.
[30] Killeen, 'Pulp Fiction', p. 50.

FOOD AND THE CARNIVALESQUE

As is becoming apparent in the discussion of existing readings of *The String of Pearls*, none of them interpret the work as a whole. While many of them concentrate on one aspect (the cannibalism, the violence, or briefly, the romance in King's case), they do not reflect on the amalgam of genres and tones in *The String of Pearls*. One essential characteristic of *The String of Pearls* that is consistently passed over is its consciously humorous and irreverent tone. Jokes range from wordplay and puns to farce and physical comedy. Not only is the humour at the surface of the text, it is self-conscious and comes close to parody. Yet, at other times, other registers become more important, such as melodrama or romance, which give rise to a different range of emotions in the reader, including pathos. The most jarring passages within *The String of Pearls* are perhaps those concerning a strange smell at St. Dunstan's Church, placed in such a way that they interrupt the main narrative in especially tense moments. Dick Collins has argued that this chapter is based on the real-life controversy of the Spa Fields' Chapel, whose graveyard became so overcrowded that the stench became unbearable, to the point that the Bishop of London refused to enter it.[31] In the reimagining of this event by Rymer, the smell at the church leads to a farcical situation where the supposed sacred become profane due to the odour. It is only further along in the story that the seemingly random interjection of St. Dunstan's Church makes sense: it is later revealed that it sits over the subterranean tunnels that Todd uses to store his victims.

One could argue that so far, scholars have only engaged with the Gothic elements of the text. They connect the text's centring of cannibalism as directly reflecting on real-world anxieties of consumption, both of accidentally consuming the dead, as well as more metaphorical consumption of the working class, like in Powell. In *Carnivalesque in American Culture* (2015), Timothy Jones writes about this issue within Gothic studies: the tendency for

---

[31] Collins, 'Introduction', pp. xxi-xxii.

academics to read Gothic texts, and their engagement with terror, 'seriously'. The Gothic text 'is thought to have a direct interest in the "real world", a significant historicity and a genuine, perhaps subversive, political engagement.'[32] The Gothic, in this view, is seen as expressing and perhaps working through anxieties of the nineteenth-century populace.[33] This tendency can directly be observed in studies of *The String of Pearls*, all of which link the text to 'real-world suffering and trauma.'[34] Jones criticises this approach when faced with carnivalesque Gothic texts, which 'tends to reduce the import of its discursive properties, so that it provides a venue for readers to stage Gothic experience before it provides a vehicle for hermeneutic effort.'[35] In other words, the pleasures these texts offer as they 'delight, thrill and amuse their audiences'[36] reflect on the Gothic reading practices and should take precedence in interpretation. As Jones stresses, this does not mean that a carnivalesque text has no impact on culture or that it stands apart from its historical context. Catherine Spooner too argues for the inclusion of feelings of pleasure and positivity within the Gothic, coining the term 'Happy Gothic'.[37] While Spooner uses this term for twenty-first century Gothic expressions, I would argue that humour has been a part of nineteenth-century Gothic fictions such as *The String of Pearls* as well.

Avril Horner and Sue Zlosnik in *Gothic and the Comic Turn* (2005) argue from a similar position. They write that some Gothic novels contain a 'parodic space'. Here their argument doubles back to the

---

[32] Timothy Jones, *The Gothic and the Carnivalesque in American Culture* (University of Wales Press, 2015), p. 16.
[33] For a critical discussion on middle-class anxieties and the Gothic, see Chris Baldick and Robert Mighall, 'Gothic Criticism', in *A New Companion to the Gothic*, ed. by David Punter (Chichester: Blackwell Publishing, 2012), pp. 267-287, pp. 279-280.
[34] Jones, *Carnivalesque*, p. 16.
[35] Jones, *Carnivalesque*, p. 8.
[36] Jones, *Carnivalesque*, p. 3.
[37] Catherine Spooner, *Post-Millennial Gothic. Comedy, Romance and the Rise of Happy Gothic* (London: Bloomsbury, 2017), p. 3.

idea that the Gothic expresses and possibly negates societal anxiety: the parodic space that opens up the face of the comic can reflect on subjectivity in modernity. It can make modernity more bearable, showing that it is 'hugely entertaining and productive as well as threatening.'[38] Here the parody – if successful – thus identifies, and subsequently neutralises possible anxieties. Killeen, as seen above, saw the 'collective loss of subjectivity' in modernity as the threat that penny bloods worked through.[39] Horner and Zlosnik's concept of parodic space provide an opportunity to reinterpret Killeen's argument. Combining these two arguments, one can say that the tearing apart of individuals in the penny blood within the parodic space does not only enact an anxiety that reflects on life in nineteenth-century modernity, but that it also shows how comic this dissolution can be – and perhaps even productive. Bakhtin's definition of the carnivalesque provides a good conceptualization of this effect: his carnivalesque contains both a life-affirming as well as a death-embracing aspect.[40] Here we are closing in on the politics underpinning *The String of Pearls*; politics which are concealed underneath 'the juxtaposition of incongruous textual effects', which 'open up the possibility of a comic turn in the presence of horror or terror.'[41]

With their reputation for escapist pleasures, penny bloods can be read as carnivalesque texts in Jones's definition. If we conceptualise *The String of Pearls* as a carnivalesque Gothic text, a text that amuses and thrills *before* it engages with societal anxieties, this raises the question: what elements of the texts are we to take seriously, and which are played for laughter? What genres are combined, and how do they work together? How does laughter intersect and influence previous interpretations, such as those formulated by Powell and Killeen? Considering the interpretations put forward by these

---

[38] Avril Horner and Sue Zlosnik, *Gothic and the Comic Turn* (Basingstoke: Palgrave Macmillan, 2005), p. 18.
[39] Killeen, 'Pulp Fiction', p. 51.
[40] David K. Danow, *The Spirit of Carnival. Magical Realism and the Grotesque* (Lexington, Kentucky: The University Press of Kentucky, 1995), p. 5.
[41] Horner and Zlosnik, *Comic Turn*, p. 3.

authors, especially Killeen's typology of the penny blood, how do laughter and violence interact? I argue that violence is used in different ways within the text, corresponding to the different registers present within *The String of Pearls*. As mentioned above, a number of scenes are farcical, and other influences include Gothic and sentimental melodrama. When is violence humorous, and when is it not? In the section below, *The String of Pearls* is read firstly in conjunction with the carnivalesque.

In his study of laughter in *Rabelais and his World* (1964), Russian literary scholar Mikhail Bakhtin writes that 'laughter and its forms represent, […] the least scrutinized sphere of the people's creation.'[42] While Bakhtin had ideological reasons for focussing on popular or 'folk' humour in his study, as he wanted to contrast the laughter of 'the people' with that of the vastly different humour of the bourgeoisie, this statement holds true for penny bloods as well. Not only is the popular form of literature vastly understudied in comparison to middle-class contemporaries, there are few comprehensive studies of popular humour in the nineteenth century overall. Whenever humour is studied, it is usually in the context of forms that are appreciated by the middle or upper classes, like wit.[43] For the purpose of this study, it is therefore important to look at other forms of (comic) entertainment the working class consumed, and what place the penny blood takes amongst those. As Tsvetan Todorov has written, 'a genre is always defined in relation to the genres adjacent to it.'[44] This is especially pertinent as multiple authors have pointed out that the penny blood is very closely related to two other genres of entertainment, the penny theatre and the Newgate novel. A third form of entertainment which is

---

[42] Bakhtin, *Rabelais*, p. 4.
[43] A nineteenth-century example is George Meredith, *An Essay on Comedy and the Uses of the Comic Spirit* (London: A. Constable, 1905 [1877]), who posited that for good comedy 'a society of cultivated men and women is required', and criticised 'the semi-barbarism of merely giddy communities' and 'idle laughers', p. 8, 30.
[44] Tsvetan Todorov, *The Fantastic. A Structural Approach to a Literary Genre*, trans. by Richard Howard (Cleveland: The Press of Case Western Reserve University, 1973), p. 27.

important to consider stands outside of the fictional, but still contains theatrical elements: public executions. This non-fictional genre of entertainment will be considered below.

The carnivalesque, a core term in Bakhtin's theory of laughter, is associated with the lower regions of the body such as the gut, and actions connected to it, like eating, drinking, and defecating. Within the context of the feast, the 'carnival celebrated temporary liberation from the prevailing truth and from the established order; it marked the suspension of all hierarchical rank, privileges, norms, and prohibitions.'[45] As food and eating are central to the plot, it is of interest to compare the scenes in *The String of Pearls* with the carnivalesque feast. The vast majority of the references to food and eating within the story reflect back to the anthropophagy. While food and drink during the carnival provides interconnectedness and community, the eating communities of *The String of Pearls* are isolated from one another. The imprisoned Ingestrie consumes multiple pies in the bowels of Mrs Lovett's pie factory in complete solitude and separation from wider society. In fact, Ingestrie initially sees himself as the ruler of a kingdom of one: 'I have no friends, and no money; she whom I loved is faithless, and here I am, master of as many pies as I like, and to all appearance monarch of all I survey; for there really seems to be no one to dispute my supremacy.'[46] In a way, this scene can be seen as carnivalesque in the way that Ingestrie, though a prisoner, finds his situation reversed because he is the lord of the pies, and 'if it is a kind of imprisonment, it's a pleasant one.' The reversal of social hierarchies is one of the core characteristics of the Bakhtinian carnivalesque. At the same time, this is an example of irony: Ingestrie's happiness at his new situation as pie-maker is contrasted with the fate of the previous prisoner, who just a few pages earlier, met a gruesome death at the hand of a 'terrific apparition'.[47]

---

[45] Bakhtin, *Rabelais*, p. 10.
[46] Rymer, *Sweeney Todd*, p. 90.
[47] 'A sudden shriek burst from his lips, as he beheld so terrific an apparition before him; but, before he could repeat the word, the hammer descended,

The camaraderie of the law clerks who eat the meat pies within the shop, quoted above, is limited by their profession. Bearing in mind Powell's capitalist critique, it is interesting that the text is very specific about whom frequents the pie shop, stating that 'mostly from Lincoln's-inn' patrons arrive, 'although from the neighbouring legal establishments likewise there come not a few; the Temple contributes its numbers, and from the more distant Gray's-inn there come a goodly lot.'[48] The introduction of Mrs Lovett's shop brings to mind other sensationalist pleasures and sets the scene for communal hedonism:

> Is it a fire? Is it a fight? Or anything else sufficiently alarming and extraordinary to excite the young members of the legal profession to such a species of madness? [...] No, the enjoyment is purely one of a physical character, and all the pacing and racing – all this turmoil and trouble – all this pushing, jostling, laughing and shouting, is to see who will get first to Lovett's pie-shop.[49]

Food in this context does not transcend class boundaries as it does within the Bakhtinian carnival. It does, on the other hand, act as a social leveller in another way. In food studies, eating animals is connected with human control and embodies a statement of human superiority.[50] While eating another person therefore can be seen as a way of exerting power over that person, anthropophagy in *The String of Pearls* is more ambiguous. The meat that is consumed could be anyone; one could be eating a judge or a postman, and either looks the same once they have been baked within a pie. The act of eating the pies does not substantially affect social hierarchies, as the eaters are unaware that they are eating human flesh. Additionally,

---

crushing into his skull, and he fell lifeless without a moan.' Rymer, *Sweeney Todd*, p. 87.
[48] Rymer, *Sweeney Todd*, p. 25-26.
[49] Rymer, *Sweeney Todd*, p. 26.
[50] Erica Fudge, 'Why it's easy being a vegetarian', *Textual Practice*, 24:1 (2010) 149-166, p. 149.

the feasting on the pies gives rise to a carnivalesque atmosphere in which everything becomes permitted, and everything becomes a joke. This effect is reached both on the level of the narrative, as we have seen above, as well as in interaction with the reader's expectations. To express this in a more theoretical way, the implied reader of the text, although it is not fully revealed until the end, is expected to know what lies behind the 'mystery meat' that appears in Mrs Lovett's basement while Todd has an unknown way of disposing the people he kills.[51] From the very beginning this possibility is suggested, as Tobias swears in the first chapter that 'I wish, sir, as I may be made into veal pies at Lovett's in Bell-yard if I as much as says a word,' to Todd.[52] This double layer, where the implied reader is in on the joke while the characters are not, creates a parodic space where cannibalism becomes carnivalesque, and even eating one's own mother becomes comic. As one of Mrs Lovett's customers exclaims: 'Lor' bless you, I'd eat my mother, if she was a pork chop, done brown and crisp.'[53]

The crowd of young law clerks that flood the Bell-yard to gain admission to Mrs Lovett's shop also brings to mind an event which might also be sufficiently alarming to excite young law clerks, to paraphrase the quote above: the raucous crowds at public executions. Though it might seem like quite a leap to go from a feast in a fictional text to a state display of law, the carnivalesque atmosphere is similar. The comparison becomes more poignant

---

[51] The implied reader is a concept defined by Wolfgang Iser in *The Act of Reading: A Theory of Aesthetic Response* (Baltimore: Johns Hopkins University Press, 1978), see in particular pp. 35-36. The implied reader is an effect of the text itself, and should not be confused by real readers – these bring their own experiences to the reading process, and can take different stances towards the text.
[52] Rymer, *Sweeney Todd*, p. 4. Todd's reaction is equally telling, in case the reader missed the significance of the statement: 'Sweeney Todd rose from his seat; and opening his huge mouth, he looked at the boy for a minute or two in silence, as if he fully intended swallowing him, but had not quite made up his mind where to begin.'
[53] Rymer, *Sweeney Todd*, p. 241.

when one sees a public execution as a stage performance and essentially theatrical – and the penny blood itself as a genre is closely related to the theatre. Throughout the nineteenth century, and especially after 1838, public executions became rarer, but their public attendance and notoriety increased.[54] While crowd estimations at this time were imprecise at best, it is assumed that many hangings in London saw tens of thousands of spectators. As observations by William Makepeace Thackeray and other contemporaries have shown, the audience at these events was diverse; they were attended both by men and women, young and old, from all levels of society.[55] The crowds at hangings have baffled critics, including Dickens, who wrote several letters on the subject, condemning the celebratory atmosphere. Historian Thomas W. Laqueur has argued that 'The crowd, and particularly the carnivalesque crowd, was the central actor in English executions.'[56] Laqueur's work is especially interesting in light of *The String of Pearls'* connection between violence and humour, and the conjunction between death and laughter. Laqueur writes:

> Through laughter, outrageous clothes, misplaced sentimentality and silence some prisoners subverted the roles assigned to them. Others [...] found themselves caught in stage disasters – grisly, generically comic foul-ups beyond their control in the technology of death. [...] There was enough variation within any one 'hanging fair',

---

[54] Thomas W. Laqueur, 'Crowds, carnival and the state in English executions, 1604-1868' in *The First Modern Society. Essays in English History in Honour of Lawrence Stone*, ed. by A.L. Beier, David Cannadine and James M. Rosenheim (Cambridge: Cambridge University Press, 1989) pp. 305-356, p. 308: 'Public executions, though smaller in number – dramatically so after 1838 – became ever grander in scale until their final abolition in 1868. Railways, better publicity and public hunger born of rarity made nineteenth-century hangings far larger and more boisterous occasions than their earlier counterparts.'
[55] V.A.C. Gatrell, *The Hanging Tree. Execution and the English People 1770-1868* (Oxford: Oxford University Press: Oxford, 1994), pp. 62-63.
[56] Laqueur, 'Crowds', p. 309.

enough laughter and comic chaos, to make them unsuitable for the imaginative realm of sublime terror, just reward, or tragedy.[57]

This quote succinctly illustrates the carnivalesque potential for prisoners, and how the crowd expects excitement in the shape of the comic in the face of death. While V.A.C. Gatrell has argued that the carnivalesque potential for reversal is limited, as both the crowd and the prisoner can never truly escape their designated roles,[58] in the context of this study it is mainly interesting how during this historical period death was enacted on a stage, where it became a form of theatre. More importantly, because of the 'laughter and comic chaos,' executions were seen as entertaining, despite their grisliness. As one spectator at a public hanging commented, at first he was uncomfortable when the condemned was brought out, but 'the actual execution was rather pleasant and satisfactory than otherwise and he went away satisfied.'[59] An additional dimension of excitement was posed by the possibility of a last-minute pardon, which could deprive the audience of its promised entertainment: 'The audience was constantly titillated by the possibility of sudden reversal.'[60] The public reaction on the hangings ranged from approbation to disapproval, depending on the crime and notoriety of the condemned, but even during solemn hangings an element of spectacle was present. It is a similar spectacle to the one the penny blood provides: a staging of gore and laughter.

Whether it is the stage of the scaffold, an account of crimes in the Newgate novel, or the penny blood, these forms of early mid-century entertainment foreground criminals and outlaws. While *The String of Pearls* contains many plots, Sweeney Todd is arguably the main character that keeps moving the story forward and receives most time on-page. This mirrors a development in nineteenth-

---

[57] Laqueur, 'Crowds', p. 319.
[58] Gatrell, *Hanging Tree*, p. 91.
[59] Quoted in Laqueur, 'Crowds', p. 324.
[60] Laqueur, 'Crowds', p. 325.

century melodrama, where an interest in evil in excess comes to dominate the genre.[61] Similarly, in an introduction to a twentieth-century edition of Newgate stories, the editor writes that the purpose of the book is to 'entertain the reader by exhibiting in these trials the extra-ordinary behaviour of men and women when their obscure lives are suddenly brought into a glare of publicity, when the thing done in secret is proclaimed from the house-tops.'[62] It is the spectacle of revealing crime and those who have committed them, and them receiving their final comeuppance (the drop from the scaffold, the receiving of a prison sentence, Sweeney Todd's reveal as murderer and his subsequent capture), that makes the narratives satisfying and provides suitable closure. Like any carnival, the revelling and law-breaking comes to an end, after which the social hierarchies are restored. In *The String of Pearls* the ending of the carnival is expressed not only by the reuniting of Johanna and Mark Ingestrie, thus satisfying the domestic plot, but also by the narrative closure of the anthropophagic plot:

> The youths who visited Lovett's pie-shop, and there luxuriated upon those delicacies, are youths no longer. Indeed, the grave has closed over all but one, and he is very, very old, but even now, as he thinks of how he enjoyed the flavour of the 'veal,' he shudders, and has to take a drop of brandy.[63]

Not only do the villains meet their end, but even those unknowing perpetrators of cannibalism are claimed by death, as they have no place outside of the carnivalesque feast. At the same time, the story resists this neat closure, not only by this single old man haunted by memories, but more notably by Ingestrie himself,

---

[61] Jacky Bratton, 'Romantic Melodrama', in *The Cambridge Companion to British Theatre, 1730-1830*, ed. by Jane Moody and Daniel O'Quinn (Cambridge : Cambridge University Press, 2007), pp. 115-127, p. 119.
[62] *The New Newgate Calendar*, ed. by Lord Birkett (London: The Folio Society, 1960), p. 9.
[63] Rymer, *Sweeney Todd*, p. 258.

who too consumed the pies during his captivity. His name, a deliberate pun on the word 'ingest', reminds the reader of the unintentional cannibalism even at the sentimental ending. Again, we can see how the text parodies its own aims: though hierarchies are restored, even in the last sentence we are reminded that our hero, despite living 'long and happily' with Johanna, has ingested human meat, by the explicit use of his last name.

In order to contextualise the cannibalism in *The String of Pearls*, it is worthwhile to consider the a few literary imaginations of anthropophagy around the 1840s. Cannibalist imagery in the nineteenth century was used in many different ways. A lot has been written on the theme of food in Dickens's texts, including the cannibalistic imagery in several of his books. In his classic study on Dickens, John Carry for example mentions how many heroes and heroines in Dickens are under threat of being eaten.[64] He also mentions the 'Captain Murderer' fairy-tale, which he argues has haunted Dickens's work.[65] In this story, 'Captain Murderer's mission was matrimony, and the gratification of a cannibal appetite with tender brides.'[66] He marries a string of women, teaching each one how to bake a pie crust. He then murders them and uses them as filling for the meat pie, which he then eats.[67] While the pie-baking might be an addition by Dickens (or, as the story goes, his nurse), it draws heavily from the folktale 'Mr. Fox', which features a similarly cannibalistic villain, though it contains no specific mention of pies.[68] While there is no evidence either for or against Rymer being aware

---

[64] John Carey, *The Violent Effigy: A Study of Dickens' Imagination* (London: Faber and Faber, 2008), p. 22.
[65] Carey, *Violent Effigy*, pp. 22-24.
[66] Charles Dickens, 'Nurse's Stories', in *The Uncommercial Traveller* (London: Chapman & Hall Ld., 1868), pp. 174-186, p. 177.
[67] From Dickens, 'Nurse's Stories', p. 179: 'And the bride looked up at the glass, just in time to see the Captain cutting her head off; and he chopped her in pieces, and peppered her, and salted her, and put her in the pie, and sent it to the baker's, and ate it all, and picked the bones.'
[68] Shuli Barzilai, 'The Bluebeard Barometer: Charles Dickens and Captain Murderer', *Victorian Literature and Culture*, 32:2 (2004), 505-524, p. 507.

of this particular story, this example illustrates a cannibalistic imagery that many people in 1840s England would at least be vaguely familiar with. Rymer's text itself is a product of this imagery, as we have seen above: it is based on the 'Rue Harpe' story, which itself was reprinted and retold several times. It was for example reprinted in the 1836 collection of tales called *Wonders of the World*,[69] as well as being retold in the 1890s in an issue of *Famous Crimes*.[70] A real-world story of possible cannibalism that often takes a central position in nineteenth-century attitudes to cannibalism is the 1845 Franklin expedition to the Arctic. In 1854 news reached England that Franklin's expedition, by then presumed dead, might have ended in cannibalism as the explorers' food had run out.[71] While the reactions to this alleged anthropophagy give an interesting insight into the meanings of cannibalism and its connection to ideas on race and national identity, it is of limited use for understanding *The String of Pearls*, since the book preceded that controversy by seven years.[72]

The elusiveness of the political dimension of *The String of Pearls* is emphasised when comparing it to a story with a similar cannibalistic imagination: Charles Dickens's *Oliver Twist*, as serialised from 1837 to 1839 in *Bentley's Miscellany*. In the second chapter, Oliver and the other boys in the workhouse have been starved so thoroughly by the economics of the board members, that:

---

[69] 'The Murderous Barber', p. 1-3.
[70] 'Tragedy in the Rue de la Harpe, Paris,' ed. by Harold Furness, *Famous Crimes*, 44 (1890[?]), pp. 115-118.
[71] Described in Alistair Robinson, 'Vagrant, Convict, Cannibal Chief: Abel Magwitch and the Culture of Cannibalism in *Great Expectations*', *Journal of Victorian Culture*, 22:4, (2017), 450-464, p. 455. Dickens responds to this crisis in Charles Dickens, 'The Lost Arctic Voyagers', *Household Words*, 2 December 1854, pp. 361-365.
[72] Dickens did not believe that cannibalism had taken place, and wrote the play *The Frozen Deep* (1856) with Wilkie Collins as a reaction to the controversy.

one boy, who was tall for his age, and hadn't been used to that sort of thing, (for his father had kept a small cook's shop,) hinted darkly to his companions, that unless he had another basin of gruel *per diem*, he was afraid he should some night eat the boy who slept next him, who happened to be a weakly youth of tender age. He had a wild, hungry eye, and they implicitly believed him.[73]

This pivotal scene foregrounds the motif of hunger that underpins the novel.[74] Hunger and appetite are dangerous forces, ominous and threatening. While the implication that a young boy (who Dickens reminds us, is 'tender') might be eaten by his fellow is comical, in the context of the circumstances in workhouses, this threat becomes real and serious. Throughout the chapter, Dickens mobilises a range of comic devices to drive home a point that is deadly serious. Eating, for Dickens, takes on a moral dimension. In *Oliver Twist*, lack of food gives rise to abominable behaviour; in *The Pickwick Papers*, which publication partially overlaps *Oliver Twist*'s serialisation, he focusses on gluttony and excess.[75] In the later *Great Expectations*, food is an important theme that connects ideas of class and nationalism.[76]

The String of Pearls too oscillates between deprivation and excess of food, but its moral and political consequences remain elusive. As seen above, the excess takes the shape of the carnivalesque feast. However, even within the carnival hierarchy is preserved, like in the case of the law clerks in Mrs Lovett's shop. Deprivation equally does not seem to carry any clear political message. In the first chapter, Todd outlines the parameters of Tobias's apprenticeship as follows:

---

[73] Charles Dickens, *Oliver Twist, or, The Parish Boy's Progress* (London: Penguin Books, 2003), p. 14.
[74] Gail Turley Houston, 'Broadsides at the Board: Collations of *Pickwick Papers* and *Oliver Twist*', *Studies in English Literature, 1500-1900*, 31:4 (1991), 735-755, p. 736.
[75] Houston, 'Broadsides', p. 736.
[76] Annette Cozzi, 'Men and Menus: Dickens and the Rise of the "Ordinary" English Gentleman,' in *The Discourses of Food in Nineteenth-Century British Fiction* (Basingstoke: Palgrave, 2010), pp. 39-69, p. 56.

> 'You will remember, Tobias Ragg, that you are now my apprentice, that you have of me had [sic] board, washing, and lodging, with the exception that you don't sleep here, that you take your meals at home, and that your mother, Mrs. Ragg, does your washing, which she may very well do, being a laundress in the Temple, and making no end of money: as for lodging, you lodge here, you know, very comfortably in the shop all day. Now, are you not a happy dog?'[77]

In the interaction between Todd and Tobias the wry comic tone is the dominant register. This tone is connected to Todd himself – whenever he dominates a scene, his cruelty and grotesqueness are expressed in a comic style. This particular quote revolves around the reversal of the expected terms of apprenticeship, combined with the mention of Mrs Ragg. Her money has no end, as there are always dirty clothes to be washed, yet the reader knows the opposite is true. A laundress will only just be able to make ends meet. If taken seriously, this scene shows how an apprentice is exploited by a violent master. In this case, Todd's appeal would disappear, as his character would approximate the real too closely. Todd is explicitly grotesque, moving beyond the human, opening up his actions as laughable, even when cruel or violent. When we are given a rare insight in Todd's motivations through the narrator, it is his greed that is brought to the forefront:

> There can be no doubt but that the love of money was the predominant feeling in Sweeney Todd's intellectual organisation, and that, but the amount it would bring him, or the amount it would deprive him of, he measured everything.[78]

---

[77] Rymer, *Sweeney Todd*, p. 3.
[78] Rymer, *Sweeney Todd*, p. 128.

In the case of Todd, greed is not a human vice or a flaw in character, but a shorthand for his monstrousness. Rymer continues:

> With such a man, then, no question of morality or ordinary feeling could arise, and there can be no doubt but that he would quite willingly have sacrificed the whole human race, if, by doing so, he could have achieved any of the objects of his ambition.[79]

Todd's monstrosity is not limited to his behaviour. His body is grotesque in its excessiveness. His mouth is described as 'immense',[80] and his hands and feet are of such size that 'he was, in his way, quite a natural curiosity'. Most remarkable, according to the narrator, is Todd's hair, which is so extraordinary that it can only be described through comparison to 'a thick-set hedge, in which a quantity of small wire had got entangled'. Even more strangely, 'Sweeney Todd kept all his combs in it – some said his scissors likewise'.[81] Todd's mouth is central to his grotesqueness. Like Bakhtin's grotesque body, Todd's mouth gapes, threatening to consume.[82] When Tobias, in the first chapter, suggests that he may be made into a pie by Mrs Lovett if he tells anyone about what goes on in Todd's shop (quoted above), 'Sweeney Todd rose from his seat; and opening his huge mouth, he looked at the boy for a minute or two in silence, as if he fully intended swallowing him, but had not quite made up his mind where to begin.'[83] According to Bakhtin, grotesque features of the body like the mouth are places where the inner and outer world are connected. In these places, the limits between the two are blurred. This can be connected to the positive and negative sides of the grotesque: its generative power and

---

[79] Rymer, *Sweeney Todd*, p. 128.
[80] Rymer, *Sweeney Todd*, p. 2. All subsequent descriptions of Todd are from this passage.
[81] In later stage adaptations Todd's hair is often distinctive but less idiosyncratic, such as Johnny Depp's black mane with a contrasting white stripe.
[82] Bakhtin, *Rabelais*, p. 317.
[83] Rymer, *Sweeney Todd*, p. 4.

rebirth, as well as its potential of death and annihilation.[84] Though Todd is always about to consume, however, it is important to note that he never does. Todd is one of the characters that abstains from Mrs Lovett's pies. Todd's enormous mouth has the *potential* to consume and therefore destroy – he is about to, threatening to, always on the verge of being the undoing of a character like Tobias, but never fully follows through on this threat. Not only does Todd's mouth threaten to eat, it also brings forth a strange laugh.

Though the mouth can also be aligned with the higher regions of the body such as the intellect through speech, laughter is connected to the lower regions such as the belly and the gut. Todd's laughter is harsh, surprising, and intrusive. It 'came in at all sorts of odd times when nobody else saw anything to laugh at at all, and which sometimes made people start again'. These 'cachinatory effusions' were 'hyena-like', and could be 'so short, so sudden' that 'people have been known to look up to the ceiling, and on the floor, and all around them, to know from whence it came, scarcely supposing it possible that it came from human lips.'[85] His laughter is unhuman, animalistic, and grotesque. It is what sets him apart. As Bergson has written, 'Our laughter is always the laughter of the group'.[86] Laughter is essentially social: laughter always constitutes a community of those who understand the joke. Todd's inhumanness is emphasised not just by the sound-quality of his laugh, but also by his exclusion from a laughing community. His laughter is one of madness, unintelligible to others. To borrow Bergson's metaphor, Todd's laughter is one without an echo within the narrative.

At the same time, Todd's laughter is comic because of the incongruity that is created within the narrative. The reader is invited to laugh at the farcical situation, where Todd has produced such

---

[84] Colin Trodd, Paul Barlow and David Amigoni, 'Introduction: Uncovering the grotesque in Victorian culture', in *Victorian Culture and the Idea of the Grotesque* ed. by Colin Trodd, Paul Barlow and David Amigoni (Aldershot: Ashgate, 1999), pp. 1-20, p. 1.
[85] Rymer, *Sweeney Todd*, p. 3.
[86] Bergson, *Laughter*, p. 6.

bizarre laughter that his customer cannot find its source, despite looking around. In a way, the reader becomes complicit in Todd's laughter. While he fails to produce an echo in the narrative, outside of the diegesis the reader's laugh mirrors his. Throughout the story the reader learns more about the source of Todd's unnatural laughter, and while other characters do not understand the significance of his outbursts, the reader does.[87] Of course, the repetition itself strengthens the joke. In this way, a paradoxical relationship is forged between the reader and Todd. Todd could have become a stand-in for every abusive master, vilified and laughed at within the narrative to temporary dispel his power, yet providing a strong social commentary at the same time. Many of Dickens's villainous figures – where ridiculed – function in this way. In the third chapter of *Oliver Twist*, for example, the chimneysweep Mr Gamfield, who applies for Oliver to become his apprentice, 'did happen to labour under the slight imputation of having bruised three or four boys to death.'[88] The humorous approach of the text towards Gamfield serves to illustrate the absurdness of the cruelties of the members of the board. Todd, on the other hand, is always too grotesque, too unbelievable to be standing in for any sort of stereotype. He is truly one of a kind, a genius of pure evil. Readers are encouraged to have an ambivalent relationship with Todd. When outlining one of Todd's many villainous schemes, the narrator for example states that 'We give Sweeney Todd great credit for the scheme he proposes.'[89] A similar principle comes into play in a long farcical sequence where Todd fights off a bunch of thieves. Not only is the comic heavily present in this scene, it is absurd and contains the innocence of a Punch and Judy show:

---

[87] When trying to sell the pearls, for example, this exchange follows: 'The pearls are worth £12,000, and I will let you have them for ten. What do you think of that for an offer?' 'What odd noise was that?' 'Oh, it was only I who laughed. [...]', Rymer, *Sweeney Todd*, p. 49.
[88] Dickens, *Oliver Twist*, p. 21.
[89] Rymer, *Sweeney Todd*, p. 123.

[...] fortunately for him there was a mop left in a pail of water, this [Todd] seized hold of, and, swinging it over his head, he brought it full on the head of the first man who came near him.
Dab it came, soft and wet, and splashed over some other who were close at hand.
It is astonishing what an effect a new weapon will sometimes have. There was not a man among them who would not have faced danger in more ways than one, that would not have rushed headlong upon deadly and destructive weapons, but who were quite awed when a heavy mop was dashed into their faces.[90]

Though the capture of Todd is the game that is shared between most of the characters, there is a strong impulse in this scene that Todd should not be stopped by *these* characters, a bunch of insignificant thieves. One wants him to survive in order to continue the main plot, and as a result, the reader likely find themselves rooting for Todd. In this scene the violence is harmless, in the way that Punch and Judy dolls might bash at each other without there being lasting consequences to these blows. Because of the lack of pain or true death, the violence becomes mocking.[91] This violence is not the intense, gory violence that Killeen describes in his study of penny bloods. Instead, the result of this battering without any emotional or physical repercussions is similar in the way it expresses a certain disconnect with subjectivity and reality. As one historian wrote about Punch, 'for whom nothing is serious, nothing worthy of respect. [...] Life is an empty joke.'[92] The jokes in *The String of Pearls* can be seen as expressing a similar emptiness. They provide no particular relief beyond the joke. Where Dickens's jokes point towards political reform and societal intervention, no such direction is given after the punchline in *The String of Pearls*.

---

[90] Rymer, *Sweeney Todd*, p. 60.
[91] Michael Byron, *Punch and Judy. Its origin and evolution* (Aberdeen: DaSilva Puppet Books, 1972), p. 24.
[92] Byron, *Punch and Judy*, p. 24.

As outlined in the introduction to this thesis, several theorists of laughter and the comic from Plato onwards have commented on how laughter implies power relations between those who laugh and those who are laughed at. Bergson saw laughter as a social corrective, 'a social gesture that singles out and represses'.[93] By this he means that the person who is ridiculed and laughed at, will cease this behaviour under the influence of that laughter. The Victorian middle class were uncomfortable with the perceived crudeness of the corrective laughter.[94] Dickens, therefore, wrote comedy in a gentler style to appeal to the middle-class sentiments, and 'thereby enlists constituencies of readership that might have been alienated by the older tastes in robust physical knockabout and comical sexual antics.'[95] As has become clear from the quotes from *The String of Pearls* above, the working-class readership had no such scruples. *The String of Pearls* pushes the boundaries of what can acceptably be seen as humorous, taking a taboo subject like cannibalism, and daring to laugh at it. Nor does it distance itself from Regency 'knockabout' humour as much as middle-class writers such as Dickens have done. Like other forms of fiction from the 1840s, penny bloods were preoccupied with having a claim to realism, ostensibly focussing on the 'hum-drummeries of reality', being 'consonant with scenes of real life'.[96] However, this close connection to reality took a different form within the penny blood than it did in more respectable fictions; *The String of Pearls* does not shy away from humorous violence. If laughter is seen as corrective, it is unclear whose behaviour is to be modified. In the above quotation, where Todd lays out the terms of Tobias's apprenticeship, the implied reader is inclined to laugh with Todd at Tobias. This mechanism becomes even clearer in the following quotation. A Mrs Wrangly enters the pie shop, looking for

---

[93] Bergson, *Laughter*, p. 87-88.
[94] Malcolm Andrews, *Dickensian Laughter. Essays on Dickens and Humour* (Oxford: Oxford University Press, 2013), p. 19.
[95] Andrews, *Dickensian Laughter*, p. 15.
[96] James, *Fiction*, p. 114.

her husband. Unbeknownst to her, he has been killed by Todd. Todd tells her:

> 'Then buy a pie, madam,' said Todd, as he held one close to her. 'Look up, Mrs. Wrangley, lift off the top crust, madam, and you may take my word for it you will soon see *something* of Mr. Wrangley.'[97]

The implied reader is complicit in Todd's laughter at poor Mrs Wrangley. Because of the dynamics of laughter, both the reader and Todd are powerful in this scene, while Mrs Wrangley is a double victim, being the target of both bereavement as well as cruel laughter at her expense. At the end of the narrative, Todd's laugh is cut short, as he is captured by the law and ultimately dies. Yet the reader's laughter never faces such punishment or abrupt closure. Through this reading of the morals of *The String of Pearls* one could argue that it is characterised by a lack of empathy and compassion, condoning horrifying treatment, perhaps as a way of externalizing real-world suffering. *The String of Pearls* is not fully typified by this description, however. Though the comic register – making a joke of abuse, violence, theft, misfortune, murder, and even cannibalism – pervades the text, it is always enclosed and juxtaposed by other genres.

THE MELODRAMATIC

One other such contrasting genre is melodrama. While the melodramatic nature of the text has been pointed out before – Mack for example calls the story 'a gruesomely compelling piece of gothic horror and melodrama'[98] – the elements that make up the melodramatic have not been studied in relation to the other tones in the text. After having studied Todd, it is useful in this context to scrutinize another main character in the text: Tobias, Todd's

---

[97] Rymer, *Sweeney Todd*, p. 244.
[98] Mack, *History*, p. xvii.

apprentice. Tobias is everything Todd is not. He is innocent, virtuous, and human; Tobias is similar to Oliver Twist in these respects. Though Tobias is not described prior to the passage quoted above ('You will remember...'), his last name 'Ragg' stands in as a descriptor, bringing to mind a poor young boy dressed in rags. This impression is strengthened by Todd's sarcastic rhetorical question, to which Tobias can only answer 'Yes, sir.' Not only is Tobias silenced and oppressed by Todd's cruelty and relative power, he is similarly silenced within the narrative. We are not given any information on Tobias that is not mitigated by Todd's overwhelming presence. While the comparison to a dog here is meant derogatorily, this echoes the 'Rue Harpe' narrative, summarised above, in which a dog is the barber's downfall. Similarly, in *The String of Pearls* a dog jumpstarts a sequence of events that eventually brings about Todd's capture. At the same time that Todd is asserting his power over Tobias, he simultaneously labels him as someone who he hates, and more importantly, fears.

In scenes where Tobias is the principal character, the tone shifts to tragic melodrama. It focusses on his physical appearance ('His cheeks were pale and sunken; his eyes had an unnatural brightness about them'[99]) as well as expressly directing the reader's sympathy:

> Oppressed with fears and all sorts of dreadful thoughts, panting to give utterance to what he knew and to what he suspected, and yet terrified into silence for his mother's sake, we cannot but view him as signally entitled to the sympathy of the reader, and as, in all respects, one sincerely to be pitied for the cruel circumstances in which he was placed.[100]

---

[99] Rymer, *Sweeney Todd*, p. 110.
[100] Rymer, *Sweeney Todd*, p. 110.

In these passages, no laughter is present or expected. These sections incorporate and rework eighteenth-century concepts of sentimentality, and like theatrical melodrama, provide a literary expression of externalization of psychological depth.[101] In melodrama, each emotional state is one of excess, and they are expressed both in words and gestures – in this case, by authorial description of Tobias's bodily state. Where Todd's cruelty requires the intermediary of comedy, Tobias's plight is emphasised. His servitude to Todd is inescapable, as Todd threatens to kill Tobias's mother unless he complies. Again, generalization into a political issue is resisted: Tobias is not kept in his place by social pressures or institutions, but by the real and immediate threat of the death of himself, his mother, or both, enacted by a monstrous villain.[102]

For Peter Brooks, the melodramatic mode – a broader category than the historic stage genre of melodrama – is a way of expressing the realism of living as a subject in a time where religion has stopped providing us with a comprehensive worldview. He calls this the 'post-sacred era'. In the 1995 preface to his seminal work from 1976, he describes melodrama as a form 'in which polarization and hyperdramatization of forces in conflict represent a need to locate and make evident, legible, and operative those large choices of ways of being which we hold to be of overwhelming importance even though we cannot derive them from any transcendental system of belief.'[103] In other words, the melodramatic is a way of addressing large concerns, such as the workings of good and evil, in such a way that 'things cease to be merely themselves, [...] they become the vehicles of metaphors whose tenor suggests another kind of reality.'[104] In its treatment of good and evil melodramatic texts can range from conservative to subversive, but the way in which the two

---

[101] Bratton, 'Romantic Melodrama', p. 119.
[102] Rymer, *Sweeney Todd*, p. 31: '(...) if you force me, by any conduct of your own, to mention this thing, you are your mother's executioner.'
[103] Peter Brooks, *The Melodramatic Imagination* (New Haven: Yale University Press, 1995), p. viii.
[104] Brooks, *Melodramatic*, p. 9.

polar opposites are interrogated in a form that uses expressive gestures, voicing of heightened emotional states, and character types that are recognisable across fictions.[105] In the scene above Tobias becomes such a melodramatic character, whose innocence and goodness are in danger of being extinguished by the evil impersonated by Todd.

Through this principle, the melodramatic scenes in *The String of Pearls* can be seen as the inverse of the humorous scenes. It is arguable whether or not melodrama is ever meant to be taken seriously, but it can be agreed on that the emotions it brings out in its audiences – when done effectively – are real. I would argue similarly for these scenes in *The String of Pearls*: they change the tone, opening space for compassion, which is incongruous with the humorous sections of the text. Bergson has written that laughter excludes all other emotions, in a way 'killing off' the potential of emotions before they can be felt.[106] This idea that the comic is antithetical to certain other emotions for example survives in Laqueur's assessment of public executions, when he writes that laughter and 'comic chaos' make public executions 'unsuitable for the imaginative realm of sublime terror, just reward, or tragedy' (quoted above). In its melodramatic mode, emotions of empathy and pathos are cultivated and allowed to flourish. However, these emotions are cut short, interrupted, by the prevalence of laughter throughout the story. This is not a problem with the text, or the result of incompetent writing. Taken together, these two modes can be seen as the negative and positive potential of the carnivalesque, both generative as well as destructive. While the negative side of the carnivalesque is concerned with death and destruction, its generative potential lies in the symbolism of rebirth. While laughter is the harbinger of the death of previous emotions, it simultaneously promises release. Nor can laughter be sustained indefinitely – within itself it already always holds its subsequent ending.

---

[105] Brooks, *Melodramatic*, p. 4.
[106] Bergson writes: 'Indifference is its natural environment, for laughter has no greater foe than emotion.' Bergson, *Laughter*, p. 4.

What does this mean for an interpretation of *The String of Pearls* as a whole? Firstly, it explains the centrality of Todd's character. The villainy of Todd, which, as argued above is cloaked in humour, pervades all aspects of the text. Only distance from this emotionally numbing humorous effect can promote other emotional modes, which is why the text constantly oscillates between character viewpoints. Unlike the mono-emotional tone of a Punch and Judy show, where all aspects of life are turned into a joke, from the law to the institution of marriage, *The String of Pearls* presents lives revolving around experiencing misery (like Ingestrie and Tobias) and the subsequent emotional release in the shape of laughter. Within the narrative world of penny fiction, both of these are inevitable, and comprise two sides of the same coin. Moreover, its incorporation of parody and melodrama reflects on the specific cultural moment of the short period in which the penny blood was popular. Like in melodrama and the Gothic, the penny blood is fascinated by personified evil, but where these are figures that inspire terror in those fictions, the penny blood villain is rarely terrifying. Todd is a grotesque figure, and his features have the potential both to terrify as well as to induce laughter. It is the second mode that dominates, as even the other characters within the narrative – who do have reason to fear him – are rarely frightened by Todd's physical presence in itself. As argued above, Todd's grotesqueness allows readers to interpret his actions as comic, despite their apparent cruelty.

I would therefore go against Killeen's assertion that within the penny blood all bodies are threatened with annihilation, and that the destruction of bodies reflects on a collective loss of subjectivity. While there is a strong argument for looking at bodies proper within the penny blood, the penny blood as a genre has a more complex relationship to violence, destruction, and the evil that perpetuates it. Of the extended cast of main characters within *The String of Pearls*, only one is actually killed by Todd in the first chapter. Due to narrative conventions, main characters like Tobias and Ingestrie might be tormented by the villains Todd and Mrs Lovett, but they will overcome this hardship and emerge victorious – and will often manage this with minimal violence. So while violence is rarely rewarded in a moral sense within the narrative, it is the paradoxical nature of the penny blood that is fascinated with evil that has caused moral outrage at the time of writing. Yet evil cannot be understood: it is impossible to empathise with Todd or Mrs Lovett. Not only are their actions perpetually cloaked in laughter, negating further emotions and empathy, they are not given the opportunity of voicing their inner psychological world in the melodramatic mode, like Johanna, Ingestrie, and Tobias are.

Romance and Domestic Romance

In the previous sections I discussed two modes of *The String of Pearls*: the comic and the melodramatic. The subject of this section is the third mode, the romantic mode. In this section I will discuss the history and significance of the genre signifier 'romance' within *The String of Pearls*, as well as showing how romance works together with the comic elements as well as the melodramatic. As outlined in the introduction, the original periodical run was subtitled 'A Romance'. In the extended and bundled collection, published in 1850, the title page shows the title *The String of Pearls; or, The Barber of Fleet Street*, accompanied by the subtitle 'A Domestic Romance'; at the start of the first chapter, however, the story is again named 'A Romance of Peculiar Interest'.[107] By its repetition it is apparent that the label 'romance' was important to communicate a certain genericity to the serial's audience. Its different iterations, however, also indicate a slippage of terms. What meaning does the word romance carry within the context of the penny blood? What is the difference between a domestic romance and a romance, or are they interchangeable terms?[108]

---

[107] James Malcolm Rymer, *The String of Pearls; or, The Barber of Fleet Street. A Domestic Romance* (London: E. Lloyd, 1850). Compare the title page and p. 1.
[108] The word 'romance', unfortunately, contains many different meanings in the English language, and to avoid confusion of terms, it is important to briefly define in what way it is used in the following section. When referring

In his survey of penny fiction, *Fiction for the Working Man*, historian Louis James follows contemporary custom in calling the stories he studies 'domestic romances'. He argues that 'the conventions of domestic romance lie within the rise of the novel in the mid-eighteenth century.'[109] In the chapter he dedicates to the 'domestic story' of the domestic romance, he writes:

> The 'domestic story' lies at the heart of almost all the penny-issue fiction published during the 1840s. Having said this, it is very hard to define what a 'domestic story' is. [...] It does not mean a tale of home life, as we would expect today. The term denotes not so much a particular subject, as an approach to the subject.[110]

What this approach is, and what subjects are suitable for the domestic romance, never becomes fully clear in his chapter. Nor does he reflect on the triple meaning of the word 'domestic': it can refer to something concerning the nation; it can refer to the home or the family; or, it can refer to domestics, servants paid to maintain a house. In the quotation above, James apparently interprets domestic in the second meaning. He discusses how the romantic love of the heroine becomes less idealistic than in chivalric romance, under pressures of the working-class readers in cosmopolitan cities seeking stories that were closer to their experiences. Yet at the same time, James adds that despite these claims of difference, 'if the romantic theme is revalued, the conventions within which it is set remain the same.'[111] A question that follows from this statement is of course, what are these romantic conventions? One can also make

---

to desire or developing love between persons, this thesis uses the term 'romantic love'. Whenever 'romance' is used, this refers to a domain of fictional works that share certain characteristics. Alternatively, this thesis also uses 'romantic mode' to refer to these common elements.
[109] James, *Fiction*, p. 116.
[110] James, *Fiction*, p. 114.
[111] James, *Fiction*, p. 116.

a case for the first meaning of the word 'domestic'; unlike the traditional romances and the 1780s Gothic romances, penny bloods are often set within Britain – *The String of Pearls*, with its pseudo-contemporary London setting, being one of them.[112] Finally, penny papers were notoriously read by the working classes, who might be domestic servants.[113] Whichever of these options was the intended sense, the word 'domestic' will have carried all three of its meanings for contemporaries.

The undeterminedness of the term romance itself complicates answering this question: as Barbara Fuchs has pointed out in *Romance* (2004), 'critics disagree about whether it is a genre or a mode, about its origins and history, even about what it encompasses.'[114] Because of the scope of this thesis, the 'romance' as a genre of narrative poems in twelfth-century France is less relevant than the thematic and formal characteristics of romance that have survived into the nineteenth century. Critic Northrop Frye has written extensively on romance, identifying the archetypes of what he calls the mythos of romance. As his research is grounded in the structuralist tradition, he seeks common elements across time, in order to answer the question of what romance *is*. Together with comedy, tragedy, and irony, he sees romance as one of the four 'mythoi' of storytelling.[115] Frye's work is less helpful as a template for deciding which texts are and are not romance than as a frame of reference, elucidating what elements are transgressed or modified by other texts like *The String of Pearls*. As we have seen, *The String of Pearls* contains several modes within itself, complicating Frye's

---

[112] David Punter, 'Scottish and Irish Gothic' in *The Cambridge Companion to Gothic Fiction*, ed. by Jerrold E. Hogle (Cambridge: Cambridge University Press, 2002), pp. 105-125. Punter uses the word domestic in this sense when referring to Gothic fictions set in the same country as its author.
[113] See Louis James, 'The Trouble with Betsy', in *The Victorian Periodical Press: Samplings and Soundings*, ed. by Joanne Shattock and Michael Wolff (Leicester: Leicester University Press, 1982), pp. 349-366.
[114] Barbara Fuchs, *Romance* (New York: Routledge, 2004), p. 1.
[115] Northrop Frye, *Anatomy of Criticism. Four essays* (Princeton: Princeton University Press, 2000 [1957]), p. 192.

theory of mythoi, which sorts texts in one or the other based on their essentialised structure. Fuchs argues, a consequence of Frye's broad reading of romance creates the opportunity to see it as more than a genre.[116] The archetypes he identifies are the narratological elements that, though not constituting romance in itself (as this category is always in flux through time, sometimes incorporating certain elements while changing others), provide a certain horizon of expectation. For Fuchs, when romance is seen as a strategy rather than a genre, 'the term describes a concatenation of both narratological elements and literary topoi, including idealization, the marvellous, narrative delay, wandering, and obscured identity, that, [...] both pose a quest and complicate it.'[117] This broad categorisation by Fuchs provides several topics that can be used to examine what constitutes a (domestic) romance in the context of the penny blood in general and *The String of Pearls* in particular.

The penny blood's engagement with the romance should be seen in the broader context of the critical discourse on the differences between novel and romance, and the contested category of 'realism' that both lay claim to in distinct ways. An early text weighing in on this debate is Clara Reeve's *The Progress of Romance* (1785), which aims 'to mark the distinguishing characters of the Romance and the Novel, to point out the boundaries of both.'[118] Near the end of the first volume, she concludes that 'The Romance is an heroic fable, which treats of fabulous persons and things. – The Novel is a picture of real life and manners, and of the times in which it is written.'[119] In advertisements for the penny stories sold by Edward Lloyd, the publisher of *The String of Pearls*, the categories bear little distinction. Lloyd's Weekly London Newspaper for example advertised as containing 'Tales, Romances, and Novels of intense interest,' listing several titles without discerning which belongs to any specific

---

[116] Fuchs, *Romance*, p. 5.
[117] Fuchs, *Romance*, p. 9.
[118] Clara Reeve, *The Progress of Romance*, Vol. I (Colchester: W. Keymer, 1785), p. vi.
[119] Reeve, *Progress*, I, p. 111.

category.[120] Despite attempts to separate the two, lack of differentiation between the novel and romance can be found in critical literature into the 1850s, like in the *History of English Literature* (1853) by William Spalding.[121] The discussion flared up again in the 1880s with commentaries defending romance against the realist novel.[122] As Margaret Doody argues, the critical discourse surrounding the romance and the novel is not without moral stakes, and ultimately the novel came to stand for a progression towards realism in English literature.[123]

Whether a story was seen as a 'novel' or a 'romance' was influenced by whether the work was valued by its critics.[124] It is this cultural work of categorising and determining origins of different strands within fiction that Ian Duncan describes when he writes about the romance revival: 'the major aesthetic enterprise of a broad, mixed, contentious cultural movement between 1750 and 1830 culminating in what has been called "the invention of tradition".'[125] The romance as a long-standing tradition, out of which the novel grew as a more rational form of fiction, is a cultural construction that was fully embedded in British society by the end of the nineteenth century. Late-eighteenth-century commentators, like Clara Reeve, who states that 'Romances are of universal growth, and not confined

---

[120] *Lloyd's Weekly London Newspaper*, 17 May 1846, p. 11.
[121] Andrew Sanders, 'Victorian Romance: Romance and Mystery' in *A Companion to Romance from Classical to Contemporary*, ed. by Corinne Saunders (Oxford: Blackwell, 2004), pp. 375-388, 377.
[122] Anna Vaninskaya, 'The Late-Victorian Romance Revival: A Generic Excursus', *English Literature in Transition, 1880-1920*, 51:1 (2008), 57-79, p. 64.
[123] In Fuchs, *Romance*, p. 9: 'Margaret Doody argues that critics working in the Anglo-American academy essential invented the distinction between novel and romance in order to imagine an English origin for what was a much older form. In this schema, she argues, literary theory adopts as its gold standard the notion of progress towards realism.'
[124] Fuchs, *Romance*, p. 104.
[125] Ian Duncan, *Modern Romance and Transformations of the Novel. The Gothic, Scott, and Dickens* (Cambridge: Cambridge University Press, 1992), p. 4.

to any particular period or countries', lay the groundwork for this myth.[126] At the height of the penny blood in the 1840s, however, the debate surrounding the two terms had not yet been resolved in the favour of the novel, and romance, especially in the shape of the novels by Sir Walter Scott, still held some critical regard.

Because of the contested nature of romance, it makes sense how its proponents defended the domestic romance by drawing on claims of realism. Louis James quotes the assessment of George Dibdin Pitt, who wrote penny bloods and was the first to adapt *The String of Pearls* for the theatre, of how penny bloods are 'consonant with scenes of real life'; another contemporary commentator states that the domestic romance is occupied with the 'hum-drummeries of reality'.[127] Taking stock of the plot of a story like *The String of Pearls*, it is clear that these commentaries do not mean to claim that a villainous plot rendering citizens into meat pies can be found in the 'hum-drummeries' of daily life. What these claims refer back to is the history of the romance, and its roots in high culture and an idealistic portrayal of the upper layers of society. Advertisements of domestic romances illustrate this. Although Lloyd's advertisements contain both the terms novel and romance, in advertising individual stories, they usually default to the subheading 'New Romance'. The term domestic romance is reserved for the accompanying text. For example, an 1846 advertisement, about six months before the start of *The String of Pearls*' run, reads:

> E. Lloyd has great pleasure in announcing to his patrons and the public that he has succeeded at an enormous expense, in purchasing the copyright of a New Domestic Romance, […] entitled AMY; On Love and Madness. Which, for exciting incidents, development of plot, and strikingly-drawn characters, far exceeds any romance hitherto published in this or any other country.[128]

---

[126] Reeve, *Progress*, I, p. xv-xvi.
[127] James, *Fiction*, p. 114.
[128] *Lloyd's Weekly London Newspaper*, 17 May 1846, p. 11.

The appeal of the (domestic) romance was not its limitation to a domestic setting, like a novel of manners, but how the characterisation and use of language closely approximated 'real life' for its readers. Rather than using the 'lofty and elevated language' Clara Reeve ascribes to the romance, the realism of the domestic romances of Edward Lloyd can be found in more contemporary use of language and incorporation of characters who are not of aristocratic birth. Whether or not the actions of characters in penny bloods are actually more realistic – however this may be defined – is less important than the fact that they were perceived to be so. Comparatively, plots were praised for being well-developed, aiming to please the reader by promising excitement rather than education.

The desire to create a new romance, combining a more contemporary sentiment of its characters with a familiar structure, echoes the development of the Gothic romance several decades earlier. In the second preface of *The Castle of Otranto* in 1765, the text that is generally seen by scholars as the starting point of the Gothic romance due to its self-proclaimed status to be such, Walpole writes that 'it was an attempt to blend the two kinds of romance, the ancient and the modern.'[129] He identifies ancient romance as 'all imagination and improbability', while modern romance followed nature too closely, limiting imagination. The improbability of ancient romances, according to Walpole, is mainly caused by their characterisation: 'The actions, sentiments, conversations, of the heroes and heroines of ancient days were as unnatural as the machines employed to put them in motion.' In combining the two, he writes:

> Desirous of leaving the powers of fancy at liberty to expatiate through the boundless realms of invention, and thence of creating more interesting situations, he wished to

[129] Horace Walpole, *The Castle of Otranto and Hieroglyphic Tales*, ed. by Robert L. Mack (London: Everyman, 1993), p. 7. Subsequent quotes are from the same page.

conduct the mortal agents in his drama according to the rules of probability; in short, to make them think, speak and act, as it might be supposed mere men and women would do in extraordinary positions.[130]

It bears remarking that throughout the second half of the eighteenth century, under influence of an increasing middle-class readership, fiction had been moving towards settings of a contemporarily recognisable world, rather than the Elizabethan romantic convention of an idealised and remote setting.[131] For the contemporary reader, therefore, it was mainly the romantic elements of the story – an aristocratic villain, problems of heritage, and supernatural events – that would stand out to its audience.[132] Walpole's self-aware typology, as Deborah Russell argues, inspires subsequent authors to create narratives that combine the marvellous and realism in varying ways.[133] Note how in this quotation Walpole touches on how using the marvellous element of what he calls the ancient romance opens up 'more interesting situations', a concern that lies at the heart of the serialised penny romance, and echoes Lloyd's advertisement proclaiming 'exciting incidents'. The domestic romance repeats the sentiment that became a key moment in the history of the Gothic romance, which enjoyed its heydays between roughly 1760 and 1820 – although the interpretation of penny writers in the 1840s results in a different narrative than their predecessors'.

Claims of realism in the romance genre are entangled with the concept of 'history'. In the discussion above I touched on how Reeve sees romance as a historical genre: a genre of texts that can be found

---

[130] Walpole, *Otranto*, pp. 7-8.
[131] David Punter, *The Literature of Terror. A History of Gothic Fictions from 1765 to the present* (Harlow: Longman, 1996), p. 21.
[132] Punter, *Terror*, p. 44.
[133] Deborah Russel, 'Gothic Romance' in: *Romantic Gothic*, ed. by Angela Wright and Dale Townshend (Edinburgh: Edinburgh University Press, 2016), pp. 55-72, p. 56.

across cultures and times. A common conception of romance in the second half of the eighteenth century was based on the idea that romance was a genre of 'barbaric' origin. In his *Letters on Chivalry and Romance* (1762) Richard Hurd writes that romances 'had their origin in the barbarous ages.'[134] Reeve, similarly, grounds romance in 'rude and barbarous ages' where they 'resided in the breath of oral tradition.'[135] Ian Duncan has aptly remarked that every construction of romance is one of romance revival: 'an active cultural work of the discovery and invention of ancestral forms'.[136] Walpole's second preface shows this rediscovering and reshaping in progress. In order for him to claim a new form of romance, he first needs to typify an 'ancient', historical version. In addition to this cultural work, romance plays with temporality by using historical settings. In 'Of History and Romance' (1797), William Godwin considers the narratological possibilities of romance in describing history. He argues that only by 'an exchange of real sentiments, or an investigation of subtle peculiarities' can lead to understanding of history, rather than dry recounting of dates of events.[137]

> The writer collects his materials from all sources, experience, report, and the records of human affairs; then generalises them; and finally selects [those elements] which he judges most calculated to impress the hear [hearts?] and improve the faculties of his reader.[138]

Like Reeve, Godwin sees the historical setting of a romance as an opportunity for the reader to learn about history, aided by the sensibility and the personal genius of the author – as long as they

---

[134] Richard Hurd, *Letters on Chivalry and Romance* (London: A. Millar, 1762), p. 2.
[135] Reeve, *Progress*, I, p. iii.
[136] Duncan, *Modern Romance*, p. 7.
[137] William Godwin, 'Of History and Romance' (1797), <http://www.english.upenn.edu/~mgamer/Etexts/Godwin.history.html> [accessed 26 September 2022].
[138] Godwin, 'Of History and Romance'.

are 'under proper restrictions and regulations they will afford much useful instruction, as well as rational and elegant amusement.'[139] Detractors of romance, on the other hand, object to these stories on moral grounds, and turn the historical argument around. James Beattie, in his essay 'On Fable and Romance', points out the dangers of reading romance, which not only are overall 'unskillfully written', they 'tend to corrupt the heart' and 'stimulate the passions'. He continues that 'a habit of reading them breeds a dislike to history, and all the substantial parts of knowledge; withdraws the attention from nature, and truth; and fills the mind with extravagant thoughts, and too often with criminal propensities.'[140] These examples illustrate the opposite ends of an ongoing debate throughout the mid-eighteenth century up to the end of the eighteenth century. The debate was less about romance specifically, than it was about the low status of fiction during this period.[141]

So how does history figure in romances themselves? Many influential Gothic novels of the 1790s, the decade that saw the height of Gothic novel publishing, are set in some vague distant past outside of Britain; examples include Ann Radcliffe's *Mysteries of Udolpho* (1794) and Matthew Lewis's *The Monk* (1796). As Gothic scholar Fred Botting argues, the historical setting is oppositional to the (perceived) rational present. He writes that 'romance, imagined in the darkness of history, encourages and assuages threats to propriety, domesticity and social duty.'[142] The Gothic novel shows a fascination with feudalist times, exhibiting both a curiosity as well as fear. The blurring of boundaries, including those of time, marks these texts; curses sustain throughout generations, the past haunts characters, all the while present and contemporary worries and

---

[139] Reeve, *Progress*, I, p. xv.
[140] James Beattie, 'On Fable and Romance' in *Dissertations Moral and Critical* (London: W. Strahan & T. Cadell, 1783), pp. 505-574, p. 573-4.
[141] Robert Miles, *Ann Radcliffe. The Great Enchantress* (Manchester: Manchester University Press, 1995), p. 35.
[142] Fred Botting, *Gothic* (London: Routledge, 2014), p. 3.

anxieties cross into the texts.[143] In the Gothic romances at the end of the eighteenth century, history is the stage of terror, a temporality in which the marvellous is connected to superstition and terrifying. The Gothic thrives on a paradoxical relationship to history; David Punter writes that Gothic history 'presents its own distortions and exaggerations while simultaneously playing a part in claiming to expose the distortions of history imposed by a generally accepted ideology or a falsely unproblematic narrative of the past.'[144] In the early nineteenth century, the historical romance is reshaped by Scott. Scott is influenced by the Gothic novel, using gothic settings, but tones down the terror, and the marvellous returns. According to Botting, in Scott:

> The romance tradition is used with a degree of ironic detachment: the past and its gothic trappings provide the background for romanticised [...] adventures that are often used self-consciously as signs of youthful enchantment and folly. [...] Romances thus provide a way of modifying the eighteenth-century novel of manners and morals by flavouring it with the charms of adventure and superstition that are kept at a distance from the bourgeois values of professionalism, industry and legality in the present.

He concludes this section by claiming that Scott 'tames the excesses of gothic romances by assimilating it within acceptable literary bounds.'[145] As Punter interprets it, Scott is interested in the mythologies of the past, rather than projecting new ones onto the past – and by explaining the motivations of his characters, his work does not contain the blurring and distorting of perspective characteristic of the 1790s Gothic.[146] In an essay by Scott written in

---

[143] As Botting writes, 'Eighteenth-century values were never far from the surface in these tales of other times.' Botting, *Gothic*, p. 58.
[144] Punter, Scottish and Irish Gothic, p. 109.
[145] Botting, *Gothic*, p. 92.
[146] Punter, *Terror*, p. 141, p. 143.

the 1820s, he weighed in on this debate on romance and the novel in a piece on romance for the Encyclopedia Britannica. To Scott, romance is not limited to tales of chivalry, war, and the middle ages; the essence of romance is that its interest 'turns upon marvellous and uncommon incidents.' Novels, on the other hand, he defines as not-romance, writing that they are 'a fictitious narrative, differing from the Romance, because the events are accommodated to the ordinary train of human events, and the modern state of society.'[147] Although Scott was highly influential and changed the common perception of what constituted a 'romance', broadly speaking the popular literature of the 1830s and 1840s sees the return of certain Gothic elements while acknowledging a debt to Scott's writing.[148]

Unlike the majority of Scott's historical romances,[149] *The String of Pearls* is set in a recent past – 1785. Its readers would recognise the London which Rymer describes; he explicitly refers to London landmarks. There is little to no historical detail in *The String of Pearls*, and therefore its historicity is a reference to the mythical element of romance: its claims on realism through the retelling of 'real history' in a narrative form. This is not necessarily true for all penny bloods; their settings vary wildly, from historical scenes set in Britain, to contemporary stories in exotic locations. The preface to the 1850 collected and extended edition makes further claims of realism. It assures us that Sweeney Todd existed, and that 'the record of his crimes is still to be found in the chronicles of criminality of this country.'[150] This statement is plausibly vague, giving the illusion of a real-world reference while at the same time giving such little information (what chronicles?) as to being impossibly checked. It plays into the sensationalism of the penny press, and is partially self-referential: Lloyd published Newgate calendars, listing criminals and their crimes. It offers a tantalising promise to the reader – perhaps Todd's exploits can be found in one of the Newgate

---

[147] Walter Scott, *The Prose Works of Sir Walter Scott, Bart*, Vol. IV (Edinburgh: Robert Cadell, 1834), p. 129.
[148] Punter, *Terror*, p. 140.
[149] An exception is *The Antiquary* (1816), which is set in the 1790s.
[150] Rymer, *String of Pearls* (1850), preface.

calendars? The preface also encourages readers to compare familiar landmarks to the story:

> The house in Fleet Street, which was the scene of Todd's crimes, is no more. A fire, which destroyed some half-dozen buildings on that side of the way, involved Todd's in destruction; but the secret passage, although, no doubt, partially blocked up with the re-building of St. Dunstan's Church, connecting the vaults of that edifice with the cellars of what was Todd's house in Fleet Street, still remains.[151]

Again, there is an undercurrent of irony in this statement: Fleet Street also happens to be the address of Lloyd's publishing business. Every claim to realism doubles back upon the fictional empire built by Lloyd. I would argue that this claim to realism is essentially comic, and that it ties in with the comic style of the story, described above. It requires a discrepancy between what is written, and a knowingness between the writer and their readership. Over time, this state of 'being in on the joke' seems to have faded. In 1939, for example, a column appeared in *The Times*, writing that 'many people believe that there once lived in Fleet Street a demon barber called Sweeney Todd. So firmly is this opinion held, that his career of crime is taken for granted.'[152] Similarly, a 2007 book promises to uncover the 'real', historical Todd.[153] The programme notes of a 2004 production of Sondheim's *Sweeney Todd* even invents a biography of Todd's life, including a tragic back story of poverty and a mysterious disappearance of his parents when he was twelve.[154]

The String of Pearls contains strong traces of a romance narrative in its construction, especially in how the plot is driven forward by the eponymous string of pearls. This object is the catalyst for

---

[151] Rymer, *String of Pearls* (1850), preface.
[152] Mack, *History*, p. 76.
[153] Peter Haining, *Sweeney Todd: The Real Story of the Demon Barber of Fleet Street* (London: Anova Books, 2007).
[154] Mack, *History*, p. 79.

important interactions between the main characters, including the death of Ingestrie's confidant by the hands of Todd in the first chapter. The failed delivery of the pearls to Johanna is the starting point for the pursuit of Todd by Johanna, aided by Colonel Jeffery and the magistrate. The narrative is shaped by a quest: 'a sequence of minor ventures leading up to a major or climacteric adventure, usually announced from the beginning, the completion of which rounds off the story.'[155] Within a traditional romance, the quest is both a goal within itself as well as essential to an emotional resolution – for example, in winning a certain object, a knight might be rewarded with a noblewoman's heart. In *The String of Pearls*, these two aspects of the quest are split between the pearls and a hidden, second quest: the rescue of Ingestrie. The pearls are first introduced in a monologue by Lieutenant Thornhill, as he contemplates the bells of St. Dunstan's church:

> I have got to see the ladies, although it's on a very melancholy errand, for I have got to tell them that poor Mark Ingestrie is no more [...] He is dead and gone, poor fellow, and the salt water washes over as brave a heart as ever beat. His sweetheart, Johanna, though, shall have the string of pearls for all that; and if she cannot be Mark Ingestrie's wife in this world, she shall be rich and happy, poor young thing, while she stays in it.[156]

The string of pearls is thus imbued with significance: it rightfully belongs to Johanna, Ingestrie's lover, a token not only of his love, but it also replaces the economic stability which their marriage would have implied. *The String of Pearls* omits how Ingestrie obtains the pearls. It operates from the assumption that the appearance of wealth from the colonies needs no explanation, while occluding the

---

[155] Frye, *Anatomy*, p. 186-7.
[156] Rymer, *Sweeney Todd*, p. 4-5.

actual work and circumstances of its production.[157] When the story of Ingestrie seeking his fortune is told to Johanna by Colonel Jeffery, it foregrounds gold rather than pearls in the shape of 'a river which deposited an enormous quantity of gold dust in its progress to the ocean.'[158] In Rymer's vision of India, natural resources are present to be taken by whomever; yet the pearls might not be Indian after all, since Ingestrie's ship never reaches its destination before it sinks, and Ingestrie hands Thornhill the pearls for Johanna. Colonel Jeffery later tells her that 'where he got them, I have not the least idea, for they are of immense value.'[159]

The pearls signify domesticity – a happy house and hearth – which explains why they become obsolete when true domesticity is reached. In the final chapter, Ingestrie's identity is revealed to Johanna. Soon after, they are remarked to be married, thus fulfilling the emotional closure of the quest of romantic love, while the initially valuable object of the string of pearls loses its significance. The only mention of the pearls in the epilogue is in the last sentence:

> Johanna and Mark Ingestrie lived long and happily together, enjoying all the comforts of an independent existence; but they never forgot the strange and eventful circumstances connected with the String of Pearls.[160]

This quotation illustrates the importance of the pearls for the narrative in terms of giving rise to events, but its true value lies in enabling the reunion of Johanna and Mark, not any value imbued within the object. The retrieval of the pearls is therefore unnecessary and not described – they have served their purpose within the

---

[157] For wealth/treasure and late nineteenth-century imperial romances, see Laura Chrisman, *Rereading the Imperial Romance* (Oxford: Clarendon Press, 2000), especially pp. 29-32, 57-59.
[158] Rymer, *Sweeney Todd*, p. 41.
[159] Rymer, *Sweeney Todd*, p. 45.
[160] Rymer, *Sweeney Todd*, p. 259.

narrative. As Johanna tells Colonel Jeffery, she 'cares very little for them [...] so little, that it might be said to amount to nothing.'[161]

A quest structure presupposes a hero, for it is the hero that must achieve a certain goal. In *The String of Pearls*, the archetypical role of the hero is fractured and carried by several characters. The quest is pursued by Johanna, Colonel Jeffery, and the magistrate. Tobias, though close to Todd, is largely powerless and unaware of the quest; this is consistent with the assessment in the above section on the melodramatic that he is the prime figure of pathos and victimhood. King states that Mark Ingestrie takes on the role of the captured Gothic heroine, while Johanna is an active character and therefore corresponds to the hero, effectively creating a gender reversal of the trope.[162] Like the Gothic heroine, Ingestrie is 'moved, threatened, discarded, and lost.'[163] He is shipwrecked, survives, and upon his return to England is under the false assumption that Johanna is no longer faithful to him. At this point he takes employment in Mrs Lovett's pie factory, a Gothic space where he is imprisoned and lost to his family and friends. In a second reversal of the Gothic trope of an imprisoned heroine, it is not a patriarch who threatens and confines Ingestrie within, but Mrs Lovett. As seen in the discussion of Marxist interpretations above, there is a strong argument for reading Ingestrie's imprisonment concurrently with threats to conditions of labour workers. At the same time, however, *The String of Pearls* parodies Gothic tropes, engaging both with the history of the romance in its Gothic configuration, as well as reconciling its humorous tone with these tropes. Considering the scope and nuances of the fractured quest in *The String of Pearls*, Ingestrie's imprisonment does not neatly fit this reversal, as this statement overlooks the resolution to Ingestrie's imprisonment. By placing himself underneath a sheet of meat pies on the lift that carries the pies from the factory into the shopping space, Ingestrie effectively

---

[161] Rymer, *Sweeney Todd*, p. 62.
[162] King, 'Literature of the Kitchen', p. 44.
[163] Kate Ferguson Ellis, 'Can You Forgive Her? The Gothic Heroine and Her Critics', in *A New Companion to the Gothic* ed. by David Punter (Chichester: Wiley-Blackwell, 2012), pp. 457-468, p. 459.

frees himself. His escape requires no facilitation by a Gothic hero – Johanna and her champions merely show up to Mrs Lovett's shop once he has already freed himself, to complete the second objective of the quest after already having apprehended Todd (the initial quest). *The String of Pearls* is therefore not quite as radical as King suggests; Johanna, though an active character, is at the same time surrounded by men who take on the brunt of the questing. The story contains a fractured quest, and its associated archetypical roles are spread over multiple characters as a result.

The quest structure illustrates how the structure of the story encodes Todd's downfall. His role is limited to that of antagonist, who is pitted against the hero(es) in a dialectical structure.[164] Although Todd is an active, important character that enjoys much time on-page, he has no quest of his own. His goals are unclear; there is the sense that he is hoarding wealth until some point in the future for his 'retirement'. This goal is not particularly convincing in light of Todd's greed; it seems unlikely that any amount of wealth would satisfy him. Todd's 'retirement' is less an abstaining from crime than it is another hurdle for the heroes, as he is threatening to slip away. After selling a fake string of pearls, Todd states:

> He has lost his pearls, and lost his money. Ha, ha, ha! That is glorious; I will shut up shop sooner than I intended by far, and be off to the continent. Yes, my next sale of the string of pearls shall be in Holland.[165]

Todd's potential escape increases the tension, as at this point of the story Johanna has disguised herself as a boy and acts as Todd's assistant – the resolution of the quest is within reach, if only Todd does not evade capture. His role is to frustrate and postpone the main quest – which he succeeds in even more spectacularly in the extended version of *The String of Pearls*, where he eludes capture for over 750 pages. Mrs Lovett, the other main villain of the story, acts

---

[164] Frye, *Anatomy*, p. 187; Fuchs, *Romance*, p. 6.
[165] Rymer, *Sweeney Todd*, p. 236.

as an extension of Todd. When she is no longer useful to Todd, he decides that he 'must dispose' of her, as he 'can think of no other mode of silencing her'; to this end he has procured poison, which he 'held up between him and the light with a self-satisfied expression.'[166] Although Mrs Lovett's relationship with Todd seems symbiotic, as their collaboration is mutually beneficial, Mrs Lovett is ultimately subservient to Todd, the main antagonist. As Fredric Jameson writes of romance, 'the hero's enemies reduce themselves to so many emanations of the villain.'[167] This dynamic is even more obvious in the character of Mr Fogg, the owner of the asylum Todd sends Tobias to in order to get rid of him. Fogg is little more than an extension of Todd's power, following his orders to kill Tobias – prevented only in this goal by Tobias's escape from the asylum.

Part of the traditional culture of chivalry that Hurd describes as the basis of the traditional romance is the interaction between knights and aristocratic ladies, revolving on the concepts of gallantry and chastity, respectively.[168] Although later romances move away from the medieval setting, traces of the idealizations of the main characters, and appreciation of gallantry and chastity can still be found in the nineteenth-century romance. In *The String of Pearls* Johanna, despite being of relatively humble middle-class birth, is 'a creature of the rarest grace and beauty.'[169] In the second chapter, 'The Spectacle-Maker's Daughter', she is introduced by her innocence and chastity, which are signified by her age: 'eighteen, but she looked rather younger.' In nineteenth-century convention, the appearance of the heroine hints at her character.[170] The descriptions of heroines change throughout the mid-century,

---

[166] Rymer, *Sweeney Todd*, p. 236.
[167] Fredric Jameson, 'Magical Narratives: Romance as Genre', *New Literary History*, 7:1 (1975), 135-163, p. 147.
[168] Hurd, *Letters on Chivalry*, p. 17-18.
[169] Rymer, *Sweeney Todd*, p. 10. All subsequent descriptions of Johanna in this paragraph are from this page, unless otherwise specified.
[170] Jeanne Fahnestock, 'The Heroine of Irregular Features: Physiognomy and Conventions of Heroine Description', *Victorian Studies*, 24:3 (1981), 325-350, p. 325.

particularly between 1830 and 1860 from vague impressions to cataloguing specific facial features.[171] Rymer's description of Johanna is a combination of idealised womanhood ('there was nothing of the commanding or the severe style of beauty about her, but the expression of her face was all grace and sweetness') and some more concrete descriptions of hair of 'glossy blackness' and eyes 'of a deep and heavenly blue.' These splashes of colour in an otherwise vague description are reminiscent of the descriptions of Scott's heroines, whose heroines sport 'a profusion of hair of play gold' or 'jetty ringlets.'[172] Johanna stays true to Ingestrie, walking away from the awkward declaration of love of a shop boy.[173] Later she is described as being 'qualified, to love once, but only once.'[174] In later chapters, various characters respond to Johanna's chastity with gallantry; the most notable character in this regard is Colonel Jeffery, who aids Johanna in finding Ingestrie. Though chivalry indicates a 'good' character who will aid the quest rather than oppose it, in *The String of Pearls* chivalry no longer indicates the protagonist as it did in medieval romance. Ingestrie elicits sympathy in his helplessness, and exhibits few chivalrous values. Jeffery, though chivalrous, does not gain Johanna's hand in marriage and fades into the background by the end of the narrative.[175]

The quest is foreshadowed in Johanna's introduction by her emotional state, expressed with melodramatic flourish:

---

[171] Fahnestock, 'Heroine', p. 328.
[172] Rose Bradwardine and Flora MacIvor from *Waverly* respectively. Quoted in Fahnestock, 'Heroine', p. 327.
[173] Sam, who works in her father's store, declares: 'I means that I won't stand it; didn't I tell you, more than three weeks ago, as you was the object of my infections? Didn't I tell you that when aunt died I should come in for the soap and candle business, and make you my missus?' After which Johanna simply leaves the room 'for her heart was too full of grief and sad speculation'. Rymer, *Sweeney Todd*, p. 16.
[174] Rymer, *Sweeney Todd*, p. 33.
[175] It is possible to read the strong emotional relationships between Ingestrie and Thornhill, and Thornhill and Jeffery as queer, further complicating the romance structure of the story.

> There was a touch of sadness about her voice, which, perhaps, only tended to make it the more musical, although mournfully so, and which seemed to indicate that at the bottom of her heat there lay some grief which had not yet been spoken – some cherished aspiration of her pure soul, which looked hopeless as regard completion – some remembrance of a former joy, which had been turned to bitterness and grief: it was the cloud in the sunny sky – the shadow through which there still gleamed bright and beautiful sunshine, but which still proclaimed its presence.[176]

The melodramatic imbues the quest with emotion: that which saddens Johanna will be solved in the narrative, leading to her eventual happiness. It is telling that the final chapter does not detail Todd's capture (this being the penultimate chapter), but rather Johanna's reunion with Mark, thus metaphorically banishing the shadow from Johanna's emotional landscape. Melodrama is closely related to romance – Fredrick Jameson goes as far saying it could be considered a 'degraded form of romance'[177] – but I would argue against collapsing the two. While a characteristic of both is a preoccupation with a conflict between good and evil, its treatment of these themes takes different forms. Both of these expressions can be read in *The String of Pearls*. A romantic struggle between good and evil takes the form of the battle against Todd (Tobias considers Todd 'the arch enemy of all mankind'[178]). At the same time, the rescue of Ingestrie is a melodramatic struggle. One is concerned with the eradication of evil for its own sake, while the other is motivated by the personal. Of course, many combinations and expressions are possible concerning these conflicts, and *The String of Pearls* exemplifies how a text can contain both, recognisably separate while being interlaced within the plot structure. Perhaps, rather than saying *The String of Pearls* contains a fractured quest, it is more

---

[176] Rymer, *Sweeney Todd*, p. 10.
[177] Jameson, 'Magical Narratives', p. 140.
[178] Rymer, *Sweeney Todd*, p. 147.

accurate to say it contains both a romantic as well as a melodramatic quest, which occasionally overlap in the plot.

From this brief discussion of the romantic in *The String of Pearls*, we can posit that the penny blood both draws upon established meanings of romance, familiar to their audience, as well as adding to, or reworking these tropes, as signalled by the adjective 'domestic'. Usage of both the label 'romance' in its title as well as incorporation of the romantic mode within the penny blood is not marked by an extreme departure or antithesis, nor necessarily one of parody, but more by an engagement with and adaptation of romantic motifs inherited from older forms of fiction. The comic, in addition to its characteristics outlined above, fits within the structure of the romantic neatly as a quest-delaying device: while a reader might want to know more about the main characters' journey, instead they are presented with a section on a strange odour in St. Dunstan's church; Johanna is frustrated in her attempt to consider her lost lover in a melodramatic manner by a comic interlude driven by the drunk Reverend Mr Lupin.[179] Even at the sentimental ending of the story the comedy persists – the pun of Ingestrie's name now too envelops Johanna after their marriage. The comic elements are not a detraction, but a conscious strategy, working together with both the romantic and the melodramatic to construct the patchwork of tones within *The String of Pearls*.

CONCLUSION

This chapter has demonstrated that current readings of *The String of Pearls* focus on certain aspects of the story, not allowing for a full appraisal of the generic elements that constitute the text. While the text inherits the quest structure from romance, this is intertwined with melodramatic flair, providing a foil of heightened emotion against the transgressive humour of the cannibalist consumption of

---

[179] 'She seemed like one prepared for death; and she hoped that she would be able to glide, silently and unobserved, to her own little bed-chamber [...]', Rymer, *Sweeney Todd*, p. 63.

Mrs Lovett's pies. Within the carnivalesque atmosphere of Mrs Lovett's shop, which is foregrounded in the text through descriptions of its hedonistic pleasures, the power relationships remain ambiguous, resisting a straight-forward reading of the capitalist consumption of working-class bodies. The humour of *The String of Pearls*, which dares to laugh at cannibalism, at violence and murder, pushes against what was considered acceptable humour during the early Victorian period. This chapter shows that the violence that is identified as the core aspect of the penny blood is part of the carnivalesque pleasures of the text. At the same time, the transgressive potential of the laughter is limited by the melodrama that intersperses the story. The melodrama provides a neat return to domesticity at the conclusion of the story, signalling that the carnival has come to an end. Overall, *The String of Pearls* is a more complex text than current scholarship has allowed, containing contrasting and contradictory elements that create a dynamic story with a broad emotional register.

Chapter Two

Valentine Vaux by Thomas Peckett Prest

INTRODUCTION

One of the most prolific writers of penny bloods was Thomas Peckett Prest. Little is known about his life; while Dick Collins estimates his death at around 1849,[1] bibliographer Helen Smith attributes several works to him into the 1850s,[2] and states his death as June 1859.[3] Although attribution is frequently difficult, Prest is often identified by references to one of his early successful titles, *Ela, the Outcast* (1840). Smith estimates that Prest wrote, edited, or collaborated on almost a hundred titles for Edward Lloyd, the majority of them penny bloods.[4] Prest started his career with Lloyd by writing criminal biographies, inspired by Newgate style publications, such as *History of the Pirates of All Nations* (1836-7), and *Lives of the Most Notorious Highwaymen, Footpads, Etc.* (1836-7). Prest moved on to specialise in plagiarisms of popular fiction, including

---

[1] Collins, 'Introduction', p. xxxii.
[2] Smith, *New Light*, p. 16-18. Smith attributes works to Prest up to 1857.
[3] Smith, *New Light*, p. 5.
[4] His work also includes some song collections, as Prest was a composer in addition to an author. For more information about Prest as songwriter, see Marie Léger-St-Jean, 'Thomas Peckett Prest and the Denvils' in *Edward Lloyd and His World. Popular Fiction, Politics and the Press in Victorian Britain*, ed. by Sarah Louise Lill and Rohan McWilliam (New York: Routledge, 2019), pp. 114-131.

plagiarisms of Scott, William Herrison Ainsworth, and several Dickens plagiarisms like *The Sketch Book, by 'Bos'* (1836-7), *Nickelas Nickelbery* (1838), *The Penny Pickwick* (1839), and *The Life and Adventures of Oliver Twiss, the Workhouse Boy* (1839). He also plagiarised Henry Cockton's serial *The Life and Adventures of Valentine Vox, the Ventriloquist*, which Robert Tyas published in a monthly format by from 1839 to 1840. *The Adventures of Valentine Vaux*, as Prest's version was titled, was published in weekly instalments from 1839 to 1840 under the pseudonym 'Timothy Portwine.' Prest typically took the main characters and key events from the original, rewriting them for the tastes of the working-class readership of Lloyd's penny issues. Discussing a plagiarism of Dickens's *The Pickwick Papers*, Louis James characterises the kind of changes made in the retelling: 'The whole level of comedy is altered. [...] For comic restraint physical slapstick is substituted wherever possible.'[5] This statement and James's subsequent discussion values this substitution negatively; the underlying judgement being that farcical humour is of lesser quality than Dickens's. This thesis does not subscribe to this assumption, and instead focuses exactly on these instances of 'low' humour, arguing that these scenes are interesting in their own right. As James has argued, the study of these plagiarisms provides insight into how penny fiction differs from its middle-class relative, as the two can readily be compared.[6] By analysing the changes Prest made to Cockton's work – especially in tone and humour – this chapter shows how laughter functions in the penny blood. Specifically, it delineates what the essence is of humour, and how it contrasts with the humour of stories for a middle-class reading public.

The predominant theme of both *Valentine Vox* and *Valentine Vaux* is that of ventriloquism: a skill of projecting one's voice across space and emulating it to make it sound like other people or animals. In both stories the main character, Valentine, is highly proficient at

---

[5] James, *Fiction*, p. 57. James judges plagiarists for what he perceives as their 'false facetiousness', calling them 'cocky' (quotes in original) for 'they did not have Dickens's delicacy of touch.' (pp. 58-9)
[6] James, *Fiction*, p. 51.

ventriloquism, and plays tricks on those around him which lead to farcical situations and laughter. In order to analyse these humorous scenes, it is therefore important to contextualise ventriloquism and its fascination to the early Victorians. The first section of this chapter will therefore be dedicated to a short discussion of perceptions of ventriloquism in the first half of the nineteenth century. In the following, these insights are discussed in context of both *Valentines*, highlighting its use for comic value; this situation is contrasted with an earlier Gothic novel featuring a ventriloquist character, *Wieland: or, The Transformation* by Charles Brockden Brown (1798). Where ventriloquism is used for humorous purposes in the *Valentines*, the voices in *Wieland* are perceived as threatening and terrifying. Finally, the chapter focuses on the meaning of laughter in *Valentine Vaux*; it questions who laughs at what, and what this means for the penny blood as a genre.

VENTRILOQUISM AND HISTORY

The word ventriloquism is derived from the Latin *venter* and *loquor*, literally meaning speaking from the belly. In the book *I Can See Your Lips Moving* (1981), a history of the performance art, the American practitioner and author writes:

> ventriloquism is a vocal illusion. [...] The name is misleading, as ventriloquism does not require any physical abnormality. The ventriloquist does not speak from the stomach, except that he employs his stomach muscles in the same manner as an actor or singer does, to assist the diaphragm to give vocal and tonal strength to the voice.[7]

To confuse matters, this ventriloquist (born Jack Riley in 1939), took his stage name from Henry Cockton's story, and performs and

---

[7] Valentine Vox, *I Can See Your Lips Moving. The History and Art of Ventriloquism* (Kingswood: Kaye & Ward Ltd, 1981), p. 8.

publishes under the pseudonym Valentine Vox. Leigh Eric Schmidt evocatively describes ventriloquists as 'masters at animating the inanimate; [...] bearers of aural astonishment – of sounds uncertain, confounding, low, tremulous, intermittent, and bestial.'[8] Abstractly, conceptions of ventriloquism are essentially conceptions of voice and the space in which the voice is created and possibly heard. As Steven Connor argues in his cultural history of ventriloquism, *Dumbstruck* (2004), these are connected to 'different conceptions of the body's form, measure, and susceptibility, along with its dynamic articulations with its physical and social environments'[9] over time. In other words, the perception of voice, its limitations and powers, are historically and culturally contingent. 'Voice' is a word with a wide range of meanings; in literary studies it brings to mind the 'authorial voice', or 'marginalised voices' and social agency, or perhaps Bakhtin's multiplicity of voices in the concept of polyphony.[10] In another way, ventriloquism can also be used as a philosophical tool: 'ventriloquism, or more precisely, sets of ventriloqual relationships, can be utilised as a metaphor, perhaps a paradigm, for generating ideas and organizing phenomena of key philosophical interest, particularly in the area of aesthetics.'[11] David Goldblatt, in his essay collection *Art and Ventriloquism* (2006), interprets the works of several philosophers, including Foucault and Nietzsche, through the lens of ventriloquism. Keeping these complexities in mind, this section explores the history of ventriloquism up to the nineteenth century. As will become clear, ventriloquism in its many guises is fundamentally concerned with

---

[8] Leigh Eric Schmidt, 'From Demon Possession to Magic Show: Ventriloquism, Religion, and the Enlightenment', *Church History*, 67:2 (1998), 274-304, p. 294.
[9] Steven Connor, *Dumbstruck. A Cultural History of Ventriloquism* (Oxford: Oxford University Press, 2004), p. 12.
[10] The nineteenth-century ventriloquist William Edward Love called himself a polyphonist.
[11] David Goldblatt, *Art and Ventriloquism* (London: Routledge, 2006), p. ix.

the *displaced* voice, or perhaps more specifically, voice of uncertain origin.¹²

Before the eighteenth century, the hearing of voices that do not originate from an apparent speaker had religious or supernatural connotations, in addition to the secular meaning. Diviners in ancient Greece would simulate being possessed by spirits with ventriloquism, either producing wordless moans or more sophisticated pronouncements, dependent on the diviner's personal proficiency. An Athenian priest called Eurycles, living in the fifth century BCE, was particularly skilled – some believed him to house a spirit in his stomach, while others found his performances comical.¹³ Perhaps the most well-known (and oft-mythologised) historical example is that of the priestesses called Pythia at the shrines in Delphi, who 'possessed by the presence and power of the god Apollo, acting as his mouthpiece in a condition of trance or ecstasy,' presented his oracles either in riddles or verse from roughly 700 BCE to the third century.¹⁴ Although it is unlikely the oracles at Delphi actually performed ventriloquism in the sense of producing a voice seemingly coming from another place like the belly, the Delphic oracles became known for 'engastrimytic' prophecy in the first couple of centuries of the current era.¹⁵ In early Christianity, the belly-spirits became belly-demons; theological debates revolved around whether it was possible to summon spirits, the story of the witch of Endor being a particular point of

---

12 Helen Davies, *Gender and Ventriloquism in Victorian and Neo-Victorian Fiction. Passionate Puppets* (Basingstoke: Palgrave Macmillan, 2012), p. 7; Connor, *Dumbstruck*, p. 23.
13 Vox, *I Can See*, p. 17. Eurycles is subject of a play by Aristophanes in 422 BCE, in which he 'inferred that Eurycles' voice diffusion was so well-managed that it appeared to come from another source and that he himself, in the same manner, wrote words to put into the mouths of actors,' p. 18.
14 Connor, *Dumbstruck*, p. 47. As Connor argues, the Delphic oracle has been subjected to extensive mythologizing since late antiquity, and have proven tenacious enough to require refuting in contemporary scholarship.
15 Connor, *Dumbstruck*, p. 51.

contestation.[16] Reginald Scott's 1584 *The Discoverie of Witchcraft* argues against the interpretation that witches (including the witch of Endor[17]) could summon spirits. He writes that 'Pythonists' (referring to the oracles at Delphi) 'spoke hollowe; as in the bottome of their bellies, whereby they are aptlie in Latine called *Ventriloqui*.' For Scott, these belly-speakers were malicious deceivers, who 'take upon them[selves] to give oracles, to tell where things lost are become, and finallie to appeach others of mischeefs, which they themselves most commonlie have brought to passe.'[18] Despite Scott's attempt to demystify ventriloquism, beliefs in the voices of spirits persisted in the sixteenth and seventeenth century.

By the seventeenth century, ventriloquism as entertainment became more well-known in England. A ventriloquist named Fannigus entertained the court of James I.[19] This development is apparent in Thomas Blount's 1656 definition of *ventriloquist* as 'one that has an evil spirit speaking in his belly, or one that by use and practice can speake as it were out of his belly, not moving his lips.'[20] However, under influence of the Enlightenment, the interpretation of voices moved steadily towards the secular; as Leigh Eric Schmidt notes, a rationalistic interpretation of ventriloquism

> provided a tangible way of thinking about revealed religion as rooted in illusion – that, indeed, various wonders of the devout ear such as divine calls, the voices of demonic possession, prophecy, mystical locutions,

---

[16] Vox, *I Can See*, p. 20, 25. In the First Book of Samuel of the Hebrew Bible, the witch of Endor purportedly summoned the spirit of Samuel to advise Saul.
[17] Scott writes that 'in truth we way gather, that it was neither the divell in person, nor *Samuell* : but a circumstance is here described, according to the deceived opinion and imagination of *Saule*.' Reginald Scott, *The Discoverie of Witchcraft*, ed. by Brinsley Nicholson (London: Elliot Stock, 1886 [1584]), p. 114.
[18] Scott, *Discoverie*, p. 101.
[19] Vox, *I Can See*, p. 31-2.
[20] Thomas Blount, *Glossographia* (1656), quoted in Schmidt, p. 281.

oracles, and even the sounds of shamanic spirits had their origins in vocal deceptions that empiricists could pinpoint and magicians could demonstrate.[21]

This change in attitude meant that ventriloquism in the eighteenth century increasingly became a performance art, its fantastical results relying on the skill of the performer.[22] A key work in this process was Joannes Baptista de la Chapelle's *Le Ventriloque, ou l'engastimythe* (1772), containing philosophical observations on the subject, which later were used for the 1797 entry on ventriloquism in the *Encyclopedia Britannica*.[23] De la Chapelle argued that the biological aspect of ventriloquy, like the anatomy of the mouth and acoustics, explained the phenomenon: 'ventriloquism, he concluded, was an art, a practiced technique of modulation, misdirection, and muscular control, which required neither supernatural assistance nor any special endowments of nature.'[24] In eighteenth-century England, entertainers performed as ventriloquists at travelling fairs, and in the nineteenth century they displayed their talents in theatres and playhouses. An example of a seventeenth-century performer was John Clinch, who could mimic people, animals, and some instruments, and performed at Bartholomew Fair.[25] Although previously lumped together with other performances including music and acrobatic arts, ventriloquism became a genre by itself between 1795 and 1825.[26] A popular ventriloquist in this period was Thomas Haskey, a former soldier who in 1796 performed as ventriloquist for London audiences under the name Askins. He even had his own halfpenny coin made, bearing his portrait and the inscription: 'The Celebrated

---

[21] Schmidt, 'Demon Possession', p. 274.
[22] Davies, *Gender and Ventriloquism*, pp. 38-39.
[23] Schmidt, 'Demon Possession', pp. 281-282.
[24] Schmidt, 'Demon Possession', p. 282.
[25] Vox, *I Can See*, p. 38
[26] Schmidt, 'Demon Possession', p. 294.

Ventriloquist, 1796.'[27] By the nineteenth century, ventriloquism as a performance became firmly rooted in its definition; the 1823 *Encyclopedia* entry defines it as 'an art by which certain persons can so modify their voice, as to make it appear to the audience to proceed from any distance, and in any direction' and refers the reader to physiology.[28] Although ventriloquists in this period might advertise themselves as being rare or perhaps even unique, ventriloquy was a common act in popular entertainment in the first half of the nineteenth century.[29] In 1822, the French Nicholas Marie Vattermare (stage name Monsieur Alexandre) performed a show advertised as 'The Adventures of a Ventriloquist; The Rogueries of Nicholas' at the Adelphi Theatre in London.[30] It is unclear whether Henry Cockton was inspired directly by Vattermare's stage show when writing *The Life and Adventures of Valentine Vox, a Ventriloquist*; however, it does illustrate the kind of ventriloquial performances early nineteenth-century Londoners might be familiar with. Valentine Vox (the performer, not the fictional character) argues that Cockton was inspired by the stories surrounding the ventriloquists of his time, particularly Vatermare.[31]

The dummy or puppet from which a ventriloquised voice might emanate, which is the more familiar ventriloquist act in the twenty-first century, can be traced back to late-eighteenth century performances. Despite the usage of the occasional puppet or doll, most ventriloquists advertised themselves with their ability of mimicry and that of creating a distant voice.[32] The puppet or automaton only became prevalent in the 1840s. In line with this historical context, the texts in this chapter feature ventriloquism without a dummy. The texts in this chapter capture a moment in the

---

[27] Vox, *I Can See*, p. 49-50.
[28] *Encyclopaedia Britannica: or, a Dictionary* (Edinburgh: Archibald Constable and Company, 1823), p. 547.
[29] John A. Hodgson, 'An Other Voice: Ventriloquism in the Romantic Period', *Romanticism on the Net*, 16, (1999).
[30] Vox, *I Can See*, p. 55. On page 56 Vox has included a reproduction of the original handbill.
[31] Vox, *I Can See*, p. 63.
[32] Hodgson, 'An Other Voice', paragraphs 15-22.

history of voice: while before the eighteenth century, the ventriloquial voice was ascribed supernatural meanings, and by the end of the nineteenth century voice became embroiled in discussions on technology (with the advent of inventions like the radio and the telephone), in the relatively short timeframe of the nineteenth century, voice was distinctly human. As Connor writes, ventriloquism in this interval appeared

> as the manipulation of human voices, as a dramaturgy. It is in this period that the questions *what?* and *where?* asked of the unlocated voice mutate into the question *who?* Ventriloquism becomes an affair of dramatization and colloquy, and a medium for exploring the relations between selves and their voices.[33]

As Helen Davies has pointed out, the move of the displaced voice from supernatural agents to a more secular one introduced anxiety: 'the fear of malign ventriloquial influence the masculinised ventriloquist as a potential sexual predator, the sense that human voice and agency might be appropriated by another'.[34] Another aspect of the anxiety can be read in a generally complimentary short poem written by Walter Scott after seeing a performance by Vattermare. Calling him an 'arch deceiver', he writes:

> Above all, are you one individual? I know
> You must be, at least, *Alexandre and Co.*
> But I think you're a troop – an assemblage – a mob –
> And that I, as the sheriff, must take up the job,
> And, instead of rehearsing your wonders in verse,
> Must read you the riot-act, and bid you disperse![35]

---

[33] Connor, *Dumbstruck*, p. 43.
[34] Davies, *Gender and Ventriloquism*, p. 47.
[35] From Walter Scott, 'Impromptu. To Monsieur Alexandre', in *The Poetical Works of Sir Walter Scott, with A Sketch of His Life*, ed. by J.W. Lake (Philadelphia: J. Crissy, 1838), p. 443.

While ventriloquism might be amusing, it could also incite panic and fear unto the unsuspecting. Referring to the ventriloquist as an arch deceiver implies connections to the devil. The different personas of Monsieur Alexandre are therefore not only wondrous, but also a threat; for Scott, perhaps, specifically a threat to the public order, as his escalation of the troop into a mob suggests. Ventriloquial anxieties are exploited in an early text featuring a ventriloquist, *Wieland: or, The Transformation* (1798) by the American author Charles Brockden Brown. In this novel the titular character Wieland and his family are terrorised by the ventriloquial effusions of Carwin. At the climax of the novel, it is revealed to the narrator, Wieland's sister Clara, that Theodore Wieland has murdered his wife and children because a voice (which he interprets as God's command) told him to do so. *Wieland* therefore incorporates traces of both the religious/supernatural interpretation of voices, while at the same time ascribing ventriloquial skill in secular terms to the character of Carwin. In another interpretation of the text, the ventriloquised voices can be seen as those of the displaced tribes implied by the narrative, therefore expressing indigenous anxieties.[36]

It is important to note that the voice Wieland perceives to kill his family does not originate from Carwin.[37] Schmidt argues that the novel expresses a distrust of revealed religion and the susceptibility of 'active religious imaginations', which allow the characters to interpret Carwin's voices as celestial.[38] Their credulity leaves these characters open to manipulation. Clara, for example, exhibits an ambiguous relationship with the first of Carwin's tricks. As Theodore walks up a hill on his estate, he hears the voice of his wife.

---

[36] Stefan Schöberlein, 'Speaking in Tongues, Speaking without Tongues: Transplanted Voices in Charles Brockden Brown's *Wieland*', *Journal of American Studies*, 51:2 (2017), 535-552.
[37] Robert W. Hobson, 'Voices of Carwin and Other Mysteries in Charles Brockden Brown's "Wieland".' *Early American Literature*, 10:3 (1975), 307-309, discusses whether Carwin could have been responsible for the murder-inducing voice Wieland hears.
[38] Schmidt, 'Demon Posession', p. 287.

When he returns to the house, however, it is revealed that his wife was in the company of others and had not stirred for the duration of his absence. The preoccupations of the novel's characters with the source of the speech reflects a core characteristic of voice: it has to originate from somewhere, though its spatial origin might be misperceived, a voice implies another person or agency.[39] Clara's reaction is one of excitement: 'My wonder was excited by the inscrutableness of the cause [...] It begat in me a thrilling, and not unpleasing solemnity.'[40] Theodore Wieland's reaction to the incident, however, foreshadows his later psychosis. Fearing that her brother might ascribe to a supernatural interpretation of the voice he heard, Clara writes:

> I could not bear to think that his senses should be the victims of such delusion. It argued a diseased condition of his frame, which might show itself hereafter in more dangerous symptoms. The will is the tool of the understanding, which must fashion its conclusions on the notices of sense. If the senses be depraved it is impossible to calculate the evils that may flow from the consequent deductions of the understanding. [41]

Clara fears that Theodore's senses might have been corrupted, which can only lead to a corruption of the mind as a consequence. When later both Theodore and Henry Pleyel hear the same voice, Clara concludes that: 'Here was information obtained and imparted by means unquestionably superhuman [...] An awe, the sweetest and most solemn that imagination can conceive, pervaded my whole frame.'[42] As the narrative progresses, however, the voices become uncanny and threatening. Clara hears voices coming from

---

[39] Connor, *Dumbstruck*, p. 23.
[40] Charles Brockden Brown, *Wieland; or The Transformation, and Memoirs of Carwin, the Biloquist* (Oxford: Oxford University Press, 2009), p. 32.
[41] Brown, *Wieland*, p. 32-3.
[42] Brown, *Wieland*, p. 42.

near her bed at night, threatening to shoot her, though there is no one to be seen. Her reaction is one of terror: 'My heart began to palpitate with dread of some unknown danger. [...] My terrors urged me forward with almost a mechanical impulse.'[43] The ventriloquism is 'ghostly,' disembodied speech from impossible origins.[44]

Initially focussed on the victims and their uncertainty, the latter half of *Wieland* is concerned with the motivations of Carwin, who extensively revisits earlier events from his perspective. His speech to Clara is one of confession: 'It is you I have injured, and at your bar I am willing to appear, and confess and expiate my crimes. I have deceived you: I have sported with your terrors: I have plotted to destroy your reputation.'[45] Carwin tells her of his powers of voice, but says not to know what name to give it. In a long footnote, Brown explains that Carwin's powers are those of '*Biloquium*, or ventrilocution', which he defines, to paraphrase, as the art of modifying the voice according to the variations of direction and distance, without changing one's place.[46] Brown here refers the reader to La Chappelle (mentioned above) and his physiological explanation of ventriloquy.[47] It is interesting Brown prefers the word biloquy (two voices, or double-speech[48]), as evidenced by the title of the unfinished sequel to *Wieland*, titled *Memoirs of Carwin the Biloquist*. The doubling of voices recalls the figure of the double, a trope central to Gothic fiction. Carwin's doubling blurs the boundaries of selfhood and autonomy, manipulating characters into actions. Carwin's actions ultimately stem from a lack of morals: 'Unfortified by principle, subjected to poverty, stimulated by headlong passions, I made this powerful engine subservient to the supply of my wants, and the gratification of my vanity.'[49] Despite

---

[43] Brown, *Wieland*, p. 54.
[44] Schöberlein, 'Speaking in Tongues', p. 538.
[45] Brown, *Wieland*, p. 181.
[46] Brown, *Wieland*, footnote pp. 181-2.
[47] Hodgson argues that Brown was probably familiar with La Chapelle's work through excerpts. See Hodgson, 'An Other Voice', footnote 5.
[48] Schöberlein, 'Speaking in Tongues', p. 538.
[49] Brown, *Wieland*, p. 182.

Carwin's weakness of character and the Wielands's susceptibility, *Wieland* takes an ambivalent position towards ventriloquism. As Brown's footnote reads, it is not so much a question of whether ventriloquy is possible, as experience shows that it is; the novel questions whether anyone should have this amount of influence over others.

In the time interval between the publication of *Wieland* and Cockton's *Valentine Vox* and Prest's concurrent adaptation in 1840, the ventriloquist appears sporadically in fictional texts. A Minerva Press novel called *The Nuns of the Desert; or, The Woodland Witches* (1805) by Eugenia de Acton for example features a female ventriloquist called Margaret Mervin, who poses as a witch surrounded by speaking animals (who she impressively voices). Mrs Mervin has an 'extraordinary gift of Nature; of which, indeed, she herself scarce knew either the cause or the extent;' and does not fully understand this power until she reads about it.[50] A footnote continues: 'This word *Ventriloquism*, which has been termed *supernatural*, explains all the seeming mystery of Margaret's profession.'[51] She receives her information through servant gossip, and makes predictions based on this information, which is so accurate and specific that it makes others call her a witch. The text argues that this misconception is mainly caused by ventriloquial skill being unfamiliar to the characters: 'Ventriloquism was, at that time, but little known, or his Worship would probably have traced the deception to its origin.'[52] The story relies on the explained supernatural, where uncanny events turn out to be ordinary. In an afterword De Acton writes that ventriloquism 'has, of late years, been more known than it was formerly',[53] but for readers who might doubt the events in the novel, she adds several pages on the subject in an appendix, taken from *Chambers's Cyclopedia*.[54] This entry

---

[50] Eugenia de Acton, *The Nuns of the Desert; or, The Woodland Witches*, Vol. II, (London: Minerva Press, 1805), p. 32.
[51] De Acton, *Nuns*, II, p. 32.
[52] De Acton, *Nuns*, II, p. 93.
[53] De Acton, *Nuns*, II, p. 283.
[54] De Acton, *Nuns*, II, pp. 286-296.

heavily relies on the writings of Le Chapelle, repeating the stories of several of the figures La Chapelle describes. The figure of the ventriloquist pops up in several novels at the start of the nineteenth century, repeating the themes of superstition, explained supernatural, and the danger that might be inherent to a skill that is suitable for deception. Some examples include John English's *The Grey Friar: and the Black Spirit of the Wye* (1810), Sophia Griffith's *She Would Be a Heroine* (1816), Anne and Annabella Plumptre's *Tales of Wonder, Humour and of Sentiment* (1818), Zara Wentworth's *The Hermit's Cave: or, The fugitive's retreat* (1821). In *The Premier* (1831) it is joked that a person who is not only 'a *twin* child', but also 'the *second* son of his father's *second* wife' who lives in a '*double*-bedded room of a *double* house, which happened, oddly enough, he would add, to *be* No. 2, and kept by Mr. *Doubleday*' should also be '*double*-jointed' and have 'a *double* voice, or the faculty of ventriloquism.'[55] *Society; or, The Spring in Town* (1831) by an unknown author is notable as it contains farcical ventriloquism[56] that became the predominant mode for *Valentine Vox* and *Valentine Vaux* a decade later.

---

[55] *The Premier*, Vol. I (London: Henry Colburn and Richard Bentley, 1831), pp. 64-65.
[56] To give an excerpt from the text: 'The Baronet, who had tact enough to see some cloud had passed over Fanny's spirits, which her cousin was anxious either to dispel or keep from notice, consented to do the *amiable* for the party. But as his own amusement was never long lost sight of, he commenced by giving some specimens of ventriloquism, to the evident danger of Mrs. Herford's Sèvres teacups, and not the less so, of Miss Bradford's gown, as he flung his voice into the stomach of the frightened footman, who was handing tea to her. The man's terrified face, and the rage of the lady, as she heard her name called out by the imprisoned huntsman – so he described himself to be – baffles description. Peals of laughter brought the rest of the gentlemen speedily amongst them. *Society: or, The Spring in Town*, Vol. I (London: Saunders and Otley, 1831), pp. 103-104.

FROM *VOX* TO *VAUX*

Henry Cockton's *The Life and Adventures of Valentine Vox, the Ventriloquist* struck a chord with the Victorian reading public, though it has disappeared from public consciousness in the twenty-first century. The story had a relatively long afterlife, and the reprints in the second half of the nineteenth century are reported to have sold almost half a million copies.[57] Cockton's story was serialised from March 1839 to October 1840, and received a mix of favourable and dismissive reviews from critics. *The Age* even optimistically proclaimed that 'we shall be much mistaken if he does not achieve a fame surpassed not even by C. Dickens'.[58] *Valentine Vox*'s popularity made it a target for penny press plagiarism or pastiche, and as *Vox* was still being serialised, Thomas Peckett Prest retold Valentine's story in 32 weekly instalments under the pseudonym of Timothy Portwine, published by Edward Lloyd. In 1840, the serialization was combined into a single volume with a short preface dated May 30th, 1840. The preface suggests that the serial was cut short due to Prest's bad health, despite the 'very numerous subscribers who have encouraged [the Editor] during the period occupied by the publication of this work.'[59] Penny press imitations of popular stories aimed to sell copies on the basis of name recognition – Vox and Vaux are easily confused or interchanged – while providing a cheaper format of penny weeklies rather than the more expensive monthlies. The name 'Vaux' might have been inspired by Vauxhall, the pleasure gardens in London which the character Valentine Vox attends in the course of the story. Another interpretation is that Vaux is a tongue-in-cheek echo of the French word *faux*, or false – as Valentine Vaux is a 'false' version of Cockton's story. Prest was not content to merely shorten or enliven

---

[57] According to the Routledge archives, 438,000 copies were sold between 1853 and 1902. See Robert Halliday, 'New Light on Henry Cockton', *Notes and Queries*, 41:3 (1994), 349-351, p. 349.
[58] 'Literary Notices', *Age*, 10 November 1839, p. 354.
[59] Timothy Portwine [Thomas Peckett Prest], *The Adventure of Valentine Vaux; or, The Tricks of a ventriloquist* (London: E. Lloyd, 1840), preface.

Cockton's story to suit weekly publication; *Valentine Vaux* is properly rewritten while retaining characters and incidents. It is clear that Prest had a copy of Cockton's version at hand when he wrote *Valentine Vaux*, but he retells and reimagines Cockton's scenes, often with a different inflection. What this different inflection entails is the subject of this section, which will spend some close attention to how Prest reimagines Cockton's story.

On a basic level, both *Valentine Vox* and *Valentine Vaux* are the story of a young ventriloquist Valentine, who travels to London to live with a friend of a relative, called Grimwood Goodman in the former and Septimus Bramstone in the latter. Goodman/Bramstone is a rich bachelor, whose brother and his son (Walter and Horace/Harry and Arnold) have prematurely claimed his inheritance for themselves. They perceive Valentine as a threat, and decide to secure their inheritance by committing Goodman/Bramstone to an asylum. In *Vox*, Goodman is initially released because of the guilt-stricken conscience of his brother; in *Vaux*, Bramstone is liberated by Valentine aided by several policemen. The plot points are strung together in a similar way: chapters that further the plot are alternated with Valentine seeking entertainment, usually in the form of a ventriloquial prank.

In *Valentine Vox*, ventriloquism is loosely connected to its stage origins. A travelling stage magician called Signor Antonio Hesperio de Bellamoniac ('whose real name, it may be proper to observe, was John Tod'[60]) visits Valentine's birth town and performs at a local inn. The townsfolk are amazed by the Signor's performance: 'when he came to his ventriloquism he completely astonished his audience, for never having heard anything like it before, they were in doubt as to whether there was not in him something superhuman.'[61] This leaves a significant impression on Valentine:

> Of all the magician's auditors on the great occasion to
> which we have alluded, Valentine was one of the most

---

[60] Henry Cockton, *The Life and Adventures of Valentine Vox, the Ventriloquist* (London: W. Nicholson & Sons, [1890?]), p. 13.
[61] Cockton, *Valentine Vox*, p. 14.

attentive, and that portion of the performances which struck him with the greatest force was the Signor's display of his power as a ventriloquist. Indeed, so deep an impression did it make upon his mind, that he firmly resolved to apply to the magician the following day with the view of ascertaining if it were possible for him to become a ventriloquist himself.[62]

As the Signor has already left town to avoid paying for the room he performed in and other expenses, Valentine is left to discover how ventriloquism works for himself. This, however, does not impede him:

> [A]fter trying with desperation for several days, he discovered, with equal astonishment and delight, that he in reality possessed the power of speaking with an abdominal intonation, and that zealous cultivation would cause that power to be fully developed.

Of particular note here is the 'abdominal intonation', a reference to the belief that ventriloquism stemmed from the stomach (while practitioners such as Valentine Vox, quoted above, have clarified that it stems from modulation of the vocal chords and surrounding muscles). Cockton is ambivalent about whether ventriloquism is a skill or dependent on the nature of one's body – while Valentine requires practice, he at the same time, to paraphrase, already possesses the power of ventriloquism.

> He accordingly commenced a severe course of training. He rose early every morning and practiced in the fields, and in doing so, frequently startled himself, for the power that was within him, not being quite under control, would occasionally send the sound in one place when he fully intended it to have been in another. The consciousness,

---

[62] Cockton, *Valentine Vox*, p. 15.

however, of his possessing this extraordinary power urged him to persevere, and in less than six months it was entirely at his command.[63]

Valentine's practice is reminiscent of a sequence in Charles Brockden Brown's *Memoirs of Carwin the Biloquist*, where Carwin discovers and practices the modulation of voice in a rocky glen near his father's house. Carwin models his ventriloquism after the naturally occurring echoes between the rocks, implying a connection between natural acoustics and the origins of ventriloquism, unlike the explicit stagecraft that Valentine attempts to emulate. Like Valentine, however, Carwin finds that 'What was at first difficult, by exercise and habit, was rendered easy. I learned to accommodate my voice to all the varieties of distance and direction.'[64] The language of control and submission permeates both texts – Valentine occasionally scares himself by modulations of his own voice taking a different shape than his expectation, until he learns to put it under his 'command.' Carwin similarly 'subjects' his voice 'to the command of his will.'[65]

In Prest's *Valentine Vaux*, the initiation into ventriloquism by exposure to a performance of it is absent. *Vaux*, instead, foregrounds trickery:

> This art which was so likely to prove a dangerous one to him, he had learnt from a travelling mountebank, and being an apt scholar, he was soon able to practice his tricks upon those at whose expense he felt inclined to make himself merry.[66]

---

[63] Cockton, *Valentine Vox*, p. 15.
[64] Brown, *Wieland*, p. 232.
[65] Brown, *Wieland*, p. 232.
[66] Portwine, *Valentine Vaux*, p. 5. Note that the pages 5 and 6 are missing from the Gale/British Library copy of *Valentine Vaux*. I used the copy held by the Bodleian library at Oxford, at shelfmark Pettingell 399.

The usage of the word mountebank is particularly noteworthy, denoting a person selling questionable medicines, synonymously used for a charlatan. Vaux has the power to deceive, which his mother worries might lead him into trouble when people find out they have been deluded. The mountebank is a flattening of the character of the magician from *Vox*, who in addition to being a charlatan that tricks an unsuspecting person out of their money, also exhibits valid and appreciated stagecraft. The training sequence that Cockton took from *Wieland* is not repeated in *Vaux*; it is enough for Prest to list various sounds that Valentine can imitate, including 'the frying of pancakes' and 'the braying of a jackass'.[67] Equally absent is an attempt to explain the ventriloquism, assigning it either to the stomach or the modulation of voice in the throat – while the chapter heading boasts that 'the peculiarities of our hero and his powers of ventriloquism described' will follow, this consists only of examples. The text assumes an understanding of ventriloquism, either via its source text by Cockton, or a familiarity through popular stage performers. At the same time, it has little appreciation for this 'art', which only serves for Vaux's (and our) personal amusement.

The first elaborate on-page display of ventriloquism in both *Vox* and *Vaux* is a political meeting at the guildhall (*Vox*)/town-hall (*Vaux*). This scene is a suitable starting point for a side-by-side comparison of the two versions, as it sets the tone for all subsequent tricks by Valentine in both versions. It also illustrates how, though the formal structure of the scene is similar, it is contextualised differently, and contains humour specific to the respective authors. Vox's first forays in exercising his ventriloquism draw on the connection of ventriloquism as a staged art. Cockton describes Valentine's disturbance of a political meeting at the guildhall, 'Valentine's first grand display [...] in public.'[68] This connotation is subverted in *Vaux*; Valentine's wish to attend the town-hall meeting is couched in recreational terms. 'I should like to be an observer of

---

[67] Portwine, *Valentine Vaux*, p. 5.
[68] Cockton, *Valentine Vox*, p. 15.

the absurdity', Valentine tells his mother, where he expects 'a great deal of amusement.'[69] There is less of a sense of Valentine taking the stage, and more language that points towards the idea that Valentine's observing the meeting, and his subsequent disturbing of it, is a chaos he creates for his own benefit; through his own interference, the characters he manipulates perform *for* him. An appreciation for the chaos Vaux produces is not shared by all characters. Valentine's mother assumes he will be up for 'some mischief', and that 'some mad trick or other is running in his head'.[70] The chapter in *Vaux* ends with Valentine laughing at the concern his mother and uncle expresses, and as he leaves he is 'determined to enjoy himself as much as possible at the expense of his neighbours.'[71] These two strands pervade the texts: Vox continues to have a close connection to stage performance while for Vaux the stage only figures in the background, foregrounding language of amusement and recreation. *Vox* for example includes a scene where Valentine uses ventriloquism to disturb an opera performance while dressed up as a member of the chorus,[72] he creates a scene during a Vauxhall theatre performance,[73] and pressures a conductor at the show of the Native Talent Association to sing English songs instead of foreign ones.[74]

The way the scene at the guildhall/town-hall is set up differs in the two versions. When Vaux arrives at the town-hall, the crowd is already in a state of disorder ('our hero found the greatest bustle prevailing in all directions'[75]), while the scene in *Vox* is more orderly. The chaotic crowd of Prest's version is a recurring image in *Vaux*, and will be discussed more expansively below. For Prest, the humour of the scene lies, partly, in the ridiculousness of the politicians themselves:

---

[69] Portwine, *Valentine Vaux*, p. 7.
[70] Portwine, *Valentine Vaux*, p. 7.
[71] Portwine, *Valentine Vaux*, p. 8.
[72] Cockton, *Valentine Vox*, p. 61 onwards.
[73] Cockton, *Valentine Vox*, p. 167 onwards.
[74] Cockton, *Valentine Vox*, p. 199 onwards.
[75] Portwine, *Valentine Vaux*, p. 9.

> The Tories were for electing Abel Squeak, on account of his high church principles, and the fact of his having once been heard to declare it as his solemn opinion, that all reformers were destructives. [...] As for Mr. Brownrigge Bullman, he stood well with the radical portion of the community, because in all things he was diametrically opposite to his rival in the present contest. [...] He gloried in being the very reverse of his antagonist in all things, and as if to carry this feeling to the utmost bounds, he grew as corpulent as a fatted bullock, while Squeak dwindled away in size, till he became not much larger round the waist than a farthing rushlight in the dog days.[76]

As the position that needs to be filled is that of town crier, the significance of the Tories backing Squeak, despite him being completely unfit for the role as he 'could utter nothing but a wheezing sound', indicates the absurdity of politics and its entrenched nature. These flourishes are all Prest's; in Cockton's text, the absurdity is expressed in the behaviour of the politicians. Vox immediately disturbs the meeting, in a manner that is characteristic of his *modus operandi* throughout the text. When the first speaker appears, Vox's interjection is instantaneous:

> "Gentlemen!" said Mr. Creedale.
> "Nonesense!" cried Valentine, in an assumed voice of course, which appeared to proceed from a remote part of the hall.
> "Gentlemen!" repeated Mr. Creedale, with some additional emphasis.
> "Pooh, pooh!" exclaimed Valentine, changing tone.[77]

---

[76] Portwine, *Valentine Vaux*, p. 10.
[77] Cockton, *Valentine Vox*, p. 16.

Vox's responses are of little substance; they intend to heckle and have no content beyond the speech act itself, which transgresses the social norms of a political meeting. Vox's voice disturbs, intervenes, and talks over others until the boundaries of social interactions dissolve. The candidates and speakers collapse into argument amongst themselves, and eventually police are summoned to intervene. The continuation of the scene shows Vox projecting his voice to several parts of the room, causing the police to run around in a farcically futile way. His voice is one without source, which continues to provoke everyone present, because it insists on being heard. By persistently frustrating the people present at the meeting, impersonating some who incur the wrath of others, Vox finally manages to bring about pure chaos.

> The voice of Valentine was now no longer needed. The electors were making amply sufficient noise without his aid. He therefore mounted the rostrum, partly for safety and partly with a view to the full enjoyment of the scene, and then for the first time discovered that instead of the combatants being divided into two grand political parties, as they ought to have been, they were levelling their blows with indiscriminate fury, regardless utterly of everything but the pleasure of conferring upon someone the honour of a hit.[78]

This violent climax quickly fizzles out when a group of dragoons gallop into the hall, and Valentine goes home 'in ecstacies' when he 'contemplates the result of the first grand display of his latent power'.[79] The violence in this scene is twofold; on one hand, the members of the political parties are shown to have descended into indiscriminate aggression that crosses party lines, but on the other hand they are provoked into this by the violence of Vox's interventions. The connection between voice and violence is made

---

[78] Cockton, *Valentine Vox*, p. 19-20.
[79] Cockton, *Valentine Vox*, p. 21.

explicit in the subsequent chapter, where Vox 'exercised his voice with so much violence' that it distresses his mother, causing her to think he might have 'eaten from the insane root'. We can read the scene at the guildhall as a farce – which the overt physicality and humorous tone invites. Farce contains both festive as well as violent elements in different proportions depending on the form and content of a work, and both are present in the scene. Vox's amusement then embodies the festive element of farce, while the fighting between the party members shows the violent element of farce.

Prest's version inserts another instance of ventriloquism before Vaux even arrives at the Town-hall. On his way there, he tricks a baker and a chimney sweep that are walking past, pretending that the baker laughs at the sweep.[80] The effect on the chimney sweep is immediate: '[he] set off at a running pace, and then crossing the road, he purposely brought himself in contact with the baker, who, by the violence of the shock, was very nearly sent into the kennel.'[81] A fight follows, during which it became 'impossible to say which was the baker or which the sweep, so completely had they mingled complexions'.[82] Vaux leaves these two to their fight, moving from one chaotic conflict to the other: in front of the hall, he 'found the greatest bustle prevailing in all directions.'[83] The meeting itself is described in humorous terms, including pun-filled speeches by several workmen, like an undertaker and a hatter.[84] Vaux disturbs

---

[80] '[...] speaking in a feigned voice, he bawled out "sweep!" accompanied with a loud "ha! ha! ha!" that was anything but pleasant to the lad of soot. Portwine, *Valentine Vaux*, p. 8.
[81] Portwine, *Valentine Vaux*, p. 8.
[82] Portwine, *Valentine Vaux*, p. 9.
[83] Portwine, *Valentine Vaux*, p. 9.
[84] 'Ladies and gentlemen, unaccustomed though I am to public speaking, I could not, on so *grave* an occasion as this, remain *mute*. A great duty is to be performed; an office of trust and responsibility is to be filled, and I have *undertaken* to propose Abel Squeak as a man in every way fitted to shed lustre and renown upon the dignity of common crier. It is not for me to re-*hearse* the numerous qualities that render him so peculiarly fit for this situation of honour, or to point out to your recollection to the many *black jobs*

the meeting in a similar manner to Vox, though Vox's exclamations include direct insults rather than mere interjections ('You had better take a NAP, old boy'[85]). Like in Vox, the meeting descends into a fistfight, which deserves quotation at length:

> [...] the two parties, radicals and conservatives, gladly seized the opportunity which it offered to vent the spleen they had so long fostered against each other. Separating themselves therefore into two bodies, the factions seemed determined upon trying their strength [...] At length, however, a reinforcement of constables arrived at the door of the Town Hall, who after dealing out broken heads in abundance, succeeded in forcing their way among the combatants, who they soon managed to disperse by means of the vigorous blows with which they saluted all those who happened to fall within their reach. At this moment the scene of confusion utterly baffles all description; [...] they squeezed, jostled, and thumped away at another with such hearty good will that the air was filled with sounds that might remind a spectator of bedlam broke loose.[86]

The political crowd is simply looking for an excuse to descend into violence. Prest's version contains more graphic detail of the violence, including 'broken heads' and 'vigorous blows.' It is interesting that the police meets the chaos with force, in contrast to the immediate calming effect of the dragoons' entrance in *Vox*. Authority is not recognised as such unless it matches the force of the

---

in which his adversary is well known to have engaged. I *plume* myself upon the justice of my cause, and all I hope is, that when the election is concluded, all ill nature may be *shrouded* in oblivion, and that our animosities may be *buried* in the *tomb* of all the Capulets.' Portwine, *Valentine Vaux*, p. 11, emphasis original.
[85] Portwine, *Valentine Vaux*, p. 11.
[86] Portwine, *Valentine Vaux*, p. 12.

mob. At the same time, the scene is not terrifying or truly dangerous; the 'hearty good will' signals a certain carnivalesque abandon.

As Jessica Milner Davis argues, at the heart of farce 'is the eternal comic conflict between the forces of conventional authority and the forces of rebellion'.[87] Cockton's farce, while focusing on the political members and finally dissolving rules of conduct, is less concerned with showing the absurdity of politics itself than it is with showing the humorous effects of transgressions of social norms. Unlike Prest's characterisations of the politicians and their supporters as fundamentally ridiculous as in the quotation above, Cockton rarely resorts to humorous types in *Valentine Vox*. While Vox attends and disturbs various political meetings throughout the story, including the House of Commons and the Court of Aldermen, both he and other characters express a degree of respect for authority. At the Court of Aldermen, for example, Valentine 'waited with patience until all the important questions of the day had been duly considered' before he engages in ventriloquism to 'enliven the honourable members'.[88] While the scene at the guildhall descends into a violent free-for-all, this is a rare result for Vox's ventriloquism. A majority of the ventriloquial scenes in *Valentine Vox* end with a return to order when he decides to either take pity on his target or simply bores of it and moves on. When visiting the British Museum, Valentine throws his voice in a closed stone coffin. After a long sequence where workers finally open the coffin and find no person within, the chapter closes with the wonder of the visitors and workmen:

> They still, however, tried very hard – very, very hard indeed – to reconcile the fact of their having heard the voice of a man, with the fact of no man being there; and as Valentine's appetite began to be somewhat troublesome, he left them engaged in unravelling the mystery which he perfectly well knew they were unable to solve.[89]

---

[87] Jessica Milner Davis, *Farce* (London: Methuen & Co Ltd, 1978), p. 24.
[88] Cockton, *Valentine Vox*, p. 106.
[89] Cockton, *Valentine Vox*, p. 97.

The confusion Vox gives rise to in the spectators is one of conflicting information of the senses: while sound implied there had been a man, vision contravenes this interpretation. Connor in *Dumbstruck* writes about the rise of the eyes as the dominant sense of perception over the ears, which he connects to the decline of oral culture. He writes that 'perhaps ventriloquism in general, testifies to a remarkably persistent desire to believe in the autonomy of the voice, in the power of the voice detached not only from its source, but also from its subordination to sight.'[90] Although Valentine's voice is powerful and impossible to ignore, the superiority of vision is reified through every humoristic encounter; if the victims of his pranks would only, to put it colloquially, 'believe their eyes', the farce would collapse.

The fact that the violent consequence of ventriloquism is rare throughout Cockton's story suggests that the violence itself is not the point, nor necessarily the logical result of ventriloquial intervention. The scenes induce laughter by the discrepancy of understanding: both Valentine and the reader know how ventriloquism works, but the other characters misunderstand situations or become baffled by the contradictory information they perceive. In the case of the workers and bystanders at the British Museum, for example, 'they could not conceive how a man could have escaped, nor could they believe that no man had been there.'[91] It is telling that in the recounting of the events at the guildhall, Valentine refuses to tell his mother of the ventriloquism that was the cause of the chaos, as he is 'inspired with the conviction that his power would lose a great portion of its value if its existence in him became known.'[92] The text, therefore, limits the ventriloquial potential – its success is conditional on a lack of knowledge of ventriloquism. The ventriloquist therefore does not have absolute power, despite the insistence of sound. Referring back to Davis's description of farce quoted above, the conventional authority is

---

[90] Connor, *Dumbstruck*, p. 22.
[91] Cockton, *Valentine Vox*, p. 96.
[92] Cockton, *Valentine Vox*, p. 21.

disturbed by Valentine's vocal rebellion to create laughter, but the effect is always temporary. Once the laughter has been achieved through misunderstanding, the rebellion comes to an end, and authority is restored effortlessly. The underlying logic is essentially conservative, and indicates that convention is and should be upheld after the laughter dies down, which underpins Vox's respect for authority figures in the Court of Aldermen. Prest's farce, on the other hand, heavily relies on the destructive aspect of farce. The humour of these scenes lies in their chaotic and violent endings. At the same time, it shows a similar conservatism as *Vox*, reifying convention through disturbance. The following section will take a closer look at the conjunction between violence and humour in *Valentine Vaux*, while bearing in mind how it figures in the original text by Cockton.

THE POLITICS OF HUMOUR AND VIOLENCE IN *VALENTINE VAUX*

The farce in *Valentine Vox* can readily be interpreted as humorous misinformation: if the characters had been aware of the possibilities of ventriloquism, they would correctly interpret their sensory perceptions. This interpretation cannot be directly be applied to *Valentine Vaux*; Prest is less interested in sensory misdirection than he is in the transgression of boundaries and the potential for violence and chaos that is inherent in social situations. In this section I will read the humorous scenes in *Vaux* as farce, paying particular attention to what creates the laughter, and how violence figures in these scenes. Davis summarises the fundamentals of farce as a delight in taboo-violation, 'but which avoids implied moral comment or social criticism, and which tends to debar empathy for its victims.'[93] While this statement illustrates how in farcical scenes the explicit moral is absent (unlike in the more politically explicit satire), this does not mean that farcical texts contain no political subtext. How this violence is defined, and what boundaries are seen

---

[93] Davis, *Farce*, p. 86.

as 'acceptable', are part of the politics of the text: who is laughed at, how, and to what end.

The structure of the humorous ventriloquial scenes in *Valentine Vaux* is fairly constant throughout the text. This, in itself, is part of the 'joke': as was recognised by Bergson, repetition is one of the key characteristics of comedy.[94] Bergson's theory of humour revolves around the idea of the mechanical: whenever we perceive something to be unlike real life, it has the potential to be humorous. He writes that 'the truth is that a really living life should never repeat itself. Wherever there is repetition or complete similarity, we always suspect some mechanism at work behind the living.'[95] In farce, unlikely repetition is used to increase comic value; a character getting hit in the head once is funny, but if it happens several times in a row in increasingly unlikely ways the comic effect is heightened. The narrative structure of *Valentine Vaux* functions in a similar way. The humorous scenes are highly repetitive, following the same script, which is part of the joke – the reader already knows what to expect by the precedent that has been set, only increasing the comic value. The scenes are instigated either by Valentine consciously seeking entertainment, or by him simply coming across an opportunity in a public space. Very few of his pranks occur within the domestic space.[96] This is connected to the sense of staging in *Vaux*: the idea that Valentine induces others to amuse him as if it were a performance, while he directs the action from a safe distance. The laughing audience is Valentine, with the reader as an extension of him, and often other characters, including his uncle Sam or the various groups of people Valentine encounters. The word 'crowd'

---

[94] The other processes Bergson identifies in addition to repetition are inversion and what he calls 'interference of series', in which a scene carries two oppositional meanings at the same time.
[95] Bergson, *Laughter*, p. 34.
[96] The only exception of a scene which only involves one other character in a domestic setting is a scene in which Valentine tricks an older man with whom he is sharing a room, keeping him awake by imitating animal sounds. Portwine, *Valentine Vaux*, p. 84 onwards.

in itself already has a theatrical connotation as it can also refer to a group of spectators or an audience.[97]

The humorous scenes are consistently embedded in the structure of the narrative itself. The ventriloquial pranks are confined within chapters, the chapter end providing narrative closure to the pranks themselves. At the beginning of each chapter, the narrative mentions the ongoing plot (Valentine searching for Septimus Bramstone, or planning to liberate him), then either providing substantial plot exposition, or more often than not, a diversion sought by Valentine. While in a stage-coach at the beginning of the story, for example, he is 'resolved to take the first opportunity that offered to carry his mirthful propensity into execution.'[98] The start of other ventriloquial scenes are signalled by similar phrases, including: 'he resolved to have a bit more fun at his expense,'[99] 'if he [Arnold] would be quiet they might have little amusement at the expense of this swarthy son of Israel',[100] or 'Valentine, who was always upon the look out for fun, was determined to have some at the captain's expense.'[101] After this initial resolve, he uses ventriloquism to 'throw' his voice to cause disruption. He uses ventriloquism in two ways; in the first, he uses it in a way where it sounds like someone else made an inappropriate comment. An example of this is when he heckles a chimneysweep, by making it seem like a baker ridicules him.

> At last he perceived a chimney sweep trudging on a little in advance of him, while nearly at the same distance, but on the opposite side of the way, was a baker, [...]. To Valentine this immediately offered a rich prospect for putting his peculiar talents into practice, and speaking in a feigned voice, he bawled out "sweep!" accompanied with

---

[97] Anne Hultzsch, 'The Crowd and the Building: Flux in the Early *Illustrated London News*', *Architecture and Culture*, 6:3 (2018), 371-386, p. 382.
[98] Portwine, *Valentine Vaux*, p. 16.
[99] Portwine, *Valentine Vaux*, p. 22.
[100] Portwine, *Valentine Vaux*, p. 66.
[101] Portwine, *Valentine Vaux*, p. 75.

a loud "ha! ha! ha!" that was anything but pleasant to the lad of soot. [...]
"What do you mean by running against me, you ugly man's child?" demanded the indignant baker.
"Vy I means to hinsult yer, as yer hinsulted me jist now," replied chummy, poking his nose so near to the baker's mouth that it was in evident danger of being snapped off.
"Who insulted you?"
"You!"
"When?"
"Vy jist now! Didn't yer call across the road arter me, and didn't yer set up a grin that would have frightened even a Cheshire cat?"
"It's a lie!"[102]

This kind of exchange, appearing in the first issue of the story, is typical for the comic script the other ventriloquial scenes follow. A heckle receives an instant response; the accused denies having had anything to do with it; the parties argue until they start a physical fight ('[the chimneysweep] lent the baker two or three such smart taps upon the face, that he was obliged to throw down his basket and act upon the defensive.'[103]) The second kind of ventriloquial intervention involves Valentine implying the presence of a hidden animal or person through sound. On his way to London, for example, Valentine scares a fellow coach passenger by pretending an aggressive dog is hidden in the boot.

> "And does the animal appear to be a very vicious one?" –
> "Remarkably so," replied our ventriloquist, and at the same moment a sullen growl was heard issuing from the place over which they were sitting. [...] Valentine stamped with his heel and in an authoritative voice commanded the supposed dog to "lie down." But this only seemed to

---

[102] Portwine, *Valentine Vaux*, p. 8.
[103] Portwine, *Valentine Vaux*, p. 9.

exasperate the animal the more, for immediately so violent a barking and snapping succeeded that it appeared as if the infuriated beast would break out from his place of confinement and make an indiscriminate attack upon the legs of whoever he could get at.[104]

Afraid that the vicious dog might attack him, the victim of Valentine's joke, 'regardless alike of consequences and the entreaties of his fellow passengers,' jumps out of the carriage into a pool of water resulting from a recent flood, with a 'tremendous splash that followed announced the completion of the design.'[105] Regardless of whether Valentine imitates another person or someone who is not present, the culmination of the ventriloquial scene involves a form of symbolic violence. This might be an actual fight, like in the case of the baker and the chimney sweep, but can equally involve the getting wet of the gentleman in the carriage, or a character falling into mud. This form of violence brings the ventriloquial scene to a satisfying climax, after which Valentine moves on, either physically by removing himself from the scene he created, or merely by no longer intervening.

A requirement of farcical violence is that it figures within certain limits; as Davis writes, 'The aggression is both sufficiently precise to be psychologically valid and yet sufficiently delimited to qualify as play.'[106] William Hazlitt, a nineteenth-century literary critic, wrote several lectures on comedy. His discussion on the humour of violence expands on Davis's remark:

> In what relates to the laughable, as it arises from unforeseen accidents or self-willed scrapes, the pain, the shame, the mortification, and utter helplessness of situation, add to the joke, provided that they are

---

[104] Portwine, *Valentine Vaux*, p. 18.
[105] Portwine, *Valentine Vaux*, p. 18.
[106] Davis, *Farce*, p. 85.

momentary, or overwhelming only to the imagination of the sufferer.[107]

In *Vaux*, the fleetingness of pain is induced by the momentum of the narrative: within a sentence or two, the story moves on to another topic. Spending time on the suffering of the characters would deflate the joke, and therefore it is paramount that the subjects of Valentine's pranks are removed from the narrative stage the moment they have served their purpose. Importantly, Valentine is in control of when the time for play ends, for example deciding 'the matter should not end here'[108] when he continues his ventriloquial deceptions. In another scene, when he angers an omnibus driver so much so that 'the old gentleman grew very outrageous and threatened every body with heavy pains and penalties if they dared to laugh at him', he leaves the bus, 'having had his joke out', and walks the rest of the way.[109] This example illustrates the distribution of power between the characters; Valentine determines the duration of the prank, who deserves to be pranked, and when the joke is 'done'. It is an extension of the power fantasy that Connor ascribes to Cockton's Valentine: 'a fantasy of exercising absolute control over people and events, while remaining himself absolutely invulnerable to detection and retribution.'[110] This assessment holds for Prest's Valentine as well.

The sense of play is touched upon when Valentine assuages his mother's worries by saying, 'If I love a joke there is no great crime in it, and most likely I, like other people, shall grow tired of it all in good time.'[111] He further assuages the dangers of his amusement to Bramstone, saying that 'it would be difficult to fix the perpetration of a bit of mischief upon a ventriloquist,' and that he is 'tolerably

---

[107] Hazlitt, *Lectures*, p. 16.
[108] Portwine, *Valentine Vaux*, p. 86.
[109] Portwine, *Valentine Vaux*, p. 98, 99.
[110] Connor, *Dumbstruck*, p. 320.
[111] Portwine, *Valentine Vaux*, p. 13.

secure as long as I act with my usual prudence and caution.'[112] By labelling his ventriloquial adventures 'jokes', he implies that they are harmless; the narrative supports this interpretation, for example by referring to it as a 'mirthful propensity.'[113] When Bramstone expresses concern for some of Valentine's targets, arguing that 'the matter was carried far beyond a joke',[114] Valentine assures him that his target 'has only been rightly served', and further claims that 'I can exercise my talent, without ill-nature, and that by a right effort I can raise a smile in the countenance of even the morose.'[115] The narrative justifies Valentine's pranks by drawing on the gullibility of his subjects; as Davis writes, '[i]n farce, the victim is shown both inviting and suffering ridicule, and the insult is delivered directly and physically to the person of the victim.'[116] Valentine's subjects are types that deserve the ridicule; this is made explicit for example in a scene in a stagecoach when Valentine decides 'he owed the crusty passenger a trick or two for the ill nature he had given utterance to.'[117] Even when there is no such justification present, the flatness of the characters that are defined by one or two descriptors, precludes any sympathy on the part of the reader. Prest's types are either defined by their occupation (a baker, a blacksmith, a costermonger);[118] persons who overstep their class boundaries and are therefore already ridiculous, which Prest describes as 'exquisites'; and persons who engage in politics, which again, makes them a target by virtue of the ridiculousness of politics. One such justification can for example be found when Valentine causes a dandy to be soaked in water; in this instance it is not just to Valentine's benefit that the person receives a punishment, as,

---

[112] Portwine, *Valentine Vaux*, p. 29.
[113] Portwine, *Valentine Vaux*, p. 16.
[114] Portwine, *Valentine Vaux*, p. 29.
[115] Portwine, *Valentine Vaux*, p. 29.
[116] Davis, *Farce*, p. 26.
[117] Portwine, p. 16.
[118] *Valentine Vaux* also contains two overtly anti-Semitic scenes featuring Jewish characters. I would argue the Jewish stereotypes fall under the occupational category, as their race is conflagrated with their occupation (greedy/shady salesmen).

> The punishment to which this puppy had been subjected was highly approved of by the generality of the company on board, though candour compels us to admit that there were three or four who thought our hero had gone a great deal further than he ought. But it must be remembered that the exquisite had rendered himself particularly obnoxious to the females on board, and since he was the contemptible for any other punishment, it must be allowed that he met with no more than he deserved for his insolent conduct.[119]

This quotation illustrates both how Valentine's victims are 'deserving', while at the same time giving more insight on who decides this. Valentine's actions are justified by the authorial voice ('But it must … his insolent conduct.'), as well as supported by a majority of bystanders. Yet, like Bramstone's objections, there is a small minority who think he has 'gone too far', overstepping the limit of play; the assessment made by Valentine (and the authorial commentary which underwrites his decisions) is conclusive.

Another aspect of Valentine's interruptions is Valentine's heckling in overtly political spaces: during the election for a town crier (as analysed in the section 'From *Vox* to *Vaux*'), in the House of Lords, during the meeting of the 'Sovereign People' in Kennington Common, and a socialist gathering.[120] The set-up for the scene in the House of Lords is similar to that of the election for town crier. The potential for amusement is immediately apparent to Valentine, as '[h]e had often wished for an opportunity to see our noble legislators at their work of law-making, and having frequently heard that capital sport was to be found there, he anticipated no small treat in his projected visit'.[121] Valentine attends with Uncle Sam, arriving

---

[119] Portwine, *Valentine Vaux*, p. 79.
[120] Portwine, *Valentine Vaux*, Chapter 10, 22, and 36 respectively (starting p. 49, p. 117, and p. 186).
[121] Portwine, *Valentine Vaux*, p. 50.

'just as a learned lord was reading the minister of the crown a pretty severe rebuke for the large professions they had made, and the little or nothing that had been done in the course of an unusually long session.'[122] The narrator notes that, not only did he bring this upon himself by voting down every piece of legislation that was proposed, the lowliness of the debate is underlined by his party members, as 'the more personal and insulting the learned peer became in his language, the more vehemently did his friends cheer him on, till Valentine began to think a serious outbreak must be the consequence between him and the premier.'[123] This quotation illustrates how the potential of violence between the politicians is already present before Valentine's meddling. It is similar in this set-up to the election for town crier, where the meeting is already in tumult before Valentine arrives. The politicians are described as 'rabid gentlemen', one of whom 'abus[es] his foe after the elegant style of a Billingsgate fishwoman'.[124] During the scene, Valentine interjects only twice: he initially pretends to be the Lord of the Treasury, yelling 'That's a lie!'. The chaos created by this one interruption is so significant that Valentine, usually entertained by conflict, intercedes a second time:

> Cheers and laughter now resounded through the house, and so indecorous did they become in their mirth, that at last Valentine, who was rather a liberal in opinion, gave vent to his indignation in an exclamation of "shame!" This, as our readers will easily enough suppose, was sufficient to set the whole house in a ferment, and in one instant every peer was upon his legs demanding the cause of so scandalous an interruption to the important deliberation which had called them together.[125]

---

[122] Portwine, *Valentine Vaux*, p. 50.
[123] Portwine, *Valentine Vaux*, p. 50.
[124] Portwine, *Valentine Vaux*, p. 50-51.
[125] Portwine, *Valentine Vaux*, p. 51.

Because of the repetitiveness of *Vaux*'s humorous scenes – Valentine looking for amusement, he interferes, he is amused by the reactions of his victims – the reversal exhibited in this scene is striking. Valentine's interjections are usually void of meaning; it is the act of interrupting that is the point rather than the words or sounds he creates. His exclamation of 'shame!' transgresses that pattern by voicing a judgement.[126] The laughter by the peers is presented as embarrassing, a point which is driven home by the close of the scene, when the speaker orders the gallery to close so the peers can deliberate on how to respond to Valentine's outburst:

> [C]andour obliges us to confess that Valentine and every body [sic] else thought it a very happy release to find themselves once more on the outside of the walls, within which they had beheld a scene that would have disgraced even a bear-garden. As for our hero, he was perfectly astonished at what he had seen and heard, for he had been used to suppose that there was some little order in an assembly that consisted of men who ranked among the highest and noblest in the land; instead of which he had witnessed a scene, of which the lowest portion of the community would have been thoroughly ashamed.[127]

The scene inverts the pattern set by previous scenes: when Valentine creates chaos among working-class people, this is seen as humorous and falls within the realm of play. The limits to Valentine's laughter, however, are shown when the same situation is applied to those of the upper classes ('the highest and noblest in the land'). The violence

---

[126] This distinction broadly aligns with the two reasons for heckling as identified by Mel Jordan and Lee Campbell in 'The Heckler's Promise', *Performance Paradigm*, 14 (2018), 126-140. They write: 'I identified two key reasons [why we interrupt in verbal exchange]: first, the interrupter disagrees with what is being said, and second, the interrupter seeks to "score a point" over the speaker' (p. 132). While Valentine is generally only interested in 'scoring a point', in this section he is expressing disagreement.
[127] Portwine, *Valentine Vaux*, p. 51.

that is acceptable on the streets becomes inappropriate when embodied by those of high status.

As mentioned above, *Vaux* sees politics as inherently ridiculous, and the scene in the House of Lords is an extension of that. Politics makes fools out of us, even if one is part of the upper layers of society. Yet this does not mean that difference in status becomes obsolete – not only is Prest much harsher on radical politics and socialism, the text also reiterates conventional authority through the way order is restored after Valentine's disruptions. Resistance is futile and misguided; at the protest by the Sovereign People, a radical group consisting of the 'unwashed and unshaved'[128] demanding rights, Valentine considers 'the folly of men who endeavoured by physical force to overpower a government which possesses so many and such ample means to defeat the plans of their enemies.'[129] Not only are the Sovereign People criticised by Valentine, they are not appreciated by bystanders either. The speech by one Mr Bowbell, one of the movement's leaders, is rudely interrupted:

> "I say, fellow countrymen, that we are an ill-used, despised, trodden-upon, oppressed, and tax-devoured people. our rulers have no pity for the productive classes, - of which I am proud to call myself a member. [Hear! hear!] Yes, gentlemen, I am proud to call myself one of you, and I only wish to convince you that no man can be happy till every one of us, rich as well as poor, are brought to a level with each other."
> At this period a huge hard-hearted cabbage was thrown by some unseen hand with such fatal precision, that taking the unfortunate Mr. Bowbell in the paunch, it laid him sprawling among the select few who had been admitted to

---

[128] Portwine, *Valentine Vaux*, p. 118. Quotation marks in original. 'The Great Unwashed' was a phrase originally coined by Edward Bulwer-Lytton in *Paul Clifford* (1830).
[129] Portwine, *Valentine Vaux*, p. 118.

a place on the platform. This was a levelling system that was very unpalatable to the leaders.[130]

The irony used in the second paragraph in this quotation underlines the hypocrisy of the radical leaders. While they appear to call for equality, the narrative positions the fact that the movement has self-important leaders who 'march pompously'[131] to the temporary platform as indicative of their insincerity. Unlike the peers in the House of Lords, the working class leaders and supporters of the Sovereign People are misguided and arrogant but ultimately harmless. Valentine finds their behaviour amusing, and as foreshadowed in his early consideration of the folly of men who endeavour to overpower a government, the meeting disintegrates immediately at the mention of incoming police.

The Sovereign People are treated narratively in a similar manner to the 'exquisites', both categories consisting of people who overstep their class boundaries. The socialists, however, are considered of a completely different kind. The narrative tone shifts from ironic to scathing, describing how Valentine attends a meeting of 'that truly vicious society the "Socialists"'. Rather than seeking amusement, Valentine 'though detesting the tenets of this class of men, resolved to enter the place, if it were only for the purpose of convincing himself whether men and women could be so utterly depraved in principle as report had stated.'[132] The scene is mainly concerned with 'socialist' views on marriage, which are a grotesque version of Robert Owen's stance on marriage and divorce. Owen gave lectures on the topic in the 1830s, arguing that marriages without affection should be allowed to be disbanded, to protect vulnerable women from abusive marriages as well as preventing people to become unhappy for life in unsuitable matches.[133] Exaggerated readings of

---

[130] Portwine, *Valentine Vaux*, p. 119.
[131] Portwine, *Valentine Vaux*, p. 118.
[132] Portwine, *Valentine Vaux*, p. 186.
[133] Robert Owen, *Lectures on the Marriages of the Priesthood of the Old Immoral World, Delivered in the Year 1835, Before the Passing of the New Marriage Act* (Leeds: J. Hobson, 1840), pp. 86-90.

Owen's ideas were prevalent, illustrated by the title page and preface of a pamphlet on marriage published in 1840; the title page reads 'With an Appendix, Containing the Marriage System of the New Moral World; And proving that the Author never entertained the sentiments attributed to him by the opponents of Socialism.' In Prest's reading, the socialists aim to 'prove that marriage is opposed to the happiness of mankind, and, consequently, that the sexes ought to live together in a state of nature.'[134] More specifically, the lecturer claims that 'We are for a community of goods – every thing is to belong in common to one another, and why, therefore, I ask you, should not our women be common also?'[135] To Valentine, this stance goes against 'common decency', and he is discouraged by the amount of women in the crowd, but he 'consoled himself with the certainty that there were always enough of good people in the world to very prevent any wide-spreading evil resulting from such a filthy sink of corruption.'[136]

While the Sovereign People are hypocrites that one should laugh at, the socialists are morally corrupt, aiming to 'poison' with 'pestiferous doctrines'.[137] When Valentine ventriloquially interferes, it is not with the intention to amuse, it is to vent his disapproval in a comparable way to his interjection in the House of Lords. While the peers in the House of Lords were embarrassing due to their behaviour, their legitimacy or authority is undisputed by the text. The Sovereign People try to claim authority, but their attempts are futile and laughable. Prest's socialists, on the other hand, argue against any authority except 'nature'; they are 'a free agent,' 'not bound to obey any laws, or submit himself to the control of those whom circumstances have placed above him'.[138] The leaders of the Sovereign People are revealed as hypocrites – they might claim to aim for equality, but they actually simply want power for themselves. The socialists are insidious exactly because they

---

[134] Portwine, *Valentine Vaux*, p. 186.
[135] Portwine, *Valentine Vaux*, p. 188.
[136] Portwine, *Valentine Vaux*, p. 186.
[137] Portwine, *Valentine Vaux*, p. 186.
[138] Portwine, *Valentine Vaux*, p. 187.

succeed in overstepping the boundaries of convention, especially sexual convention. The speaker, for example, is looking for a fourth partner, and to Valentine's disgust, the women in the audience show an interest in filling this position. While the structure of the scene at the socialist meeting is similar to the comic script the reader has become very familiar with at this point in the text, its tone is diametrically opposed to the usual carnivalesque humour Valentine's ventriloquial exploits express. The effect of this jarring opposition is stronger than if the narrator had suspended the comic script to insert a moralising authorial voice condemning the socialist movement (like Cockton does in his introduction to *Valentine Vox*, writing an essayistic section on asylums). The crimes of the socialists are so extreme, the text reasons, that even the trickster Valentine cannot abide their ideology. When the lecturer argues for the rights of women to separate from a husband who has for example become imprisoned, Valentine becomes the mouthpiece of conservative familial values:

> "Curses light upon the woman who would forsake the husband who has fallen into trouble!" cried Valentine, indignant at the glaring barbarism of the lecturer's views. "In difficulties a man should be strengthened and supported by the tender care of his wife, and yet there are hollow miscreants who would deprive him of this; - perhaps his sole remaining consolation upon earth!"[139]

This speech might seem surprising coming from a character who has little compassion for anyone except perhaps his benefactor, and actively goes out his way to annoy others. What Valentine is expressing in this speech is therefore not a call for wives to have pity on their husbands who might fall on hard times, but a defence of the status of monogamous heteronormative marriage as a moral obligation and a pillar of civilization. The section continues with

---

[139] Portwine, *Valentine Vaux*, p. 189.

Valentine exclaiming, 'I am, indeed, bigoted, as you call it, to the cause of virtue,' calling the lecturer's words 'language that would be a disgrace even to a barbarian.'[140]

The speech reveals Valentine's true relationship to power: he is opposed to any shift in the structures of power present in early Victorian society. Valentine is characterised as an impulsive trickster, whose 'love of mischief' often 'predominate[s] over all other feelings.'[141] Like other trickster figures, Valentine moves on the outside of the boundaries set by society. Helena Bassil-Morozow's concept of the trickster describes them as someone who 'regard[s] "order" and "peace" as forms of stagnation, as lack of movement, death.'[142] Valentine is impatient, hot-headed, and impulsive, always seeking his next source of entertainment. His presence disrupts, causes disorder, and escalates conflict. On the surface, Valentine therefore appears to embody the 'trickster spirit' that Bassil-Morozow describes, an archetype that has a long history in various mythologies. However, where Bassil-Morozow argues that the trickster questions the validity of any authority by destabilising the concept of logic and rationality,[143] Valentine's rebellions do not have this destabilising effect. Valentine, both in Prest's as well as in Cockton's version, is a trickster, a figure closely related to the picaresque hero; Connor describes their overlap as an 'openness to experience and in seeming immunity to time or change.'[144] Valentine's potential as a trickster – or as a picaresque hero[145] – is limited. His pranks only highlight how he stands apart from those he tricks. Under the pressure of Valentine's disruption,

---

[140] Portwine, *Valentine Vaux*, p. 189.
[141] Portwine, *Valentine Vaux*, p. 98.
[142] Helena Bassil-Morozow, *The Trickster in Contemporary Film* (London: Routledge, 2012), p. 7.
[143] Bassil-Morozow, *Trickster*, p. 10.
[144] Connor, *Dumbstruck*, p. 320.
[145] According to Barbara Babcock-Abrahams the term picaresque 'combines with the notion of trickery and roguish behaviour the idea of the uncertain or hostile attitude of an individual to existing society and an involvement in narrative focussed on movement, within and beyond that society.' '"A Tolerated Margin of Mess": The Trickster and His Tales Reconsidered', *Journal of the Folklore Institute*, 11:3 (1975), 147-186, p. 159.

the socialist meeting erupts in violence, only to be disbanded by the police. The subject of the following section is the interplay between Valentine, crowds, and the disciplinary role of the police in the text.

VOICE, SOUND AND THE CROWD

Large groups of people are a recurring theme in *Valentine Vaux*: crowds are mentioned twenty-seven times, and mobs an additional ten times in the text. In the nineteenth-century context, the crowd was more and more perceived as problematic; they were increasingly understood 'as a destabilising threat to social order, laced with possibly serious, revolutionary consequences,' and warranted a larger presence of constables to prevent a potential riot.[146] In political theory the French Revolution permanently changed the perceptions of crowds, making it impossible to see them as an occasional but ultimately harmless nuisance, as historian Edward Gibbon did in 1788.[147] Although extensive theories of crowds were not to be formulated and popularised until late in the nineteenth century by thinkers like Hippolyte Taine and Charles-Marie Gustave Le Bon, crowds were perceived to have the potential to become revolutionary crowds.[148] In *Extraordinary Popular Delusions and the Madness of Crowds* by Charles Mackay (first published in 1841), crowd behaviour is understood as the extension of individual human nature:

> In reading the history of nations, we find that, like individuals, they have their whims and their peculiarities; their seasons of excitement and recklessness, when they

---

[146] Matthew White, '"Rogues of the Meaner Sort"? Old Bailey Executions and the Crowd in the Early Nineteenth Century', *The London Journal*, 33:2 (2008), 135-153, p. 139.
[147] J.S. McClelland, *The Crowd and the Mob. From Plato to Canetti* (Abingdon: Routledge, 1989), p. 114.
[148] This perception was cemented by the revolutions of 1848. See McClelland, *Crowd and the Mob*, p. 6.

care not what they do. We find that whole communities suddenly fix their minds upon one object, and go mad in its pursuit; that millions of people become simultaneously impressed with one delusion, and run after it, till their attention is caught by some new folly more captivating than the first.[149]

The problem of crowds, historically, is one of control.[150] The control framework does not fully encompass the meaning of crowds in *Valentine Vaux*, where amusement drives the text. While Mackay points out that delusions on a national scale can lead to 'rivers of blood' and sow 'a harvest of groans and tears, to be reaped by posterity', this is not extended to all crowds; some of his descriptions are 'sketches of some lighter matters – amusing instances of the imitativeness and wrongheadedness of the people, rather than examples of folly and delusion.'[151] This distinction is important, as while the threat of large amounts of people and the interactions between crowds and constables are played out repeatedly in *Valentine Vaux*, and groups of people convene and dissipate continuously, they are provoked by the actions of the main characters for their own pleasure. Mackay, in his chapter 'Popular Follies of Great Cities', describes his aims in a sentence that could easily summarise Valentine's actions in *Valentine Vaux*: 'wandering through the busy haunts of great cities, we shall seek only for amusement, and note as we pass a few of the harmless follies and whimsies of the poor.'[152]

When Valentine confronts Arnold in front of Septimus Bramstone's house, which the latter had been emptying of Septimus's possessions, their fighting draws attention: 'a crowd of

---

[149] Charles Mackay, *Extraordinary Popular Delusions and the Madness of Crowds* (London: Wordsworth, 1995), p. xv.
[150] Mark Harrison, *Crowds and History. Mass Phenomena in English Towns, 1790-1835* (Cambridge: Cambridge University Press, 1988), p. 4.
[151] Mackay, *Popular Delusions*, p. xiii.
[152] Mackay, *Popular Delusions*, p. 515.

people thronged round, having been attracted to the spot by the loud tones in which the latter part of the conversation had been carried on.'[153] The crowd is an audience to the argument, but these boundaries quickly blur when Arnold punches a butcher's boy who heckles him. This lack of distinction between crowd and individual, between audience and participant, echoes Bakhtin's description of the carnivalesque crowd. He writes that 'carnival does not know footlights, in the sense that it does not acknowledge any distinction between actors and spectators. [...] Carnival is not a spectacle seen by the people; they live in it, and everyone participates because its very idea embraces all the people.'[154] While Bakhtin was writing specifically about historical celebrations, conceptualizing the tumultuous, violent crowds of *Valentine Vaux* as carnivalesque draws attention to their festive nature. Like Bakhtin's carnival, the laughter of the crowd in *Vaux* is 'gay, triumphant, and at the same time mocking, deriding.'[155] The laughter of the crowd in Vaux encapsulates this ambivalence. When Arnold punches the butcher's boy:

> a tremendous outcry was raised by the mob, and before Arnold had time to secure his safety by flight, he was seized in the arms of a study coal-porter, who, lifting him up with about as much ease as a cat would a mouse, carried him to a place where there happened to be a large collection of mud, and there deposited his burden, amidst the laughter and applause of the bystanders.[156]

Arnold is punished for his violence, mocked by the bystanders, while at the same time there is a sense of joy in the whole event. As quickly as the crowd gathers, it falls apart: 'the mob dispersed – which it did immediately upon a cry being raised that the police

---

[153] Portwine, *Valentine Vaux*, p. 110.
[154] Bakhtin, *Rabelais*, p. 7.
[155] Bakhtin, *Rabelais*, p. 11-12.
[156] Portwine, *Valentine Vaux*, p. 110.

were coming'.[157] The crowds of *Vaux* are spontaneous gatherings, small pockets of carnivalesque license that dissolve when faced with hierarchy and power as embodied by the police. As such, the mob – utilizing a word that has connotations with threat[158] – has no political power in *Valentine Vaux*, and is no danger to the established order. While violence is part of the groups of people that gather, this violence is not aimed at the state or revolutionary in its aims, and therefore should not be seen as expressing the established intellectual discourse of the dangerous crowd (though one could argue that the violent potential of them could be used as an argument for control in itself).

The carnivalesque shares many commonalities with the farcical. Farce, too, levels hierarchy, incorporates derision as well as joy.[159] While Jessica Davis's *Farce* for example does not cover Bakhtin, she does mention the Feast of Fools (a recurring theme in Bakhtin), and her description of farce as 'both aggressive and festive' echoes Bakhtin's 'gay, triumphant, and at the same time mocking, deriding' aspects of the carnivalesque.[160] While there are many differences between the two approaches – particularly as Bakhtin's work has an additional layer of meaning beyond the literary theoretical[161] – I use them as complimentary terms. The carnivalesque in this thesis retains the folk-connotation of Bakhtin's work, being applicable only when we speak of groups of people, feasting, chaos, or other essentially social themes. The theory of farce and the farcical, on the other hand, has been developed to be used in theatre studies and is particularly suited to themes pertaining to the individual or small-

---

[157] Portwine, *Valentine Vaux*, p. 111.
[158] McClelland, *Crowd and the Mob*, p. 7-8.
[159] Davis, *Farce*, p. 85.
[160] Davis, *Farce*, p. 24. Bakhtin, *Rabelais*, pp. 11-12.
[161] As Michael Holquist writes in the introduction to *Rabelais and His World*: 'At one level Rabelais and His World is a parable and guidebook for its times, inexplicable without reference to the close connection between the circumstances of its own production and Soviet [xv] intellectual and political history. At another level, directed to scholars anywhere at any time, it is a contribution to historical poetics with theoretical implications not limited by its origin in a particular time and place.' Michael Holquist, 'Proloque', in: Bakhtin, *Rabelais*, p. xvi-xv.

scale interactions. Returning to the example of the baker and the chimney sweep discussed in the section 'From *Vox* to *Vaux*', the initial fight between the two is farcical rather than carnivalesque, as it involves only themselves with Valentine as instigator/witness. The crowd, or 'the people' are absent in this scene, and therefore does not lend itself well to a carnivalesque interpretation. The boundaries between the two are porous, and rather than creating an arbitrary boundary about how many people constitutes a crowd, this thesis instead follows the language used by the texts themselves in determining what theoretical terminology is more appropriate.

As the primary readership of penny bloods were the London working classes themselves, the lived experience of people in the busy city deserves mention in this analysis. It was common knowledge in early nineteenth-century London that being present in a crowd could pose a danger to one's body – in very large assemblies like public executions, people routinely lost their lives by being trampled, falling from high observation points, or from the collapse of make-shift spectator structures.[162] The inquest after a particularly gruesome tragedy in 1807, where thirty people lost their lives in a stampede outside the Old Bailey, reveals that several parents warned or even forbade their children from attending the event, fearing for their safety.[163] Despite the police presence at public executions, these large assemblies rarely descended into riots; historian Matthew White reports that the constabulary's 'responsibilities largely involved pushing back numbers when danger was detected and in dealing with cases of pickpocketing and petty larceny.'[164] Meanwhile the policemen in *Valentine Vaux* have a heavy workload: they appear several times in the text, being tasked with dissolving chaotic crowds, as in the example above. The text exhibits a feature of Victorian life that David Churchill has described as 'police-consciousness'. Throughout the nineteenth century, the police became increasingly involved not merely in the

---

[162] White, 'Rogues', p. 140-141.
[163] White, 'Rogues', p. 141.
[164] White, 'Rogues', p. 149.

prevention of crime, but also in urban regulation.[165] The aim of this regulation was particularly to control 'nuisance,' a broad concept that could refer to anything from gambling and drinking to standing still for too long ('loitering') or children playing in public spaces.[166] The result of this increased public visibility of the police and their interference in everyday activities, was 'an awareness that one's everyday conduct in public space was subject to sanction according to prescribed norms of good order.'[167] In *Valentine Vaux*, the police too is 'part of the mental furniture,' as Churchill describes the constant possibility of surveillance on those who lived in a Victorian city.[168] Prest's police can be called at a moment's notice, implying the police are always present in the public space, or they simply show up whenever a crowd becomes too raucous.[169]

The constables in *Valentine Vaux* are surprisingly effective, often being able to return the exuberant crowds to order simply by being seen. An example of this effect can be found at the tail end of the scene featuring the meeting of Sovereign People, where Valentine's ventriloquial interjections cause a fight. Just as the two brawlers fall over the side of a platform, to the laughter of the spectators, the threat of the police becomes apparent.

> At this moment, too, a shout was again raised that a strong body of the police was coming, and as the report was on this occasion perfectly correct, every body began to look out for his own safety with surprising agility. In fact, so effectual was the report, and so greatly did it operate upon the crowd, that in a few minutes the place was nearly deserted by the thousands who had, but a short time

---

[165] David Churchill, *Crime Control and Everyday Life in the Victorian City. The Police and the Public* (Oxford: Oxford University Press, 2017), p. 98-100.
[166] Churchill, *Crime Control*, p. 117.
[167] Churchill, *Crime Control*, p. 116.
[168] Churchill, *Crime Control*, p. 117.
[169] The police occasionally even interferes in spaces beyond the streets, like at the socialist meeting, where 'In the midst of this riot a party of policemen rushed in', Portwine, *Valentine Vaux*, p. 189.

before, covered the common with a dense mass of human beings.[170]

Behind this almost instantaneous dispersal is the threat of arrest, tying in with what Churchill calls the 'culture of arrest': 'a preference for using the full extent of legal authority entrusted to the police (and sometimes exceeding that authority) in dealing with prosaic infractions against urban order.'[171] The constables therefore restore order after the disturbance of the carnivalesque crowd. Even Valentine deems it prudent to escape the possibility of arrest: 'he, wisely enough, thought that discretion the better part of valour, and having no wish to be taken up on a charge of riot and disorder, he turned from the spot'.[172] As was the case for real-life middle-class Victorians, Valentine's class only partially protects him from police scrutiny; while the working classes were often targeted specifically, the middle class was not exempt from street policing.[173] Valentine's relationship to the police, however, is more complex than simple avoidance. At the socialist meeting, for example, he reasons with a policeman to let the socialists go home despite their rioting.[174] Part of the dynamic between Valentine and the police can be explained through the sense of play that the text espouses – for the text to present itself as play, it is necessary that there is no real lasting consequence to Valentine's antics. The reader is periodically assured that his victims went home safe and sound, though perhaps slightly worse the wear as a result of their fighting, dunking, or mudding. However, it also illustrates Valentine's relationship to authority and order. He only avoids the police when he might be 'mistaken' for

---

[170] Portwine, *Valentine Vaux*, p. 122.
[171] Churchill, *Crime Control*, p. 119.
[172] Portwine, *Valentine Vaux*, p. 122.
[173] Churchill, *Crime Control*, p. 120.
[174] While this might seem surprising in the light of Valentine's stance on socialism, his argument is that 'their own absolute wickedness will ultimately wreck the frail vessel they have launched, and by suffering them to meet in darkness, and obscurity, you will do them a far greater injury than could be inflicted upon them by any punishment the laws they affect to despise, could by any possibility oppose to them.' Portwine, *Valentine Vaux*, p. 190.

one of the people fighting; when he wants to free Bramstone from the asylum he is being held in, the police immediately support his interests:

> His first act was to apply to the nearest magistrate for advice under existing circumstances, and fortunately for himself, he happened to meet with a gentleman who was willing to afford him every assistance in his power to bring the guilty parties to justice. By this person's order four policemen were desired to accompany Valentine to Prospect Villa, with instructions to remain close by, so as to be in readiness should their assistance be required.[175]

It becomes clear in this quotation that Valentine is not antithetical to authority. In fact, the police's support is easily secured, and in the following scene, he retains power and agency, while the policemen follow his directions. While Valentine and the police, at a glance, might seem to have oppositional interests (Valentine causing disorder, while the police return crowds back to order), when placed together in the pattern of the narrative, they underpin conventional authority and the inevitable triumph of order. While allowing for the fact that Valentine himself is not completely beyond the control of these forces (as he too is aware of the possibility of arrest), he affirms their validity by drawing on their authority.

> "And pray what authority do you possess to search my house?" demanded the other in a bullying tone. "Who, I should like to know can have authorised you or any body else to go over my premises without permission?" [Valentine:] "No less a personage than Mr. Clause, the magistrate."[176]

---

[175] Portwine, *Valentine Vaux*, p. 135.
[176] Portwine, *Valentine Vaux*, p. 136.

Valentine respects and supports the power invested in the police and magistrate, indicating that his temporary rebellions are not meant to go beyond any boundaries of permitted behaviour, but instead reveal where those boundaries lay and reinforce them through laughter, or lack thereof, such as at the meeting of the socialists.

Another aspect to the lived experience in early-nineteenth-century London, related to crowds, is the aural. The ever-expanding modern city was notoriously noisy; William Wordsworth describes London as a 'monstrous ant-hill' in *The Prelude* (1850).[177] The soundscape of London that Wordsworth portrays includes 'the deafening din', a 'roar' that 'continues, till at length, escaped as from an enemy' one finds a 'sheltered place'. A 'female vendor's scream' is deemed 'the very shrillest of all London cries', and street performers cause 'the uproar of the rabblement.' As these quotations illustrate, the crowd was an essential part of the London soundscape; and as the population kept growing during the early nineteenth century, the noisiness of the metropolis only increased as a consequence. Representations of city soundscapes are relatively rare in early nineteenth-century writings, usually focussing on the visual rather than the aural.[178] A similar description to Wordsworth's can be found in Dickens' *Nicholas Nickleby* (1839):

> They rattled on through the noisy, bustling, crowded streets of London, [...] Streams of people apparently without end poured on and on, jostling each other in the crowd and hurrying forward [...] while vehicles of all

---

[177] William Wordsworth, *The Prelude; or, Growth of a Poet's Mind* (New York: D. Appleton & Company 1850). The quotes are taken from pp. 177-182.
[178] Arnold suggests that 'Perhaps the rarity of descriptions of auditory experiences of the metropolis in early nineteenth-century writings is due in part to the contemporary belief in the unrecordability of sound and the absence of a coherent and effective vocabulary to describe the auditory experience of the metropolis.' Dana Arnold, *Re-presenting the Metropolis. Architecture, urban experience and social life in London 1800-1840* (Aldershot: Ashgate Publishing Limited, 2000), p. 35.

shapes and makes, mingled up together in one moving mass like running water, lent their ceaseless roar to swell the noise and tumult.[179]

In Victorian England, the noise of the city was not simply a nuisance, but also had connotations of class identity. As Peter Bailey argues, 'Freedom of noise became a defining characteristic of the English bourgeoisie, as much a mark of their nationality as their class.'[180] He continues that 'It was the city street [...] which remained the front line in the contest over noise and an alleged struggle between civilization and barbarism.'[181] *Valentine Vaux* is a particularly noisy text; not only are various scenes constructed around noise and chaos, the text itself is peppered with almost eight hundred exclamation points, creating a reading experience that is everything but restrained.[182] Noise is an indicator or excitement to be had – silence, on the other hand, indicates seriousness. In a very rare instance of Valentine's silence, this is precipitated by him 'having no wish to offend', and therefore 'he wisely forbore giving any opinion.'[183] The next moves back and forth between a festive noise and laughter and the civilizing (and quieting) influence of conventional power, embodied by the constables. Noise is not free of its barbaric connotations, yet the text revels in excessive sound.

The meaning of noise within a text is part of its generic positioning. In Gothic literature, for example, uncanny sounds are central to the genre.[184] Sound or its absence creates uncanny effects, as 'sound suggests presence even when this presence is invisible or

---

[179] Charles Dickens, *The Life and Adventures of Nicholas Nickleby* (London: Chapman and Hall, 1839), p. 307.
[180] Peter Bailey, 'Breaking the Sound Barrier: A Historian Listens to Noise', *Body and Society*, 2:2 (1996), 49-66, p. 60.
[181] Bailey, 'Sound Barrier', p. 60.
[182] The Gale OCR text of *Valentine Vaux* includes 796 exclamation points. Some of these might be errors, while others might have been missed.
[183] Portwine, *Valentine Vaux*, p. 36.
[184] Isabella van Elferen, *Gothic Music. The Sounds of the Uncanny* (Cardiff: University of Wales Press, 2012), p. 1.

intangible, and thus closely related to the ghostly.'[185] This effect of ghostly presence which ventriloquism can create is utilised in *Wieland*; in *Valentine Vaux*, however, sound is no longer uncanny. If a person is terrified at the voices or sounds Valentine creates, this fear is always mediated through Valentine's laughter. Despite *Valentine Vaux* embracing Gothic tropes such as asylum incarceration, disembodied voices, and repetition in its plot, it creates a laughter that is an expression of joy rather than fear. In the categorisations by Peter Bailey, *Valentine Vaux*'s laughter is a 'noise of merriment', rather than a 'noise of terror'.[186] While the Gothic thrives on ambiguity and liminality, *Vaux*'s characters are quick to ascribe a source to any voice or sound they come across. In a particularly silly passage set in the Tower of London, Valentine throws his voice in a statue of Henry the Eighth to frighten a family with a shockingly bad knowledge of history, calling them fools.[187]

> "Is that figure alive?" at length asked Mr. Jonas Jenkins, in a tone of mingled terror and amazement.
> "Alive, lor' bless you, not as I knows on," answered the horror-struck warder. "It's only an effigy, sir, and though I've been here for the last ten years I never heard him speak a word before, as I'm an honest man."
> "He called me a fool, at any rate," exclaimed Bob, indignantly, "and king or no king, I'm blest, if I'm going to stand that sort of caper."[188]

Even when faced with a terrifying voice coming from a statue, the characters in *Vaux* take these situations in their stride, and deal

---

[185] Van Elferen, *Gothic Music*, p. 3.
[186] Terminology paraphrased from Bailey, 'Sound Barrier', p. 51-52.
[187] A boy educated at a boarding school named Bob shares some wonderful facts about several English royalties, including: 'Edward the First was the father of George the Third, and was chiefly celebrated for his battles with Julius Caesar the Grecian hero. He was the inventor of steam guns and was surnamed the Great, though history describes him as a very little man.' Portwine, *Valentine Vaux*, p. 100.
[188] Portwine, *Valentine Vaux*, p. 101.

with the seemingly impossible at face value. Fear soon morphs into anger, a particularly ineffective anger as Bob is arguing with a statue. Unlike Cockton's characters, Prest's characters solve the aural mystery (a voice coming from an impossible place) by accepting that it is indeed coming from this place, however improbably. It is this willingness by the subjects of Valentine's pranks to 'play along' with these situations, as it were, that constitutes the humour in *Valentine Vaux*. As any ambiguity is immediately resolved in the text, however, even a voice coming from a place it should not fails to become uncanny.

Conclusion

As we have seen *Valentine Vaux* incorporates Gothic tropes, not for Gothic affect or even to parody them, but merely as a backdrop to its laughter. Ultimately, the carnival of *Valentine Vaux* is part of the same cultural moment as the 'harmless follies' that Charles Mackay describes in his non-fictional *Extraordinary Popular Delusions*. He describes the short-lived trend of exclaiming 'What a shocking hat!' in the mid-century metropolis.

> He who showed symptoms of ill-feeling at the imputations cast upon his hat, only brought upon himself redoubled notice. The mob soon perceive whether a man is irritable, and, if of their own class, they love to make sport of him. When such a man, and with such a hat, passed in those days through a crowded neighbourhood, he might think himself fortunate if his annoyances were confined to the shouts and cries of the populace. The obnoxious hat was often snatched from his head, and thrown into the gutter by some practical joker, and then raised, covered with mud, upon the end of a stick, for the admiration of the spectators, who held their sides with laughter, and

exclaimed in the pauses of their mirth, "Oh! what a shocking bad hat!" "What a shocking bad hat!"[189]

The same elements that constitute the humour of *Valentine Vaux* are present in the (supposedly) real-life 'hat' joke. The target of the joke is a person who is deemed 'not agreeable' and therefore 'deserving'. This decision is made by the crowd, generally perceived as constituted of working-class individuals. Their sport is harmless exactly because it does not spill over class boundaries; respectable middle- or upper-class members of society are 'safe' spectators to these antics, their class preventing them from ridicule. The 'exquisites' Valentine makes fun of are targeted exactly because they overstep their boundaries. The laughter of the crowd is noisy and boisterous. Mackay describes working-class humour as 'humble wit or grotesque peculiarities'.[190] Ultimately, the mud-dunking of both Mackay's crowd as well as Prest's text is a de-fanged version of the Bakhtinian laughter of the marketplace. It is regenerative, mocking, and public, but at the same time holds no threat to existing hierarchies. If anything, it distances the working-class crowds from the middle-class Valentine, reiterating their difference in standing. While there was a move during the nineteenth-century towards 'civilizing' noise, including laughter, *Valentine Vaux* is a text that revels in the noisy working-class environment, but never extends beyond it.

---

[189] Mackay, *Popular Delusions*, pp. 516-517. While this tale is probably recounted second- or even third-hand, its origin is a bit questionable, and its verity unclear, it is worthwhile to quote here to illustrate a broader contemporary humorous discourse.
[190] Mackay, *Popular Delusions* p. 515.

Chapter Three

Jack Rann by James Lindridge

INTRODUCTION

Stories of highwaymen and their exploits have captivated imaginations across several centuries. Their stories were told and retold in the shape of chapbooks, ballads, and Newgate calendars; and in the 1840s, the figure of the highwayman was incorporated in several penny serials. The subject of this chapter is James Lindridge's *Jack Rann, alias Sixteen-String Jack* (1840), published by George Purkess. Based in Compton Street in Soho, Purkess collaborated with Edward Lloyd and another London-based publisher, William Strange, on the serials *History of the Pirates of All Nations* (1836-1837) and *History and Lives of the Most Notorious Highwaymen, Footpads and Murderers, Brigands, Pickpockets, Thieves, Banditti and Robbers of Every Description* (1836-1837).[1] George Purkess senior published several penny 'domestic' romances throughout the 1840s. The database *Price One Penny* lists several of Purkess's publications,[2] though this list is likely incomplete when compared to the 1849 advertisement reproduced by John Adcock, which lists several

---

[1] Sarah Louise Lill, 'In for a Penny: The Business of Mass-Market Publishing 1832-90', in *Edward Lloyd and His World. Popular Fiction, Politics and the Press in Victorian Britain*, ed. by Sarah Louise Lill and Rohan McWilliam (New York: Routledge, 2019), p. 26.
[2] Marie Léger-St-Jean, 'George Purkess' in *Price One Penny* <http://www.priceonepenny.info/database/show_publisher.php?publisher_id=72> [accessed 26 September 2022].

penny plays, illustrated works, and over sixty romance tales 'complete for one penny' (presumably stories complete within one penny issue).[3] Very little is known about George Purkess and many of his publications seem to have been lost over time, though some of the illustrated, collected works are preserved in the Barry Ono collection, including *Jack Rann*.[4] Even less is known of the author James Lindridge; on the title page of *Jack Rann* Lindridge is identified as the author or *De Lisle* and *Tyburn Tree*. The 1848 edition of *Tyburn Tree* published by Purkess, however, names J. Dicks as the author.[5] It is possible that J. Dicks (occasionally styled Jayhohenn Deehiseekayess Esq.) refers to the London publisher John Thomas Dicks who might have used James Lindridge as an (inconsistent) pseudonym; it is also possible both of these names are pseudonyms by a currently unknown person.

Jack Rann: Alias Sixteen-String Jack is a reimagination of the life story of John Rann, an English highwayman active in the 1770s. The biographical database London Lives describes Rann as 'one of the first criminal celebrities'; as we shall see in the following section, however, the celebrity highwayman has a long history in Britain, reaching way beyond the eighteenth century, when Rann was active. His crimes were fairly standard for a highwayman of the period; he gained notoriety not necessarily because of his criminal track record, but because of his extravagant appearance after one of his arrests in 1773. He gained the nickname of 'Sixteen-String Jack' because of the number of colourful

---

[3] John Adcock, 'The Purkess Family of Dean Street', *John Adcock*, image 3 <http://john-adcock.blogspot.com/2014/04/the-purkess-family-of-dean-street.html> [accessed 26 September 2022].
[4] Purkess's son (also named George Purkess) appears as a named character in a recent true crime novel based on the 1879 death of Matilda Hacker. Sinclair McKay, *The Lady in the Cellar: Murder, Scandal and Insanity in Victorian Bloomsbury* (London: White Lion Publishing, 2018).
[5] John Adcock, 'James Lindridge', *Yesterday's Papers Archive* <http://yesterdayspapersarchive.blogspot.com/2009/02/james-lindridge.html> [accessed 26 September 2022] is a good bibliographical resource for the various editions of Lindridge's works.

ribbons attached to his breeches.[6] At a later inquest, a newspaper reports that

> Rann entered the [Bow Street] office with [more] audacity than was ever observed in any other person in the like circumstances; his irons were tied up with blue ribbons, and he had an enormous bouquet of flowers affixed to the breast of his coat.[7]

On 19th October 1774 Rann was sentenced to death, and he was executed on December 7th in the same year.[8] Like other highwaymen such as Dick Turpin and Jack Sheppard, Rann's short albeit eventful criminal career became the subject of much speculation and fabrication. After his death, two pamphlets were published containing different accounts of his life. 'An Account of John Rann, Commonly Called Sixteen String Jack' claims that Rann was born on 15 April 1752 in London, while 'A Genuine Account of the Life of John Rann, alias Sixteen String Jack' claims that Rann was born in a village in the vicinity of Bath. *Jack Rann* was published more than sixty years after Rann's death, and can be seen as part of the novelistic tradition of the highwayman novel as well as an example of popular penny fiction. It is the working-class counterpart of the Newgate novel, a generic indication used by contemporary accounts to refer to books like William Harrison Ainsworth's *Rookwood* (1834) and *Jack Sheppard: A Romance* (1839-1840), and Charles Dickens's *Oliver Twist* (1837-1839) that caused controversy around their publication. In relation to the subject of this thesis, *Jack Rann* illustrates a different relationship to the carnivalesque, the theoretical concept which, as this study has demonstrated, is key to understanding the playful disorientations of the penny blood. While it features humorous scenes of deception that are

---

[6] There seems to be some confusion about the actual number of strings. It is unclear whether there were sixteen strings in total, or sixteen on each knee.
[7] Robert B. Shoemaker, 'The Street Robber and the Gentleman Highwayman: Changing Representations and Perceptions of Robbery in London, 1690-1800', *Cultural and Social History*, 3 (2006), 381-405, p. 400.
[8] 'October 1774 (s17741019-1)' and 'December 1774 (o17741207-1)' in *Old Bailey Proceedings Online* <www.oldbaileyonline.org> [accessed 26 September 2022].

comparable to Valentine Vaux's tricks, the text also shows a preoccupation with death, execution, and crime, all themes whose political implications become clearer when reading them through the lens of the carnivalesque. Where *Valentine Vaux* exhibits a certain conservatism, the adventures of Jack Rann unsettle categories like class and authority in subtle ways, resulting from a rebellious text that revels in its carnivalesque elements. An understanding of the rich history of the cult of the highwayman is essential to discern *Jack Rann*'s place in this tradition, and will therefore be the subject of the following section. This context will provide a background for an in-depth discussion of *Jack Rann* – starting with the function of laughter and the carnivalesque in the text, before closing in on the politics of disguise and class that pervade the text. Finally, a discussion of the role of Rann's execution that ends the text shows how the text deals with questions of authority and rebellion. The complicated relationship between humour, violence, and hero-worship is the thread that runs through all of these sections, and the chapter will show that *Jack Rann* subverts contemporary assessments of authority and class.

KNIGHTS OF THE ROAD

Appreciation for highway robbers has a long history in English culture. It baffled foreign commentators, like the French Abbé Le Blanc, who remarks in the late 1730s that in England, 'a noted thief is a kind of hero, in high repute among the populace.'[9] This section will briefly highlight some of the long and diverse history of the outlaw and the highwayman to explore some of the commonalities, or core features, across time. I see 'the outlaw' as the archetype, of which highwaymen are a specific subset defined as those who intercept and rob people on the highway; the confrontation is an essential feature of highway robbery, and differentiates the highwayman from a pickpocket, who might steal purses on the road. This distinction between outlaw and highwayman is

---

[9] Cited in Gillian Spraggs, *Outlaws & Highwaymen. The Cult of the Robber in England from the Middle Ages to the Nineteenth Century* (London: Pimlico, 2001), p. 1.

not always made by other sources, and some slippage in terminology is evident across time.[10] In *Outlaws & Highwaymen* (2001) Gillian Spraggs argues that the 'national worship of the armed robber' has its roots in the medieval period.[11] The earliest preserved writing about an outlaw is a biographical Latin text about Hereward, who led a rebellion against the Normans in the eleventh century.[12] At the start of the fourteenth century, the author of the poem *The Outlaw's Song* laments being left no other choice but to embark on a life of outlawry and robbery when faced with an unfair and biased justice system.[13] This tradition most likely spans back several centuries, beyond the preserved writing we have accessible to us now. As we will see in this section, justifying robbery through necessity is a common defence used both by fictional as well as historical robbers and thieves, a justification that reflects changing circumstances and the ever-evolving legal system. Stories about outlaws have been passed on both through oral storytelling as well as written texts, being changed and adapted for their contemporary audiences. A prime example of this is the body of work surrounding Robin Hood, one of the earlier and most enduring mythical highwaymen.

Although extant manuscripts about Robin Hood from the fifteenth century differ in content and story specifics, in all of them Robin Hood is an outlaw, a leader of a gang of criminals who robbed others. Regardless of whether the tales of Robin Hood were based on a historical figure or was merely inspired by several people, the Robin Hood myth became a cornerstone of the highwayman story-telling tradition. The stories 'transform a gang of hardened highwaymen and poachers, who do not hesitate to kill even innocent children when they get in their way,

---

[10] E.J. Hobsbawm, *Bandits. Revised Edition* (New York: Pantheon Books, 1981), for example, prefers the use of 'bandit' over outlaw. In the eighteenth and nineteenth centuries, a highwayman could also be called a robber or a thief. However, not every thief is a highwayman. As explained later in this section, there was also a perceived difference between a footpad (unmounted) and a highwayman (mounted), but again, these distinctions are not static and absolute.
[11] Spraggs, *Outlaws*, p. 12.
[12] Spraggs, *Outlaws*, p. 16.
[13] Spraggs, *Outlaws*, p. 15. The exact year of publication of *The Outlaw's Song* is unknown.

into jocular, heroic, swashbuckling adventurers.'[14] As A. J. Pollard argues in his study on the earliest Robin Hood texts, the ever-changing retellings of these stories each capture a specific historical moment.[15] Analysing the specifics of the text, the way the text engages with the enduring archetypes of the highwayman or outlaw story, reveals how their audiences engaged with themes like authority, violence, and class – an approach this chapter subsequently takes with *Jack Rann* as its subject. The figure of Robin Hood and subsequent outlaws and highwaymen have routinely been interpreted as social critics. According to Stephen Knight, the 'essence of Robin Hood as an outlaw is not distance from society and its norms, but challenging contiguity with them' and the 'crucial gap of otherness between law and outlaw is the domain of the Robin Hood myth and the many narratives that constantly recreate it.'[16] Although a direct line can be drawn from Robin Hood to highwaymen like Rann, the relationship between the nineteenth-century interpretation of Rann and authority do not necessarily follow this archetypical example.

A text that constantly negotiates the tension between law and outlaw is John Clavell's *A Recantation of an ill led Life* (1628). Clavell was convicted for highway robbery, and while waiting in prison for the king to sign his pardon, he wrote a verse novel about his career as a highwayman. Though on the surface intended as a cautionary tale – Clavell meant to convince authority figures that he had truly repented – the popularity of Clavell's confessions suggest that his readers were amused by the tales told in the 'liveliest colours'. Although upon his pardon and subsequent release from prison Clavell never turned to highway robbery again, he also sees his criminal exploits as part of his fame,[17] displaying the inherent ambiguity of his confessions themselves. Clavell's accounts in *Recantation* should not be taken at face value in light

---

[14] A. J. Pollard, *Imagining Robin Hood. The Late-Medieval Stories in Historical Context* (Abingdon: Routledge, 2004), p. 82.
[15] Pollard, *Robin Hood*, p. 16.
[16] Stephen Knight, 'Introduction' in *Robin Hood in Greenwood Stood. Alterity and Context in the English Outlaw Tradition*, ed. by Stephen Knight (Turnhout: Brepols Publishers, 2011), p. xi.
[17] Spraggs, *Outlaws*, p. 149.

of the conflicting interests in part of its creation, but it is an important literary artefact, part of the large body of highwayman literature. It touches on several tropes that are familiar to fictionalised accounts of historical highwaymen: the wish for glory, the swearing of oaths of brotherhood within the robber's band, the use of disguise to avoid capture, and the importance of a highwayman's horse. Not only does Clavell's list of disguises serve as a practical purpose, for Clavell they also serve as the highwaymen hiding their true (moral) self:

> But first pluck of your visards, hoods, disguise,
> Masks, Muzles, Mufflers, patches from your eyes,
> Those beards, those heads of haire, and that great wen,
> Which is not natural, that I may ken
> Your faces as they are [...][18]

As we shall see below, the trope of disguise takes a comic dimension in Lindridge's *Jack Rann*, while at the same time questioning what a 'true' self entails. Clavell refers to highwaymen as 'Knights of the Rodes' or 'High-way Lawyers', tongue-in-cheek terms that were still in use to describe highwaymen by the nineteenth-century.[19] The defining characteristic of a knight of the road was his horse – unlike the footpad, disdained by Clavell – the highwayman robbed while mounted. The 'knight of the road' designation points towards an important aspect of the highwayman: one relating to (self-appointed) class status. Highway robbery held a certain glamorous appeal in the public eye, partially because of its history. Clavell writes that some might 'Concei[ve] that it is a gentile course' and 'Some Gentlemen perhaps, before they knew / The poornesse of this way, to serve their neede / Have more then [sic] once attempted some such deede.'[20] In the centuries preceding the seventeenth, men of high birth who had no way to provide for

---

[18] John Clavell, *A Recantation of an ill led Life. Or A discouverie of the High-way Law.* (London: Richard Meighen, 1628), pp. 12-13. The original spelling of Clavell's text has been preserved, but the long s has been shortened and the u replaced with a v for increased readability.
[19] Clavell, *Recantation*, p. 12.
[20] Clavell, *Recantation*, p. 13.

themselves might turn to highway robbery, which made highway robbery gain a gentile reputation. The nobility-turned-robber for example appears in Thomas More's *Utopia* (1516), where the 'noblemen who live idly like drones off the labour of others' get rid of their retainers, usually lower nobility, in time of scarcity or peace. More's character Raphael Hythlodaeus states 'Just as thieves are not bad soldiers, soldiers turn out to be enterprising robbers, so nearly are these two ways of life related.'[21]

Material changes such as improvements to England's infrastructure, the increased inland trade, and the invention of the flintlock pistol, lead to highway robbery being perceived as a growing problem in the seventeenth century.[22] Attitudes to robbers and highwaymen had always been ambivalent, oscillating between praising them for their courage and vilifying them for their role as disturber of the social order. As Robert Shoemaker has shown, between the 1720s and mid-century, the public debate regarding thievery 'crystallized into two contrasting images: the violent urban street robber, and the polite gentleman highwayman.'[23] As we shall see, the paradoxical class distinction of the gentleman highwayman is a cornerstone of Lindridge's characterization of Jack Rann. While a 'street robber' (a designation first appearing in in print in 1722[24]) was deemed exceedingly dangerous, the gentleman highwayman were thought only to resort to violence when they were forced to, like when capture was imminent. Clavell, in the early seventeenth-century, already argues that the highwayman is reluctant to use violence, and instead intimidates his victims.[25] The lack of violence exhibited by highwaymen was thought to be a particularly English characteristic; as Spraggs writes, 'from the seventeenth century onwards we find a growing tendency for the English to congratulate themselves

---

[21] Thomas More, *Utopia*, ed. by George M. Logan and Robert M. Adams (Cambridge: Cambridge University Press, 2002), pp. 56-57.
[22] Robert B. Shoemaker, 'The Street Robber and the Gentleman Highwayman: Changing Representations and Perceptions of Robbery in London, 1690-1800', *Cultural and Social History*, 3 (2006), 381-405, p. 382.
[23] Shoemaker, 'Street Robber', p. 382.
[24] Shoemaker, 'Street Robber', p. 386.
[25] Spraggs, *Outlaws*, p. 155.

on the *lack* of genuine violence displayed by their [highway] robbers.'[26] In a pamphlet attributed to Daniel Defoe titled 'An Effectual Scheme For the Immediate Preventing of Street Robberies' from 1731, the author claims that 'Violence and Plunder is no longer confin'd to the Highways', but instead has spread to the London streets, where 'the whole Body of the Inhabitants seem alarm'd and uneasy.'[27] According to the pamphlet, highway robberies are incredibly violent in 'most Parts of *Europe, Great Britain* and *France* only excepted.'[28] The author states that 'the *English Highway-men* generally rob with more Civility and good Manners than is practis'd abroad, and with something of Generosity; not murdering those they attack, and frequently bidding the Ladies not be frighted, and telling them they will do them no Harm'.[29] In essence, both real highway robbers and fictional ones claimed a certain level of 'civility' during the seventeenth century. When the idea of civility became supplanted by 'politeness' during the eighteenth century, 'it was only a matter of time before highwaymen began to portray themselves as polite.'[30] The 'gentleman highwayman' had a brief zenith in mid-eighteenth century, through robbers like James Maclaine who robbed Horace Walpole in 1749; by the 1770s, however, the ideal had lost its persuasiveness to the majority of middle- and upper-class audiences.[31] When Jack Rann stood trial in 1774, the 'gentleman highwayman' was already in decline, and while the Newgate ordinary described him as bearing a 'genteel carriage' and handsome in appearance,[32] James Boswell accused him of 'foppery in his dress'.[33] While actual highwaymen like Rann could no longer claim gentility to the same level of success like James Maclaine did and the public discourse became more critical of all robbers, some of the gentleman highwayman's reputation

---

[26] Spraggs, *Outlaws*, p. 156.
[27] [Daniel Defoe?], 'An Effectual Scheme For the Immediate Preventing of Street Robberies', (London: J. Wilford, 1731), p. 9.
[28] Defoe, 'Effectual Scheme', p. 29.
[29] Defoe, 'Effectual Scheme', p. 30.
[30] Shoemaker, 'Street Robber', p. 393-5.
[31] Shoemaker, 'Street Robber', p. 396, 399.
[32] Shoemaker, 'Street Robber', p. 400.
[33] Quoted in Shoemaker, 'Street Robber', p. 400.

survived both in fiction as well as non-fiction. Condemning the French, Mary Wollstonecraft in 1794 claims that 'in England, where the spirit of liberty has prevailed, it is useful for an highwayman, demanding your money, not only to avoid barbarity, but to behave with humanity, and even complaisance.'[34]

The most popular eighteenth-century fictional highwayman appears in *The Beggar's Opera* (1728) by John Gay. This amalgam of different dramatic genres ran for sixty-two nights in its first season, and was retroactively named a 'ballad opera'.[35] Largely inspired by the life of Jonathan Wild, a notorious criminal who both took stolen goods off criminals while occasionally selling out those who did no longer bring him a profit to the law (earning him the nickname 'Thief-taker General'), *The Beggar's Opera* revolves around a highwayman, Captain Macheath, and Peachum (a Wild-like figure), who aims to impeach Macheath. The plot mainly involves Macheath attempting to elude the law, while being aided or sold out by his various mistresses. Macheath does not actually commit any robbery during the play, relying on the archetype of the highwayman familiar to its audience. *The Beggar's Opera* revels in its low-life main characters and reversals of common morality. Descriptions of the characters, therefore, should be read with this irony in mind. Mrs Peachum is charmed by Macheath's manners, stating that 'there is not a finer Gentleman upon the Road than the Captain!'[36] In a later scene, Mrs Peachum compares marrying to a highwayman to marrying to a Lord (and in the context of the play, both are equally undesirable). Peachum responds that the 'Captain looks upon himself in the Military Capacity, as a Gentleman by his Profession.'[37] Macheath likes to think of himself as a soldier, whose kinship he claims when he calls them 'the other Gentlemen of the Sword'[38], earning his money through courage and

---

[34] Mary Wollstonecraft, *An Historical and Moral View of the Origin and Progress of the French Revolution; and the Effect it Has Produced in Europe* (London: J. Johnson, 1794), p. 516.
[35] Hal Gladfelder, 'Introduction', in John Gay, *The Beggar's Opera and Polly*, ed. by Hal Gladfelder (Cambridge: Cambridge University Press, 2013), p. vii-viii.
[36] Gay, *Beggar's Opera*, p. 9.
[37] Gay, *Beggar's Opera*, p. 14.
[38] Gay, *Beggar's Opera*, p. 28.

violence. One of the members of his gang claims that whatever they 'win' is theirs 'by the Law of Arms' and 'the Right of Conquest'.[39] Macheath is praised by other characters for his 'Personal Bravery' and 'fine Strategem'[40]). The two are collapsed in a negative light when Mrs Peachum later states that 'A Highwayman's Wife, like a Soldier's, hath as little of his Pay, as of his Company.'[41] The use of military titles is a common trope in highwayman fiction; in 1830, the main character of Edward Bulwer's *Paul Clifford* also styles himself as 'Captain Clifford'. Lindridge draws upon this tradition when calling Jack Rann the Captain of his band of robbers, providing a certain amount of legitimacy for his exploits.

Macheath is defined by objects and roles that were associated with highway robbery. When swearing his love to Polly Peachum, he claims, 'May my Pistols miss Fire, and my Mare slip her Shoulder while I am pursu'd, if I ever forsake thee!'[42] Without horse or pistol, a highwayman would lose his livelihood, and the importance of the horse in particular is already signalled in Clavell's text. He warns innkeepers that highwaymen can be recognised by the extraordinary care they request for their horses: 'They must be strangely drest, as strangely fed / With Mashes, provender, and Christians bred.' When questioned they will sing their horse's praises, 'Crying, they doe deserve it, and that they / By their good service will their cost repay.'[43] Dick Turpin's mare Black Bess particularly took hold of the public's imagination, popularised amongst others in William Harrison Ainsworth's *Rookwood*. As we will see in the next section, *Jack Rann* too incorporates the exceptional bond between the highwayman and his horse in its text, providing its own exceptional black mare called Sue.

Eighteenth-century highwaymen like Dick Turpin and Jack Sheppard are, according to Spraggs 'a fairly late arrival in the history of the English robber', and they are best understood as 'a survival from an earlier time'.

---

[39] Gay, *Beggar's Opera*, p. 25.
[40] Gay, *Beggar's Opera*, p. 21.
[41] Gay, *Beggar's Opera*, p. 19.
[42] Gay, *Beggar's Opera*, p. 22.
[43] Clavell, *Recantation*, pp. 46-47.

In light of these findings, the eighteenth century 'might more reasonably be seen as a period of decadence and decline' rather than 'as the heyday of the robber'.[44] While this might be true when looking at the outlaw/robber throughout the last millennium, for eighteenth-century English city-dwellers the public executions and their accompanying broadsheets, pamphlets, and other criminal biographies were a significant part of the cultural discourse. These texts were read widely, from servants to the middle classes; broadsides could be priced as high as a shilling, or as little as two pence for a cheap pamphlet.[45] While accounts of criminal lives have often been characterised as a specifically working-class entertainment, there is evidence that a significant portion – if not the primary – audience of these texts were middle class.[46] Crime writing proliferated across class boundaries and different genres, and focusses on crime and its perpetrators rather than detection. When characters do come in contact with law enforcement, the legal system is often revealed to be corrupt or unfit for purpose.[47] While Newgate calendars continue to be published through the start of the nineteenth-century, the highwayman in fiction is briefly relegated into a secondary role, such as the banditti that proliferate in Gothic writings like Ann Radcliffe's. In the 1830s and 1840s highwayman fiction sees a brief revival in public discourse through the Newgate novel controversy.

The relationship between authority and the outlaw or robber has always been rife with tension. While the Robin Hood tales were performed both for aristocratic as well as peasant audiences, late-medieval critics were unimpressed by the popular tastes for outlaw tales. They disapproved of the 'profane stories, dissolute innuendo,

---

[44] Spraggs, *Outlaws*, pp. 11-12.
[45] Andrea McKenzie, 'The Real Macheath: Social Satire, Appropriation, and Eighteenth-Century Criminal Biography', *The Huntington Library Quarterly*, 69:4 (2006), 581-605, p. 591.
[46] McKenzie, 'Macheath', p. 591. See also Philip Rawlings, *Drunks, Whores, and Idle Apprentices: Criminal Biographies of the Eighteenth Century* (Cambridge: Cambridge University Press, 1992), p. 4.
[47] Ian A. Bell, 'Eighteenth-century crime writing', in *The Cambridge Companion to Crime Writing*, ed. by Martin Priestman (Cambridge: Cambridge University Press, 2003), pp. 7-18, p. 9.

disrespectful jokes' which were 'leading good Christians, and lawabiding subjects, astray'.[48] These late-medieval criticisms echo throughout the centuries in various shapes, being repeated in the critical outrage against the Newgate novel. Primarily a journalistic construct, the 'Newgate novel' was a generic designation assigned to some late-1830s and 1840s novels about criminals, robbers, and highwaymen (often inspired by Newgate calendars), most notably including Bulwer's 1830 *Paul Clifford*, William Harrison Ainsworth's *Rookwood* (1834) about Dick Turpin and the immensely popular *Jack Sheppard* (1839-40), and Charles Dickens's *Oliver Twist* (1837-9).[49] As Lyn Pykett has argued, 'critics of Newgate fiction deplored its mixing of high- and low-life characters, and the combining of high- and low-class characteristics in a single character.'[50] Even though the middle-class Newgate novels were too expensive for most working-class readers, 'they are linked with these readers in a discourse of social hierarchy that equates low income and low ethics.'[51] Due to changing reading practices in the 1830s, prioritizing critical detachment over sympathy,[52] the compassionate depiction of criminal characters in the Newgate novels indicated a danger to correct reading practices. Additionally, the controversy expresses anxiety over uncontrollable reading audiences.[53] As we have seen directly in the case of *Valentine Vox* and *Valentine Vaux*, in the 1830s and 1840s, middle-class texts would be plagiarised or rewritten for penny magazines, or they were adapted for the stage (sometimes before a serialization had even reached its conclusion). Critics assumed that lower-class readers were particularly vulnerable, reading the criminal accounts sympathetically,

---

[48] Pollard, *Robin Hood*, p. 9-10.
[49] Lyn Pykett, 'The Newgate novel and sensation fiction, 1830-1868', in *The Cambridge Companion to Crime Fiction*, ed. by Martin Priestman (Cambridge: Cambridge University Press, 2003), pp. 19-39, p. 21.
[50] Pykett, 'Newgate Novel', p. 29.
[51] Cassandra Falke, 'On the Morality of Immoral Fiction: Reading Newgate Novels, 1830-1848', *Nineteenth-Century Contexts*, 38:3 (2016), 183-193, p. 185.
[52] Falke, 'Morality', pp. 188-189.
[53] Avid A. Ibitson, '"A book in his hand, - but it couldn't be a prayer-book": The Self-Awareness of William Harrison Ainsworth's Newgate Novels', *Journal of Victorian Culture*, 23:3 (2018), 332-349, pp. 333-335.

which was 'facile, fun, and potentially dangerous because it could escape cognitive control.'[54]

To nineteenth-century commentators, the eighteenth-century robbers were therefore significant in their corrupting influence, even across time. Despite the cultural anxiety around Newgate novels themselves, it might be said that penny theatre adaptations in particular were a cause of anxiety for contemporaries. In his *Extraordinary Popular Delusions*, Charles Mackay devotes a chapter to the 'Popular Admiration of Great Thieves'. Although the exploits of thieves have a broad and timeless appeal ('it is certain that the populace of all countries look with admiration upon great and successful thieves'), Mackay blames the theatre for continually renewing the interest in thieves and corrupting its audience:

> In fact, the theatre, which can only expect to prosper, in a pecuniary sense, by pandering to the tastes of the people, continually recurs to the annals of thieves and banditti for its most favourite heroes. These theatrical robbers; with their picturesque attire, wild haunts, jolly, reckless, devil-may-care manners, take a wonderful hold upon the imagination, and, whatever their advocates may say to the contrary, exercise a very pernicious influence upon public morals.[55]

To Mackay, it is the stagecraft specifically ('with the aid of scenery, fine dresses, and music'[56]) that induces impressionable young into a life of crime – fiction authors or poets are harmless, according to Mackay ('here there is no fear of imitation'[57]). Mackay's anxiety mainly revolves around the penny theatres, whose audiences are described like they are already a hairbreadth away from crime: 'chiefly frequented by striplings of idle and dissolute habits' tales of criminals 'give pleasant lessons in crime to their delighted listeners [...] for the amusement of those who will one

---

[54] Falke, 'Morality', p. 183.
[55] Mackay, *Popular Delusions*, p. 525, 533.
[56] Mackay, *Popular Delusions*, p. 536.
[57] Mackay, *Popular Delusions*, p. 536.

day become its imitators'.[58] The penny theatre-goers Mackay so despises would have a significant overlap with the reading audience of Lindridge's *Jack Rann*, a cheap text that capitalised on the public's interest in highwayman tales, regardless of the moral outrage of middle-class commentators. It is in this cultural landscape that it was published: in the period from the late 1830s up to the 1840s, the appetite for tales about outlaws seemed insatiable, and writers drew their inspiration mainly from Newgate Calendars and biographies of eighteenth-century criminals. While a commentator like Mackay found the fascination of the working classes with criminals disturbing because of the possibility of 'imitators', the prevalence of highwayman tales in penny fiction raises the question of why it appealed to its audience. In other words, how is the figure of the historical highwayman reconfigured and represented in a penny text such as *Jack Rann*? Faller has argued that the eighteenth-century highwayman as represented in criminal biographies is a 'failed satirist,' a figure whose politics are unfixed and are open to opposite interpretations.[59] Is the fascination with highwaymen in the 1840s a remnant of seeing criminals as liberators from an oppressive society? Is a figure like Jack Rann, then, a rebel venerated for his actions? If his actions are meant to be satirical, who is the target of the satire? In the following section I will argue that the highwayman in early Victorian penny fiction was far from a straight-forward critic of class and authority.

JOHN RANN, HIGHWAY ROBBER

Very little is known of the historical John Rann; like Faller describes in his book about criminal biographies, criminals themselves 'sank quickly out of sight' of the public consciousness, while 'what ripples they made, or did not make' become the subject of studies like Faller's.[60] These

---

[58] Mackay, *Popular Delusions*, p. 536.
[59] Lincoln B. Faller, *Turned to Account. The forms and functions of criminal biography in late seventeeth- and early eighteenth-century England* (Cambridge: Cambridge University Press, 2008), pp. 186-187. McKenzie, 'Macheath', p. 594.
[60] Faller, *Turned to Account*, p. 2.

'ripples' are the textual legacy of a convicted criminal like Rann. After Rann's execution, two biographies are published which become the basis of later accounts of his life and crimes. Faller identifies Rann as arguably the last 'classic' highwayman to receive biographical attention in this way.[61] *A Genuine Account of the Life of John Rann, Alias Sixteen-String Jack* names Bath as his place of birth.[62] This version is repeated almost verbatim in *The Malefactor's Register* in 1779[63] and extracted again in 1795 in *The New and Complete Newgate Calendar*, even including the same lengthy footnote advertising a pamphlet on love and courtship.[64] Rann also appears in *The Old Bailey Chronicle*, a collection 'Properly arranged from the Records of the Court' by James Mountague.[65] Apart from the two criminal biographies, another important text of Rann's legacy is a play by William Leman Rede, *Sixteen String Jack* from 1823. These works illustrate a tendency that Faller identifies as a flattening of the public understanding of the criminal: 'the actual complexities of their lives, as people were aware of them at the time they died, are not at all to be found in works that later took them as centers of attention.'[66] This tendency can be seen at work around the most recognizable symbol connected to Rann: the brightly coloured ribbons that are attached to his breeches. His dress becomes an empty signifier, only used to identify Rann in texts like Rede's and Lindridge's, while none attempt to explain *why* Rann eccentrically tied sixteen ribbons to his breeches. This relative emptiness of characterization allows these figures to take on mythical proportions, being reinserted in various narratives without a stable 'core' of

---

[61] Faller, *Turned to Account*, p. 127.
[62] *A Genuine Account of the Life of John Rann, Alias Sixteen-string Jack* (London: Bailey, [1774?]), p. 6.
[63] 'A full and particular Account of the Life and extraordinary Transactions of John Rann, otherwise Sixteen-Strings Jack, who was hanged for a Robbery on the Highway,' in *The Malefactor's Register; or, New Newgate and Tyburn Calendar* Vol. V (London: Alex Hogg, 1779), pp. 138-146.
[64] William Jackson, Esq., *The New and Complete Newgate Calendar; or, Villany Displayed in All its Branches*, Vol. V (London: Alex Hogg, 1795), pp. 138-146.
[65] James Mountague Esq., *The Old Bailey Chronicle; Containing a Circumstantial Account of the Lives, Trials, and Confessions, of The Most Notorious Offenders, Who Have Suffered Death, and Other Exemplary Punishments*, Vol. IV (London: S. Smith, 1788).
[66] Faller, *Turned to Account*, p. 20.

personality or historical detail that needs to be maintained. Because of this, Lindridge easily borrowed entire scenes and characters from Rede's play, inserting them in the middle of his own narrative. This recycling and re-incorporation of different texts in the penny blood illustrates the patchwork nature of the genre: Lindridge's *Jack Rann* includes songs, criminal biography, and theatre in a cannibalization of genre and narrative. While some of these are identified in this chapter, it is very likely Lindridge has creatively borrowed from more sources.

Faller recognises three different types of highwaymen as they are presented in criminal biographies: the hero, the buffoon, and the brute. Faller traces various polarities along which lines these types fall, including: humorous/serious, attractive/repulsive, minimal suffering/maximal suffering.[67] These oppositions provide a starting point for analysing the text. Are Jack's adventures described in humorous, or serious terms? Is he an attractive hero (worthy of emulation or admiration), or a repulsive brute? Since it is a given that a highwayman will commit robberies, do these cause minimal or extensive suffering? In this section, these questions will be answered through a close reading of the first robbery committed by Jack in the text. This will reveal how Jack as a character functions in a text that is fundamentally carnivalesque, celebrating reversal and laughter. Examining how laughter is created, reveals the underlying politics of the text, which in turn informs us what the significance is of the highwayman figure in 1840s penny fiction. In this section, I will first give a summary of the plot of *Jack Rann*; then, I will do a close reading of the first scene in which Jack commits a robbery, examining how humour functions in this scene. Finally, this section will look at the influences of the picaresque on its structure, and how Lindridge positions his own text in comparison to other highwayman fiction. These narrative-level concerns will provide the context for more in-depth analysis of important themes in the following sections.

It is difficult to give a succinct summary of Lindridge's *Jack Rann*, as many of its episodes are only loosely connected. It starts with the eponymous Jack as a peasant boy of sixteen years old, selling food at the

---

[67] See Faller, *Turned to Account*, pp. 125-148.

Bath market. While Jack and the local poacher and reputed thief Luke Jones taunt the local squire from atop his property wall, the squire steps onto the ice of the frozen lake, which breaks under his feet. While Luke laughs, Jack jumps into the lake to save the drowning man. The event introduces Jack to several key characters as he is welcomed into the house by the squire's brother-in-law, a merchant from London called Mr Malcolm. He meets the young Miss Isabel Malcolm and Lady Dashfield, both of whom become infatuated with Jack. The event awakens pride in Jack, who is no longer content with being a food seller, and after being betrayed by Luke Jones, he flees from his parents' house and leaves for London. While in a fistfight with 'some young cockney vagabonds', the carriage of the Earl of Dashfield and Lady Dashfield drives past, and the Earl decides to take him on as a valet. Lady Dashfield cheats on her husband with Jack, an act which is observed by Elinor Roche,[68] who informs the earl. He rushes home to find the lady of the house in Jack's arms, and when he attempts to shoot him, he accidentally shoots Lady Dashfield instead. Jack flees, being taken in by a gang of thieves, who introduce him into a life of crime. Lady Dashfield is eventually killed by the earl, who seeks revenge from Rann, and becomes the main villain of the story. Jack participates in a string of humorous robberies and spends his time drinking and exchanging farcical stories with his fellow gang members. The causal relationships between the series of robberies are tenuous at best, and events often repeat themselves. Jack rescues Miss Malcolm from being carried off by the Earl of Dashfield twice. Jack is captured and stands for trial three times, being released twice while the third time leads to his execution. One event that stands out in the string of robberies committed by Jack is an elaborate deception which attempts to surpass Dick Turpin's legendary ride to York, spanning several chapters. Jack creates an illusion, aided by two of his gang members, that he rode from London to Newcastle in one night. This prank increases his already apparent fame with the public, further increasing attempts to apprehend him. Despite his earlier flirtation with Miss Malcolm, Jack marries Elinor Roche and, under influence of the Malcolms, attempts to

---

[68] Roche was an accomplice of the real-life John Rann. Lindridge uses her name, but the character is not based on the historical Roche.

emigrate to the Americas and start anew. The newlywed Ranns, however, suffer shipwreck only a couple of days out of Liverpool, and Jack is reunited with his gang one last time, before he is finally captured by soldiers led by Sir John Fielding. Jack is convicted of theft, the decisive testimony given by the Earl of Dashfield. Jack spends his last days in Newgate as 'guest', rather than a prisoner, and entertains several of his friends until his solemn execution terminates the narrative.

Farce plays an essential role in Jack's picaresque adventures. Like Valentine's pranks in *Valentine Vaux*, Jack's robberies are cast in a comic light through the usage of farcical tropes that minimise perceived suffering of the victims of the farce. While Jack commits crimes (unlike Valentine's interjections which cause disturbances, but are not against the law), the text takes a carnivalesque attitude that interprets property crime as a joke. The first robbery Rann participates in illuminates how humour functions within the narrative: how laughter is created and at whose expense. The scene introduces several important themes that are repeated in the subsequent robberies, like social deception, comic violence, and being a good-natured victim. The robbery takes place at an inn, one of the many drinking spaces that populate the text. The transient and socially equalising nature of the inn, where travellers from different classes mingle and move on, lends social ambiguity to Jack.[69] The focus on alcohol consumption, a thoroughly corporeal pleasure, brings to mind connotations to feasting and the carnivalesque. The association between drinking and humour is particularly on the surface in this scene. As Jack and Clayton, a fellow robber, enter the inn, the landlord is introduced as a comic stereotype of a drunk: 'his round rubicund face ornamented with such a brilliant specimen of a "jolly nose," as would leave not a shadow of doubt in the beholders mind, [sic] that the tapster had a strong partiality for the liquors he dispensed.'[70] The landlord's propensity to drink his own wares make him a suitable victim for the ensuing prank. Clayton and Rann, using the fake names Clifford and

---

[69] Susanne Schmid, 'Eighteenth-Century Travellers and the Country Inn' in *Drink in the Eighteenth and Nineteenth Centuries*, ed. by Susanne Schmid and Barbara Schmidt-Haberkamp (London: Pickering & Chatto, 2014), pp. 59-70, p. 62.
[70] Lindridge, *Jack Rann*, p. 46.

Allspice respectively, terrify the landlord, accusing him of providing them with sub-par drinks. They claim he gave them 'water and brandy' instead of 'brandy and water', and that he deserves 'a good horse-whipping for daring to dispense such disgusting stuff.'[71] While the landlord is described to be 'panic-stricken' and 'horror-struck', the scene exhibits a sense of playfulness. Clayton and Rann are merely acting; there was nothing wrong with their drinks, and the reader is in on the 'joke' that the landlord is in no real danger despite his fear. The scene escalates when Clayton demands to 'forbear corporeal punishment only upon one condition': that the landlord brings a bottle of Hollands[72] and rum.

> Pouring half of the brandy and water from out of each vessel, [Clayton] deliberately filled them up with an equal admixture of Hollands and rum; then beckoning the landlord, he bade him, on the pain of instant flagellation, to drain them instantly to the dregs.[73]

The landlord complies after Clayton gives him a 'smart lash with the whip', and falls down 'dead drunk', passing out because of the excess of alcohol. The landlord's self-indulgence is what instigates his downfall, a humorous reversal that creates laughter. That this sequence is meant to be comic is explicit in the text: when the landlord collapses, 'a burst of laughter greeted the fall.'[74] For good measure, the joke is repeated several times over, including his wife calling him a 'drunken beast' and 'pummelled [him] soundly,' and the ostler, in an idiosyncratic accent, exclaiming 'Hollo! What drunk agin!'[75]

As in the farce discussed in *Valentine Vaux*, the innkeeper deserves the ridicule he receives. As the butt of a joke in a farce, the 'victim "asks for"

---

[71] Lindridge, *Jack Rann*, p. 48.
[72] Hollands is used here to refer to the spirit mainly distilled in the Netherlands and Belgium called *jenever*, similar to gin.
[73] Lindridge, *Jack Rann*, p. 48.
[74] Lindridge, *Jack Rann*, p. 49.
[75] Lindridge, *Jack Rann*, p. 49.

punishment by their stupidity', and as a result, is 'tortured shamelessly'.[76] To briefly recall Faller's typology of the highwayman along the lines of humorous/serious, attractive/repulsive, minimal suffering/maximal suffering, it becomes clear that Jack is a humorous hero. His actions are considered ludic, and despite the presence of suffering imposed on the landlord, his suffering is considered negligible and deserved. Although his actions generally might not be considered as quite heroic, he is nevertheless a sympathetic and attractive character. In Faller's taxonomy, Jack falls between the archetypes of hero and buffoon. I would argue that this ambivalent heroism is typical of the hero in the penny blood: part of the perceived realism of the penny blood is how its heroes and their acts are more mundane than the epic feats of the classic hero.[77] Jack is no Robin Hood – he robs only for his personal gain rather than for some higher cause – yet his robberies do not make him a repulsive character. This is illustrated in the continuation of the scene: after the fainting of the landlord, Jack and Clayton rob the other gentlemen present in the inn.

The squire and two other gentlemen present in the inn, who laugh at the landlord's humiliation described above, become the target of the robbery.

> On [Clayton's] return to the parlour, he was greeted with a peal of laughter, the squire declaring it was "the richest joke he had ever seen."
> "And the beauty of it is, gentlemen, it is not the only spree I intend to have to-night; Jack, guard the door, and the first man that disobeys my orders, shoot him through the head."[78]

While the squire and the gentlemen were the audience before, they now become the subject of the second joke (or 'spree' in Clayton's words). The incongruity between the previous joviality and the intense physical threat uttered in immediate succession create a comic effect. At the same

---

[76] Davis, *Farce*, p. 26.
[77] For a discussion of the characteristics of the classic hero, see Dean A. Miller, *The Epic Hero* (Baltimore: The Johns Hopkins University Press, 2000).
[78] Lindridge, *Jack Rann*, p. 50.

time, it implicates the threat of violence and robbery into the comic vocabulary of the narrative by their concurrence. Robbery, in *Jack Rann*, is humorous business. While two of their victims struggle, one of them admonishes his companions to simply hand over their valuables. He is cooperative:

> "Don't let me detain you, gentlemen – I perceive it is useless to deceive you," and saying these words, he placed his watch and purse upon the table; "they are the only valuables I have about me – if you doubt my word, search me."
> "I'll be d — — d if I do!" said Clayton, "I should hope I know an honest man when I see him; thank you sir – your'e [sic] a gentleman;" and he bowed politely, "much obliged to you."[79] The other returned the salutation good-humouredly, and by way of a joke, observed that he "hoped soon to have the pleasure of meeting him again," a wish in which both Rann and Clayton joyously concurred.

Being a well-behaving participant in the robbery earns the man respect from Rann and Clayton, and as a result, better treatment; he is not searched, unlike his companions. This character 'plays along' with the joke, and therefore does not invite ridicule and violence in the way the innkeeper does. Not only does cooperation lead to less violence, in the carnivalesque text, playing along is seen as honourable, deserving of the classification of a 'gentleman'. It points towards the class politics that are present in the text: a true gentleman does not mind being stolen from. Jack overwhelmingly steals from rich middle-class and small country gentry. When he does take money from working class individuals, it is often freely given. On the surface, this is related to the 'suffering' that robbery causes; it is assumed, by the text, that the middle class and gentry can stand having some money taken off them without any particular hardship. It is easier to laugh at victims that are not significantly harmed. The lack of harm is an important limit on the use of physical violence as well; the quotations above clearly show how Rann

---

[79] Lindridge, *Jack Rann*, p. 52.

does not shy away from violence. However, he constantly admonishes his fellow highwaymen not to use violence. When planning the robbery of a house, they plan 'to decamp without doing any violence, disturbing any of the house, or committing any further depredations.'[80] Jack's repeated insistence of 'no violence' defines the limit of play – 'no violence' means no *lethal* violence, which would ruin the joke. The consequences of Jack's robbery of the middle class and gentry go beyond the humorous: by constantly blurring the boundaries of property and possessions, by intruding into private spaces and taking objects that are owned by others, Jack symbolically claims their social status for himself. The doubleness that this creates, of both belonging and not belonging, constitutes the humorous uncertainty that the text exploits over and over. The carnivalesque delight of the text shows several of Rann's victims enjoy being robbed by him. After having already been robbed by Rann and Clayton once, the squire claims that 'nothing would give me greater pleasure than to see [Sixteen-string Jack] and Clayton seated at my table.'[81] This joy is not merely one of perverse pleasure – it is an expression of admiration and recognition of an equal. How class functions in the text is the subject of the next section. Before discussing this in more depth, however, it is useful to briefly consider two significant influences on the text: the picaresque mode, and a self-conscious recognition of other highwaymen stories.

The farcical scenes that intersperse the more serious plotlines like Lady Dashfield's death are more integrated into the overall narrative than they are in *Valentine Vaux*; where Valentine's exploits never moved beyond the boundaries of their respective scenes, Rann's robberies are often loosely connected to the main antagonists in some way, or feature returning characters rather than an ever-revolving collection of victims, like in Vaux's case. The storytelling is inspired by picaresque fiction of the eighteenth century, like Henry Fielding's *Jonathan Wild* (1743) and criminal biographies of thieves. Faller notes that thief narratives consist of series of events that resist coherent and logical organisation. He writes

---

[80] Lindridge, *Jack Rann*, p. 91.
[81] Lindridge, *Jack Rann*, p. 163.

that 'they do not tend to rise in the intensity of their violence or humour.'[82] The picaresque, as conceptualised as a literary style, features an anti-hero engaging in a string of (often humorous) episodes.[83] According to Ulrich Wicks, 'the picaresque mode satisfies our impulse for a vicarious journey through chaos and depravity'.[84] This journey is particularly visible in a story like *Jonathan Wild*, where the titular character engages in various forms of depravity throughout the story. *Jack Rann* draws from the picaresque tradition the episodic format, defined by Wicks as follows: a confrontation out of need (for Rann, this is usually his need to steal to ward off poverty), some scheme to satisfy that need, a complication that endangers the picaresque hero's safety, and the extrication, or the entanglement if he is caught.[85] In other words, Rann's adventures usually follow the pattern of some vague motivation like needing money, a scheme for robbing a person or household, some complication in the form of discovery, and either his heroic escape from the situation, or his capture. Even though *Jack Rann* is not a first-person account, as the majority of picaresque fiction, Jack resembles the *picaro*, the traditional picaresque anti-hero, who is a 'pragmatic, unprincipled, resilient, solitary figure who just manages to survive in his chaotic landscape', whose 'essential characteristic is his inconstancy – of life roles, of self-identity – his own personality flux in the face of an inconstant world.'[86] Although the picaresque legacy is clearly visible in the organisation (or perhaps more accurately, its lack thereof) of the text, Lindridge departs somewhat from the formula through partial embedding of Jack in a social context. In criminal biography, the

---

[82] Faller, *Turned to Account*, p. 126.
[83] The picarasque can also be narrowly defined as a group of texts from sixteenth- and seventeenth Spain and their translations and adaptations across Europe. According to Harry Sieber, who takes a narrow view of the picaresque, for example, 'After the eighteenth century in Europe it is no longer possible to speak of picaresque novels, and even [...] of a 'picaresque theme'. Harry Sieber, *The Picaresque* (Abingdon: Routledge, 2018), p. 60.
[84] Ulrich Wicks, 'The Nature of Picaresque Narrative: A Modal Approach', *PMLA*, 89:2 (1974), 240-249, p. 242.
[85] Wicks, 'Picaresque', p. 244.
[86] Wicks, 'Picaresque', p. 245.

highwayman is generally depicted as individual, even if it was well known that he was part of a gang.[87] Lindridge, however, overwhelmingly shows Jack accompanied by fellow thieves, with Jack in a leadership position. While the traditional *picaro* is defined by his position as outsider, the constant negotiation between belonging and exceptionalism determines Jack's character. This is most clearly visible in regards to his class status, the subject of the next section. This inconsistent self-identity is mainly expressed by the class-uncertainty the text expresses through the trope of disguise. Like most picaresque characters, Jack does not develop or change significantly in the narrative, despite outside pressures to do so.[88]

Jack Rann's carnivalesque aspects are not limited to farcical robbery scenes – the text consciously plays with genre expectations, drawing upon the supposed reader's knowledge of other highwayman heroes. Jack is referred to as 'BOLD AND BRAVE JACK RANN!' (capitalization original) on the first page. Lindridge wastes no time to position Rann in comparison to other legendary highwaymen, simultaneously establishing the narrative to be in the tradition of highwayman literature that revels in the illegal accomplishments of robbers, rather than condemning them.

> Yes, SIXTEEN-STRING Jack – at once the bravest, most daring, dashing, and intrepid highwayman; whose glorious exploits on the road were unequalled; whose adventures and spirits threw the boasted valour of Dick Turpin and Claude du Val far, far into the rear – was once a peasant boy, and drove a donkey, laden with eatables, through the good city of Bath.[89]

---

[87] Faller, *Turned to Account*, p. 178.
[88] Alleen and Don Nilson summarise six characteristics of the picaresque novel. See Alleen and Don Nilsen, 'Literature and humor', in *The Primer of Humor Research*, ed. by Victor Raskin (Berlin: Mouton de Gruyter, 2008), pp. 243-280, p. 253.
[89] Lindridge, *Jack Rann*, p. 3.

Within the first chapter, Jack wishes to turn into a highwayman, exclaiming: 'Yes, let me but cross the back of a gallant steed – let me but feel want behind my back and a chance before my face, and with mask covered face and pistol in hand, show me the man that dare refuse my STAND AND DELIVER.'[90] Rann invokes all of the highwayman tropes the nineteenth-century readership would be familiar with: a horse, pistol, disguise, combined with essential phrases like 'stand and deliver'. Not only does this section serve as introduction to Rann as a character, but it also positions the text generically through the foregrounding of the highwayman theme, and the tone implies that *Jack Rann* is a celebration of a highwayman. The text is conscious of its generic context, placing itself in the textual tradition and claiming superiority over even Dick Turpin's legacy. When Jack is compared to Turpin, he responds:

> "Equal to Dick Turpin," dried Jack, with a sneer in the curl of his handsome lip. "Equal! ha, ha, ha! if ever I was driven on the road [...] it shall be to raise a name that shall last in the pages of history as long as the word Highwayman lives in the English language – shall last, ah! until DICK TURPIN'S name, like his body, shall be mouldered and forgotten."[91]

This wish to surpass Turpin drives one of the most elaborate pranks described in the text: instead of the mythical one-night ride from London to York, Jack wishes to convince the public that he rides from London to Newcastle within one day. This legendary feat, which 'rendered' Turpin 'King of the Tobymen' (a word meaning highwayman), Rann 'will perform another that shall crown me their Emperor!'[92] Rann announces that,

> I am quite conscious as you are, gentlemen, that none but a madman, or fool-hardy idiot, would attempt what I have proposed. But, by artifice and stratagem, we may contrive to

---

[90] Lindridge, *Jack Rann*, p. 10.
[91] Lindridge, *Jack Rann*, p. 10.
[92] Lindridge, *Jack Rann*, p. 237.

make it appear as if the act was performed, without "Sue's" lifting a leg.[93]

Instead of Rann riding this distance, three of his gang members, Jared, Clayton, and Sheppard disguise themselves as him and ride parts of the route on black mares similar to Sue, robbing one of their henchmen in predetermined places during the same night. The ruse is successful, further increasing Rann's popularity with the wider public, and fulfilling his wish to exceed Turpin's feat. Lindridge includes a fictional paper extract, parodying sensational reporting ('Daring outrage and burglary!', 'Unprecedented effrontery!!!').[94] The fake ride from London to Newcastle subverts Jack's heroism, revealing it to be all sensation without substance. This sequence mocks the fictional public's desire for more outrageous stories about highwaymen – even if they are not based in truth. At the same time, this gentle mockery also includes the target audience of the text itself: readers who wish to be entertained by stories about highwaymen. It is here where the carnivalesque potential of the text resides, the unsettling uncertainty of exactly who is the subject of the comedy. As Bakhtin has argued, the carnival is all-encompassing, without a distinction between stage and audience. He writes, 'Carnival is not a spectacle seen by the people; they live in it, and everyone participates because its very idea embraces all the people.'[95] *Jack Rann* exploits this relationship to facilitate an atmosphere of licentiousness, breaking down categories of identity.

This blurring can be witnessed in a humorous interlude during Clayton's part of the ride to Newcastle. In a country inn, he encounters a travelling showman who owns several animals, including a baboon 'dressed up in a scarlet coat, with hat and feathers, so that to an unscrutinizing eye it seemed like a miniature resemblance of wild Kit Clayton.'[96] Not only does the baboon drink a glass of ale and smoke a pipe in imitation of humans, he is mistaken for a human by the locals. Clayton improves the illusion by tying a handkerchief in front of the

---

[93] Lindridge, *Jack Rann*, p. 238.
[94] Lindridge, *Jack Rann*, p. 287.
[95] Bakhtin, *Rabelais*, p. 7.
[96] Lindridge, *Jack Rann*, p. 271.

baboon's face, and uses him as a decoy while he escapes from a hue and cry himself. After a chaotic string of increasingly unlikely events, Rann accidentally leaves a bag of money outside of a labourer's house, who was about to be incarcerated for debt. Finding a bag of a hundred guineas left behind by the distressed baboon, the incident 'had accidentally the effect of adding greatly to the fame of Sixteen-string Jack', as whenever Rann comes up in conversation, the labourer 'always related, with feelings of gratitude, the benevolent act which he conceived the highwayman had performed; and thus, without any cost, our hero earned a character for liberality, little inferior to that achieved by Turpin himself.'[97] Earlier the narrator states that 'Jack Rann was all generosity – far more prone to good intents and generous deeds, than evil ones'.[98] As the public perception of Jack's liberality is based on a complete comical misunderstanding, and has little to do with Rann himself, this scene undermines the text's own claims. Furthermore, the disguised baboon raises questions about what it means to be perceived – how visual cues lead to classification, and how they relate to the self. These questions are the subject of the following section.

DISGUISE, HUMOUR, AND CLASS

The use of disguise in *Jack Rann* is not an anomaly – it is a common feature across the highwayman tradition. Clavell names several ways of highwaymen disguising themselves (quoted above), and connects the use of disguise with cowardice. While disguise can be malicious or grotesque, the disguise in *Jack Rann* most often takes the shape of comic disguise, leading to farcical situations of misrecognition. At the same time, the text displays its anxiety surrounding class and class perceptions most acutely through disguise. To make sense of how disguise functions in the text, it is worthwhile to consider the literature on masquerade, which provides an understanding of the meaning of disguise in a social context. In *Masquerade and Civilization* (1986), a study of the

---

[97] Lindridge, *Jack Rann*, p. 282.
[98] Lindridge, *Jack Rann*, p. 8.

carnivalesque in the eighteenth century, Terry Castle places the notion of the self as central concern at the heart of the masquerade.[99] Castle states: 'The pleasure of the masquerade attended on the experience of doubleness, the alienation of inner from outer, a fantasy of two bodies simultaneously and thrillingly present, self and other together, the two-in-one.'[100] I argue that this experience of doubleness is an essential part of how disguise functions in *Jack Rann*. It is this doubleness, a presence of both humble birth and an outer body signifying gentle status, that is continuously present in the text, particularly in the character of Jack. This section will therefore discuss two aspects of the way Lindridge incorporates disguise in the narrative: how it gains its humorous dimension through sensory disruption, as well as the class anxiety that is expressed by uncertain classification of individuals.

The usage of disguise is ubiquitous in *Jack Rann*; Jack utilises his 'favourite disguise of a country gentleman'[101] to gain admission to various spaces, like middle-class households or Newgate prison without suspicion. The disguises evoke a sense of play-acting. When returning to the squire's home that he has robbed before, Jack and his gang disguise themselves as 'a thoroughbred gentleman':

> Mike shall be General O'Blunderbuss, [Clayton] Viscount Neverwag, a very aristocratic personage indeed, and I will be my Lord Swipes; a little bit of a libertine [...] We shall each, therefore, have a cue. O'Brien, all bluster, yourself all gentility, and myself all fal de ral, which is about as lovely a character as any fool like myself could wish to pourtray. [sic][102]

The disguises are so effective, in fact, that Jack rhetorically questions whether they could not 'so equip ourselves that our own mothers, if they

---

[99] Terry Castle, *Masquerade and Civilization. The Carnivalesque in Eighteenth-Century English Culture and Fiction* (Stanford: Stanford University Press, 1986), pp. 4-5.
[100] Castle, *Masquerade*, pp. 4-5.
[101] Lindridge, *Jack Rann*, p. 155.
[102] Lindridge, *Jack Rann*, p. 159.

mounted spectacles and all, would fail to know us?'[103] In *Jack Rann*, disguise is a visual deception – it depends on the other party seeing and recognising certain markers of class. Although disguise can also involve the assuming of a different voice (so important to the humour in *Valentine Vaux*), the disguise in *Jack Rann* relies solely on surface presentation. Laughter is created by the various incongruities created by the gang members pretending to be members of the upper class. The largest joke of all, however, is when people speak about Jack Rann, the highwayman, to Jack himself, not realizing it is him. Disguised as Lord Swipes, the squire praises Sixteen-string Jack as someone 'who for real bravery might challenge the world.'[104] This joke, repeated in various forms in the narrative, invites laughter at the inability of the characters to see what is right in front of their eyes.

According to Dror Wahrman, it is 'identity play' that is the essence of the masquerade: 'In the process, the boundaries of every category of identity were explicitly and frequently played with.'[105] In *Jack Rann*, it is mainly class that is subjected to play; other categories, like race, nationality, and gender, are far less common in the narrative, though not absent. While historical masquerades generally kept this play within 'the boundaries of ludic make-believe', 'the potential for less containable exposure of the limits of identity categories was never far from the surface'. I argue that disguise in *Jack Rann* functions similarly; while masquerade is embedded in farcical sequences, its repercussions speak to anxiety about class boundaries. In the eighteenth century, the levelling and mixing of all kinds of social levels in the masquerade caused 'anxiety about the undermining of actual social distinctions'. Wahrman writes that 'eighteenth-century depictions of the genteel masquerading as peasants and laborers were nervously entwined with reputed instances of peasants and laborers [...] passing as members of the gentility and gate-crashing the festivities.'[106] Rann, being of peasant birth, constantly intrudes in middle-class social spheres by wearing a disguise. In the

---

[103] Lindridge, *Jack Rann*, p. 159.
[104] Lindridge, *Jack Rann*, p. 163.
[105] Dror Wahrman, *The Making of the Modern Self. Identity and Culture in Eighteenth-Century England* (New Haven: Yale University Press, 2006), p. 159.
[106] Wahrman, *Modern Self*, p. 159.

following we will look at how Rann's class is perceived by other characters in the text, and the role disguise plays into it.

In the sequence largely inspired by Rede's play (see the section above), Jack assumes the title of Count Chantrais, and disguises himself: 'being now habited in the dress then worn by aristocrats, he looked the very *beau ideal* of a perfect gentleman.'[107] The disguise causes those around him to treat him accordingly, as 'the whole company for each seemed to strive to outdo the other in heaping praises and honours to him.'[108] Although Jack, as Count Chantrais, becomes a common visitor in the household, he is aware of his welcome being completely dependent on the disguise. To a fellow highwayman he says, 'It is not me that he welcomes, he worships wealth and rank, and would spurn a beggar from his door.'[109] The way Jack here refers to himself as being without wealth and rank suggests that this self signifies beyond his disguise both as nobleman as well as his highwayman persona. As a highwayman, he enjoys a certain rank, being called 'Captain' by his gang members, and even being recognised as a fellow military man by Captain Manby.[110] Yet, the categories of highwayman and gentleman are opposites, comically brought together:

> "You are a gentleman, sir," said the Beau, with a bow of exquisite grace.
> "I am, sir," answered our hero, with equal politeness, "OF THE ROAD, and therefore as a preliminary measure, am under the necessity of demanding your money or your life."[111]

The Beau later calls him 'the most gentlemanly vagabond I ever met in my life!'[112] The text suggests that neither highwayman nor gentleman are Rann's 'true' identity; Rann says that 'for the spree of the thing [I must]

---

[107] Lindridge, *Jack Rann*, p. 142.
[108] Lindridge, *Jack Rann*, p. 142.
[109] Lindridge, *Jack Rann*, p. 147.
[110] Lindridge, *Jack Rann*, p. 152.
[111] Lindridge, *Jack Rann*, p. 135.
[112] Lindridge, *Jack Rann*, p. 135.

shake off the Count and appear in propria personæ as the play writers say – as Sixteen-stringed Jack the dashing knight of the road,'[113] speaking about both his presentation as Count and as highwayman in the same terms. In a different scene, Jack is disguised as a nobleman, and then reveals himself to be a highwayman. Yet, these categories are reversed when Jack later states: 'We are not here as thieves to-day. No, sir, for once in our lives we can afford to play the gentleman.'[114] While underneath the disguise of the nobleman, Jack 'appear[s] like magic in his habiliments,' the instability of these categories are illustrated by the ease with which Jack can 'play' any role.

After the robbery of the squire and his friends in the inn, discussed at length above, the Earl of Dashfield urges the squire to give a description of Rann to aid his apprehension. The squire describes Rann and Clayton as follows: 'all I know is they're both devillish good looking fellows – polite in their behaviour and exhibiting in their costume and carriage, the true born gentlemen'.[115] The squire, a landed part of the gentry, recognises Rann and Clayton as 'true born' gentlemen, regardless of their actual status at birth. It suggests that one can be 'true born' despite blood relations, their class instead depending on a nebulous constellation of values and behaviours, including dress and conduct. Conduct is essential to Miss Malcolm's defence of Rann when he is captured as a thief, pleading to her father:

> "Father, dear, dear father, do not let this cruel injustice be done to this brave, good, and generous, gentleman; I am indebted for more than life; it was his generous aid saved me from dishonour; [sic] it was his generous aid, his matchless daring intrepidity, that rescued me from the villains toils; [sic] he is innocent of this crime, father: he is worthy of your warmest, most devoted thanks! Oh, Rann, dear Jack, for God's sake remove this mystery; convince these men of your innocence, demand your freedom."[116]

---

[113] Lindridge, *Jack Rann*, p. 147.
[114] Lindridge, *Jack Rann*, p. 163.
[115] Lindridge, *Jack Rann*, p. 100.
[116] Lindridge, *Jack Rann*, p. 118.

The 'mystery' Miss Malcolm refers to here is the incongruous presentation of Rann as both highwayman and gentleman. She asks Rann to solve this dilemma, and claim honourable status – which includes disavowing being a highwayman and therefore being innocent of the crime of robbery. It is distressing to Miss Malcolm that 'my generous deliverer, my gallant protector, [is] to be dragged to prison like a thief,'[117] and yet Rann refuses to defend himself or his innocence. He is brought to prison 'without a word being spoken by Jack Rann.'[118] This reluctance to speak can be read as Rann failing to resolve the tension of identity the scene displays: it is impossible for him to claim innocence, therefore forfeiting his claim to gentility at the same time.

A pivotal character who represents the upper class in the narrative is the earl, who acts as the villain of the story. This paradox is explicitly evoked by Jack, as he tells the earl: 'you are the representative of a nobleman, without a spark of true nobility in your carcase; the effigy of a man, with the body of a beast, and the heart of a villian [sic].'[119] The earl's depravity opens him up to farcical ridicule. The farce specifically targets his class-consciousness. After the liberation of Miss Malcolm from the earl's coach by Rann and Clayton, the earl is left with a coachman with a broken arm, and two labourers paid by Clayton to 'catch his lordship's horses, and convey the carriage and its occupants to the Red Lion,'[120] a nearby inn. The earl refuses to drive himself ('I'll see you d—d first – not while I am able to keep a coachman to do it for me'[121]), and lets the labourers take the reins. The labourers are utterly useless ('A couple of novices never sat behind a living horse'), managing only to confuse the horses, 'nine times out of ten' leading them straight into the hedges lining the road.[122] The labourers finally decide to lead the horses themselves, but this is futile as well.

---

[117] Lindridge, *Jack Rann*, p. 118.
[118] Lindridge, *Jack Rann*, p. 118.
[119] Lindridge, *Jack Rann*, p. 346.
[120] Lindridge, *Jack Rann*, p. 74.
[121] Lindridge, *Jack Rann*, p. 92.
[122] Lindridge, *Jack Rann*, p. 93.

> They had not proceeded a hundred yards before another accident occurred; the cord which connected the harness to the carriage, from the unskilful manner in which it was tied, came unfastened, and the vehicle was left in the road, whilst the men and horses went plodding carefully forwards; the latter right glad doubtless to be relieved from the cumbersome machine.[123]

After this comic interlude, there is no other option but for the earl to get involved beyond yelling insults at the labourers. The farce culminates with the joke: 'so Robert, Earl of Dashfield, as he so vauntingly described himself, was compelled to submit to the degradation of leading his own horses.'[124] It is the earl's pride that is his downfall: he could have driven himself, but he refuses to engage in any labour, which he finds beneath him. This attitude causes him immense frustration, and ultimately, having to walk on foot to the closest village, a further degradation.

Despite being noble by birth, the earl is far from virtuous. When a squire urges him to 'stick more faithfully to matrimony' and leave Miss Malcolm alone, he responds:

> "Matrimony!" echoed his lordship, "is cant fit for plebeians, and are words never made for the aristocracy. Pho! it disgusts me! Would I had never heard its name!"[125]

At another point, he is described moving with 'impetuous action more characteristic of a maniac than a man,'[126] drawing attention to his lack of aristocratic bearing. The figure of a decadent and licentious aristocrat would be familiar to the 1840s reader of penny bloods; five years later, Reynolds' *Mysteries of London*, a tale populated by misbehaving

---

[123] Lindridge, *Jack Rann*, p. 94.
[124] Lindridge, *Jack Rann*, p. 95.
[125] Lindridge, *Jack Rann*, p. 99.
[126] Lindridge, *Jack Rann*, p. 103.

aristocrats, would gain immense popularity. [127] Even when the aristocrats in *Jack Rann* are not directly malicious, they are wasteful or useless at best. Describing the entrance to a squire's house, flanked with 'two high towers' of stone, the narrator quips: 'Why erected, except it were to furnish employment, or to lavish money away, no tongue could tell.'[128] At a different point in the story, Rann witnesses a boating accident at Richmond where a young woman falls into the water and is ostensibly drowning.

> "Poor thing!" was the exclamation of some gentleman riding near Jack; but, beyond commiseration, nothing was offered. Rann, whose whole nature glowed with generous impulses, was however not so apathetic; [...][129]

Rann of course saves the damsel, who turns out to be his childhood sweetheart, Mary Colville, the daughter of a lawyer. Unlike the gentleman, who only observes and comments on the accident, Rann acts as a protector to women.

This event illustrates how Rann's identity is not merely about class – it is also about masculinity and what form of masculinity is acceptable within the narrative. Rann's masculinity is not grounded in the domesticity that became the centrepiece of nineteenth-century masculinity.[130] It is his independence, physical strength, skill as an

---

[127] For a more general discussion of anti-aristocratic sentiment in Britain, see Antony Taylor, *Lords of Misrule. Hostility to Aristocracy in Late Nineteenth- and Early Twentieth-Century Britain* (Basinstoke: Palgrave Macmillan, 2004).
[128] Lindridge, *Jack Rann*, p. 160.
[129] Lindridge, *Jack Rann*, p. 140.
[130] Ralf Schneider succinctly describes the domestic masculine ideal as the figure of the paterfamilias, 'the breadwinner who struggles most of his time in the world of business, competition, and strife, to return home to find rest in a beautiful environment, arranged for him and presided over by the angelic presence of his wife and mother to his offspring'. Ralf Schneider, 'The Invisible Center: Conceptions of Masculinity in Victorian Fiction – Realist, Crime, Detective, and Gothic', in *Constructions of Masculinity in British Literature from the Middle Ages to the Present*, ed. by Stefan Horlacher (New York: Palgrave Macmillan, 2011), pp. 147-168, pp. 150-151.

equestrian, and courage that constitute his appeal, all forms of masculine prestige. The Earl of Dashfield hires Rann early in the narrative as a valet, and describes him as 'handsome as Adonis, strong as Hercules, and as courageous as a lion.'[131] These traits, and Rann's unstable status as a gentleman criminal, stand at odds with the masculinity espoused by male characters like Mr Malcolm and Captain Dashfield. Rann shows no remorse or self-consciousness surrounding his chosen profession, until it clashes with the comfortable domesticity of the Malcolms. He overhears Miss Malcolm in her sleep, calling him 'my own beloved Jack Rann – so noble, so generous, so kind, so true!'.[132] Then,

> For the first time Jack felt a pang that shivered his whole frame with all the panic and potency of an electric shock, that she should be so deceived – that he should be the despicable thief – the highwayman – the robber that he was: he cursed the strange fatality, that, instead of being in her father's house an honoured guest, he should be there as a disreputable thief![133]

It is the perversion of the role he wishes to take within their home (that of a guest) that causes the brief moment of regret and reflection. Domesticity is continually rebutted and complicated in the text – Rann resists entreaties to conform to middle class values, urging him to give up his highwayman ways. Captain Dashfield, the heir of the villainous Earl and Miss Malcolm's suitor, attempts to convince him that the life of a highwayman 'does not near approach in happiness the life led by an honest man,' and tries to win him over 'to a life of industry and the path of rectitude,' which is a 'life of quietude, ease, and comfort'.[134] Jack argues that domestic life does not suit him; he is 'naturally of a restless disposition,' and without excitement 'should die of *ennui*'.[135] Emigration is positioned as a possible antidote to the tedium of middle-class

---

[131] Lindridge, *Jack Rann*, p. 28.
[132] Lindridge, *Jack Rann*, p. 112.
[133] Lindridge, *Jack Rann*, pp. 112-113.
[134] Lindridge, *Jack Rann*, pp. 356-357.
[135] Lindridge, *Jack Rann*, p. 357.

domesticity, ('Why, in America, Jack, freed from all the trammels of European manners, you might build yourself a house, wander, gun in hand, over miles and miles of forest ground literally swarming with game'[136]). Rann marries Elinor Roche on the ship taking him to Liverpool, the departure point of the emigration vessel. In the conversation between Mr Malcolm and Rann, he concedes to domesticity:

> "Marriage is a serious step to take," said the good old gentleman, smilingly, "have you calculated the extra expense, and extra duties that would devolve upon you if saddled with a wife?"
> "I have weighed and considered all, sir," responded Jack, ["]and am firmly convinced the extra duty would not only be a pleasureable [sic] one but a profitable one likewise." […]
> "And you think then, notwithstanding your fickle and wayward heart, notwithstanding the unnatural ferocity for which your enemies have given you credit, you would not be found wanting in love for your spouse, or in parental tenderness for your children."
> "No, no," said Jack; "vile and unfeeling as I may have been, I am not so bad – not so unnatural as that."[137]

Mr Malcolm, himself a paterfamilias and successful purveyor of middle-class respectability here induces Jack into that sphere. Despite Rann's fickleness and 'unnatural ferocity', he too can become respectable if only adhering to the familial constraints. Despite Rann's spiritedness (described by himself as 'more blood than brains'[138]), deemed unnatural in the domestic sphere, he does not completely disavow matrimonial feeling, which would position him completely outside of respectability; this stands in direct contrast with the Earl's outburst, quoted above. Rann's domestic happiness collapses before it even begins, however. Rann never manages to leave England: the ship that is supposed to take

---

[136] Lindridge, *Jack Rann*, p. 357.
[137] Lindridge, *Jack Rann*, pp. 373-374.
[138] Lindridge, *Jack Rann*, p. 354.

Jack and his newly acquired wife, Elinor Roche, to America, suffers shipwreck just two days after departure. He immediately returns to his highwayman ways, even reuniting with his trusty mare, Sue. Soon after the shipwrecking he is captured and sentenced to execution, effectively cutting him off from any chance of domestic bliss at the end of the narrative.

The text questions: what makes a man a gentleman? Is it birth, values, conduct, or the perceptions of others? Can Jack Rann be a gentleman despite his low birth? The importance of the issue is underlined by the fact that, despite the general comic tone of the text, Jack's relationship to gentility is never ridiculed. The issue of class is never fully resolved, revealing class to be an unstable category, with repercussions possibly even beyond the carnivalesque text. Despite the farcical tone of the earl's degradation at having to lead his own horses, it foreshadows a far more serious scene towards the end of the text. Jack demands that the earl apologise to Miss Malcolm for his repeated attempts to abduct her, as well as insisting the earl's household be present so 'they may reap a lesson from your disgrace, and learn how despicably mean, man in his baser qualities may reduce himself.'[139] Unlike the farcical sequence, no laughter is found in this scene. When the earl refuses to apologise, Jack takes a 'massive riding whip' from a servant, 'stripped his coat from his back,' and whips the earl in front of his own household: 'he applied the thong with such vigour to the sides, back and legs of the unfortunate earl, that he danced and screamed with agony,' '[…] writhing like an eel in his agony, and completely black in the face.'[140] Unlike the earlier playful reversals, the narrative here confirms Jack's superiority over the earl, in a scene that does not rely on disguise or subterfuge. The earl is the lowest of the low, 'a scoundrel , who deserves to have his ears slit, and be put in the pillory, as a mark for all the offal and filth of London,' and Jack takes on the role of justicial authority, 'teaching him, that right must not always be trespassed upon with impunity even by the mighty.'[141] In a wider sense, then, disguise in *Jack Rann* figures in the space between society's perceptions of individuals and the class system

---

[139] Lindridge, *Jack Rann*, p. 346.
[140] Lindridge, *Jack Rann*, p. 347.
[141] Lindridge, *Jack Rann*, p. 346, 347.

as a structure of power. Jack's ability to 'pass' as a gentleman despite his birth allows him to unsettle and upset conventional power to a certain degree, becoming powerful enough to whip the earl in his own home without consequence. Yet, this ability to unsettle has a definitive limit: the promise of execution that defines the ending of the narrative.

THE SHADOW OF TYBURN

The threat of execution is an integral part of the English highwayman tradition. For Clavell in 1628, this threat was quite immediate, as he was awaiting his pardon from capital punishment. In highwayman fiction, too, execution – often at Tyburn, though not necessarily – plays a significant role. Execution crowds have intrigued scholars with their often paradoxical and inconsistent emotional states.[142] Crowds could be boisterous, celebratory, mournful, or contrarian, depending on public opinion of the person scheduled for execution. In *The Beggar's Opera* Polly evokes a melancholy scene when she contemplates her husband's possible demise:

> Methinks I see him already in the Cart, sweeter and more lovely than the Nosegay in his hand!—I hear the Crowd extolling his Resolution and Intrepidity!—What Vollies of Sighs are sent from the Windows of *Holborn*, that so comely a Youth should be brought to disgrace!—I see him at the Tree! The whole Circle are in Tears!—even Butchers weep!—*Jack Ketch* himself hesitates to perform his Duty, and would be glad to lose his Fee, by a Reprieve.[143]

This monologue features many of the common images of public hangings in London: the cart that transports the prisoner, the flower they were often given on their way to execution,[144] the crowd, the hanging

---

[142] See for example Laqueur, 'Crowds', and Gatrell, *Hanging Tree*.
[143] Gay, *Beggar's Opera*, p. 21.
[144] Gay, *Beggar's Opera*, see footnote p. 194.

tree, the legendary executioner Jack Ketch, and the slightest chance of a reprieve at the last minute. While the audience might lament and grieve, the role of the criminal was to face his death with courage. Macheath is resigned to his fate; in Air 57, he goes, 'undismay'd', stating that 'Contented I die'.[145] This fictional bravery was drawn on and referred to by several real-life convicted highwaymen.[146] The threat of execution – an expression of state power over the individual – therefore looms over highwayman fiction. In *The Beggar's Opera*, Macheath is reprieved in a metafictional joke to suit 'the Taste of the Town,' undermining the fictionalised author's intention of including a 'Moral.'[147] As foreshadowed throughout the narrative, Jack Rann received no such reprieve in Lindridge's *Jack Rann*. This decision seems to have been deliberate – the 1823 play by Rede, which Lindridge borrows from liberally, does reprieve Jack at the end of the narrative. While Laqueur has argued that public executions allowed for carnivalesque crowds: executions 'were more risible than solemn as they lurched chaotically between death and laughter.'[148] Lindridge's Jack Rann embodies laughter in the face of death, yet its execution scene does not contain a crowd that can be read as carnivalesque. In this section we will look more closely at the text's philosophy of dying, the relationship between Jack and authority, and how Jack's rebellion persists beyond his execution through carnivalesque renewal.

While many characters refer to death by hanging throughout the text, the most comprehensive philosophy regarding execution is posited by Clayton in his 'dessertation on death' [sic]. He summarises the life of a highway succinctly with three words: 'STRUGGLE! — GUGGLE! — BUBBLE!'[149] He explains that '"Struggle," exemplifies the vicissitudes of his chequered life: "Guggle," is the only sign he gives of pain in death: and "Bubble," closes the career of the man, as a bubble on a stream of water bursts and leaves no trace behind.' This inevitable cycle, Clayton argues, is not to be feared:

---

[145] Gay, *Beggar's Opera*, p. 64.
[146] McKenzie, 'Macheath', p. 596.
[147] Gay, *Beggar's Opera*, p. 69.
[148] Laqueur, 'Crowds', p. 309.
[149] Lindridge, *Jack Rann*, p. 90.

[...] every man must die, and never a man will die before his allotted time; for us the glorious death of a public execution is reserved, and what more fitting to expiate the life of sunshine than a gay and sudden exit, eh? [...] What happy dogs we ought to be then, to escape the physicing, blistering, pain and torment, of the infernal doctors with the miserable death that follows it; to leap at once into eternity, wafted thither by the tears, sobs, and prayers of a pitying mob. My boy, to the really brave, death can have no terrors.[150]

Clayton's view on the life and death of the highwayman goes further than 'dying game'; the eighteenth-century ideal of the criminal facing his death with courage.[151] All of human existence is condensed into the humorously irreverent words of struggle, guggle, and bubble, drawing attention to the bodily functions that accompany execution. The lack of extended suffering in the form of a long illness serves as one last boon after a 'life of sunshine' enjoyed by the highwayman. In this interpretation, the aspect of punishment is absent – as no man dies before his time (an assumption drawing on theological determinism), a faster death is more desirable than a slow one. Clayton defers the authority for execution away from the state, submerging it instead in a vague debate about predestination that denies its interpretation as judicial and political ritual, as Foucault has described public executions.[152] Rather than execution being seen as the expression of 'the dissymmetry between the subject who has dared to violate the law and the all-powerful sovereign who displays his strength,'[153] execution is refigured as a mercy. This denial of state and judicial power is typical of the relationship of the text with authority and law. While the highwaymen

---

[150] Lindridge, *Jack Rann*, p. 90.
[151] McKenzie, *Tyburn's Martyrs*, pp. 191-192. McKenzie describes the 'game' criminal as 'the bold and dashing highwayman or street robber who dressed like a beau, drank like a lord, and went without tears or trembling to the gallows.'
[152] Michel Foucault, *Discipline and Punish. The Birth of the Prison*, trans. by Alan Sheridan (New York: Vintage Books, 1995), pp. 48-49.
[153] Foucault, *Discipline*, p. 49.

are subject to the consequences of their actions in the light of law and convention, their understanding of these realities subverts their meaning. The highwayman's 'guggle', the last sound he will make when hanged, is thoroughly profane, and drowns out any conversation about the validity of state authority.

While Clayton's 'dessertation on death' from the highwayman's perspective is irreverent and practical, the emotional resonance is displaced from the highwayman to the crowd. The criminal remains stoic and without regret, in contrast to the 'tears, sobs, and prayers of a pitying mob'. The crowd appears several times as an emotional foil to the rational strictness of law and authority. Not only do they appear at the final theatre of the scaffold, they are an integral part of Rann's examinations at court. When Rann appears in front of magistrate John Fielding for the first time,

> A crowded court was awaiting our hero's arrival, for already had the fame of his adventures been blazoned throughout the metropolis. His daring intrepidity also formed no unimportant portion of his fame, and the old police office at Bow-street was crowded with many ladies in fashionable attire.[154]

The crowd is an essential part of Rann's status as a celebrity criminal, meta-fictionally supporting the text and Jack's adventures as admirable and entertaining. The crowds in *Jack Rann* are generally undefined – the 'ladies in fashionable attire' here are middle- to upper-class women charmed by Jack's courage and exploits, implicitly confirming his masculinity. The emotions of the crowd are heavily in Rann's favour and contrast with the solemnity of the legal proceedings; during the squire's testimony against Rann, 'the mob having in their admiration of the prisoner and the detestation of prosecutor favoured him with a shower of mud, stale cabbage, an occasional dead kitten, and such concomitants as might be anticipated from the remoteness of Covent Garden.'[155] This popular displeasure in the face of state authority undermines its

---

[154] Lindridge, *Jack Rann*, p. 119.
[155] Lindridge, *Jack Rann*, p. 119.

legitimacy, turning it into a farcical tableau where an 'occasional dead kitten' is thrown without repercussions to those who participate in this communal display of dissatisfaction. The dynamic between crowd and state is reminiscent of Eric Hobsbawm's definition of social banditry, where outlaws 'whom the lord and state regard as criminals' are 'considered by their people as heroes' and 'men to be admired, helped and supported.'[156] In fact, the scene 'assumed more the look of a triumph than a trial, thousands of people being in waiting without, who rent the air with shouts of admiration at the appearance of Jack.'[157] The crowd rejects the state authority, refusing to interpret Rann's appearance as accused, inserting themselves into the judicial ritual to honour him.

However, if Jack is a champion of the people, it is not immediately clear what his rebellion represents. Unlike the crowd, Jack does not show any emotion. Nor does he play the role of the penitent criminal. Inspired by the historical John Rann, the fictional Jack appears in eccentric dress; 'his iron's [sic] were decorated with blue ribbons, and at his breast he wore a magnificent nosegay.'[158] Instead of respecting the squire's authority, Jack responds to his testimony with an insult ('I must confess I have never had the pleasure of looking at your ugly mug, and to tell the truth although its [sic] before a crowded audience I shouldn't care to look upon his like again.')[159] Jack's brushes with the law bring us to the one exception to the narrative's irreverent attitude to authority: 'the acute and sagacious magistrate, Sir John Fielding,'[160] who oversees Jack's trail, and returns later in the narrative.[161] Jack is acquitted because of lack of evidence, yet Fielding warns him to change his ways: 'from your gay appearance here to-day, I am positive, if not actually criminal you are advancing with the companionship of bad men; I beseech you […] to

---

[156] Hobsbawm, *Bandits*, p. 17.
[157] Lindridge, *Jack Rann*, p. 119.
[158] Lindridge, *Jack Rann*, p. 119.
[159] Lindridge, *Jack Rann*, p. 120.
[160] Lindridge, *Jack Rann*, p. 119.
[161] The historical Rann also had several run-ins with Sir John Fielding. See Edward Duncan, 'John Rann, d. 1774', *London Lives* <https://www.londonlives.org/static/RannJohnExecuted1774.jsp> [accessed 26 September 2022].

forsake these bad companions.' Jack's response is respectful, if not exactly submitting to Fielding's advice. He answers, 'I thank you sincerely and kindly for your words, Sir John, that I will follow them I cannot promise, but that I will not lose sight of them I promise most sincerely, most faithfully.'[162] Despite the text's mockery of trial and law in general, it stops short at mocking Fielding, who formed the Bow Street Runners police force as his brother Henry Fielding's assistant, and became a magistrate at Bow Street after Henry's death. The admiration for John Fielding stands in contrast to the attitude towards constables in the text. Colledge, the youngest member, describes 'the charlies' as 'cosy enough in their boxes as their beds.' He continues: 'Wise fellows! They take care of themselves and leave City to take care of itself.'[163] Irreverence has its limits, and the figure of Fielding, who is mythical in his own right, sticks out as appearing unscathed from a text that revels in mockery.

Fielding's exceptionalism within the text sets him up as the perfect counterpart to Rann. At the end of the narrative, it is Fielding who captures Jack:

> "John Rann," said Sir John Fielding, in a solemn voice, for in the person before him, he at once recognised the young man who had been placed before him at Bow-street, "you are my prisoner, armed with the warrant of the king, I arrest you on the charge of highway robbery." [...]
> Jack saw at once the odds were against him. "Sir John," he said, frankly extending his hand, which the worthy magistrate took and shook heartily, "I am your prisoner, and it gives me some pleasure in this dark hour to confess so, for you are the only man in England worthy of taking me."
> "My duty is a painful one, Mr. Rann," said the good man, a tear of commiseration appearing in each eye, "but it must, nevertheless, be fulfilled."[164]

---

[162] Lindridge, *Jack Rann*, p. 128.
[163] Lindridge, *Jack Rann*, p. 108.
[164] Lindridge, *Jack Rann*, pp. 400-401.

The handshake between Rann and Fielding is an equalising gesture, implying their mutual respect and to a certain degree, equal rank. The exchange has the air of a sports match, in which Jack has lost with dignity. The 'tear of commiseration' that Fielding displays is the only suggestion of the high stakes of Jack's capture, while at the same time imbuing Fielding's character with the compassion and emotion that legal proceedings lack. If persecution is a game, Fielding is a worthy opponent, and Jack's eventual capture does not constitute a negation of all the adventures that preceded the capture. Once Jack has declared his loss and gives his word not to escape, Fielding dismisses the soldiers present at the scene. Jack and Elinor 'walked arm and arm down Fleet-street',

> Sir John walking by the side, and freely conversing with them, so that they bore the appearance of three friends in social conversation. They entered Newgate by the governor's private door, who attended upon them from that time up to the day of their trial as if they were respected guests on a visit of ceremony with him.'[165]

Fielding treats Jack and Elinor as his social equals, and despite Jack's crimes and low birth, he is treated as a guest during his time in Newgate. The relationship between Jack and authority, as embodied by Fielding, is therefore complex: although the narrative ends with his capture, Jack retains his paradoxical status as gentleman highwayman even while incarcerated in Newgate, a position legitimised by the fictional Fielding.

This resistance to casting Jack as penitent and regretful criminal underpins the narrative's carnivalesque interpretation of state power. While on the surface the order is restored by the end of the text by way of Jack's execution, the text manages to unsettle conceptions of authority by casting Jack's life in an alternative light. Unlike Fagin in *Oliver Twist*, Jack is not plagued by regret or distress. Fagin, a 'receiver of stolen goods' and gang leader 'raved and blasphemed,' and 'howled and tore

---

[165] Lindridge, *Jack Rann*, p. 402.

his hair' while he awaited his execution in a cell in Newgate.[166] Jack, in contrast, receives visitors in 'a private apartment allotted to him by the governor' and cautions his friend that 'what can't be cured must be endured' and he might 'as well laugh as pine [his] time away' in Newgate.[167] Fagin is tortured not only by the threat of death, but also by his guilty conscience:

> [H]e started up every minute, and with gasping mouth and burning skin hurried to and fro, in such a paroxysm of fear and wrath, that even [his guards] – used to such sights – recoiled from him with horror. He grew so terrible at last in all the tortures of his evil conscience, that one man could not bear to sit there, eyeing him alone, and so the two kept watch together.[168]

Jack's conscience is clear, however, because he has not committed murder, merely property-related crimes: '[were] my hand stained in blood to the wrist, He might have terror for me [...] but, thank heaven, it is for no murder that I am about to suffer, [...] and for the rest, why should I care?'[169] This positioning as the act of murder as the only true crime or sin is an inheritance from the criminal biography, obscuring or at least trivialising his other crimes.[170]

If anything, his last few days act as a capstone to a life well-lived, spent in quiet contemplation with loved ones. Not only do Fagin's and Jack's incarcerations differ on a personal level, the two texts show two different approaches to execution. While Dickens famously criticised public executions, especially the festive attitude of the crowds present at

---

[166] Dickens, *Oliver Twist*, p. 445.
[167] Lindridge, *Jack Rann*, p. 403.
[168] Dickens, *Oliver Twist*, p. 446.
[169] Lindridge, *Jack Rann*, p. 408.
[170] As Faller writes, '[W]here the murderer is made to stand for all criminals and indeed all sinners, the thief becomes a special case.' Faller, *Turned to Account*, p. 175.

them, he was in favour of capital punishment away from public view.[171] While *Jack Rann* makes no explicit political statement towards abolition, it does suggest that the state's power to enact a death penalty is not legitimate: in the words of Captain Dashfield, 'if they hang you, Jack, it will be cold-blooded murder in reality.'[172] Despite being faced with one of the harshest punishments one can be convicted of,[173] Jack's rebellion is one of courage. The text describes how 'his undaunted carriage, and flashing eye, told of a spirit that the law, in all the majesty of its terrors, had no power to bend or break.'[174] Though Rann must die, he refuses to repent, with 'extraordinary nerve and unflinching behaviour' that 'sustained him to the direful end.' He stands firm even under religious pressure: 'The minister prayed, preached, and besought, with all the energy of a fanatic, in order to bend, what he termed, our hero's stubborn spirit.'[175] Jack's refusal to play the role of the penitent prisoner is his final rebellion, a symbolic stance against the pressures to conform to state-sanctioned morality.

Jack is supported in this resistance by the crowd at his execution. Unlike the carnivalesque crowds that attend the executions of highwaymen and murderers, as described for example by Dickens and Thackeray, the crowd at Jack's is mournful:

> Every head uncovered – every eye moistened – every heart full to bursting with grief, as they gaze upon the devoted young man, in all the pride and bloom of manly beauty, so soon to

---

[171] Andrew Smith, *Gothic Death 1740-1914. A Literary History* (Manchester: Manchester University Press, 2016), pp. 108-110, 117.
[172] Lindridge, *Jack Rann*, p. 408.
[173] The only harsher punishment was reserved for those convicted of treason, who might be beheaded and quartered instead of hanged.
[174] Lindridge, *Jack Rann*, p. 405.
[175] Lindridge, *Jack Rann*, p. 407. For the role of penitence and religion at Tyburn, see McKenzie, *Tyburn's Martyrs*, Chapter 5 'The Ordinary's *Account*: Confession and the Criminal' and Chapter 6, 'Dying Well: Martyrs and Penitents', pp 121-156, 157-190.

perish ignominiously before their eyes.
Oh, God! That such scenes should be.[176]

The description is reminiscent of the melancholy scene from *The Beggar's Opera* quoted at the start of this section. Although the crowd does not celebrate in carnivalesque feasting, the outpouring of sympathy and emotion gives Rann the appearance of a martyr, unjustly becoming the victim of state violence. Not even the speech that Jack gives at his execution manages to convey true regret or piety. He warns the crowd not to follow in his footsteps to save them 'from sin and destruction': he urges them to 'be honest', 'turn away from the path of sin', and to 'be sober' as 'drink fetters the soul'.[177] It stands in contrast to Jack's own words only spoken a couple of chapters earlier, where he describes execution as 'sav[ing] a wondrous sum in doctor's fees':

> [Death by hanging] is the shortest cut to heaven I know of. So hang me, I'll spin my gay career to the end, and when the times comes to snap my thread of life, let it be done by an hempen neck-cloth.[178]

Jack's last-minute pandering to public execution as a warning against crime only serves to give the narrative a safe façade of didacticism, while taken as a whole, its contents do not support any such messages. Even in the preface, Lindridge describes Rann's life as a 'gay career' whose 'acts of gallantry' could fill 'many an exciting page.'[179]

Taken as a whole, *Jack Rann*'s relationship to law and authority is one of carnivalesque negation. Life is a game, and laws are merely rules to be broken. Not only is *Jack Rann* a carnivalesque text, the role it plays within the tradition of stories about highwayman emphasises Jack's journey as part of a cycle. As Fuller writes about criminal biographies:

---

[176] Lindridge, *Jack Rann*, p. 412.
[177] Lindridge, *Jack Rann*, p. 412.
[178] Lindridge, *Jack Rann*, p. 356.
[179] Lindridge, *Jack Rann*, p. 1.

criminals [...] were made to play the central role in rituals of sacrifice and renewal. Their necks safely wrung, processed and packaged in ways that declared them fit for public consumption, criminals lived their lives over in readers' imaginations, committed their crimes and met their deaths, again and again.[180]

This immortality granted by the public to those who were condemned to die was one of the main issues of capital punishment for Dickens, who feared that the flurry of posthumous publications in the wake of executions would endanger the social order.[181] For a text like *Jack Rann*, this means that despite the relative closure of the text due to the execution that terminates the text, Jack's death is merely part of a cycle of 'sacrifice and renewal', as expressed by Fuller, whereby the subversion as embodied by the text persists outside of its boundaries, functioning through a process of death and literary resurrection. Despite Jack's neck being 'safely wrung', the social order is not restored at the end of the narrative; there is always a possibility of his story being retold, repackaged, or revived, preserving its potential to subvert authority even beyond this version's Jack Rann's literary death.

CONCLUSION

In this chapter I placed Lindridge's *Jack Rann* within the context of the historical highwayman tradition as well as its related field of literary production, such as criminal biographies and the picaresque. On the surface, Jack's characterisation is reminiscent of Valentine Vaux, especially when considering the importance of enjoyment: 'few possessed a soul more open to enjoyment of every description than his.'[182] Yet where Prest's *Valentine Vaux* is an essentially conservative text, *Jack Rann* undermines authority and unsettles class distinctions. Its carnivalesque attitude with Jack at its epicentre turns crime into a game,

---

[180] Faller, *Turned to Account*, p. xi.
[181] Smith, *Gothic Death*, pp. 116-117.
[182] Lindridge, *Jack Rann*, p. 138.

where playing along is rewarded and joy is found in being robbed. Jack occupies the paradoxical position of gentleman highwayman, and despite being of low birth, is recognised and treated as a gentleman by several authority figures in the narrative, including the middle-class Mr Malcolm and the magistrate Sir John Fielding. Yet the question of Jack's class is never truly settled: the text questions whether the gentleman is a disguise, or the highwayman, and floats the possibility that both these positions are. Not only class, but authority is unsettled by the carnivalesque implications of the narrative as well. The text shows no particular appreciation for aristocrats, nor is execution seen as a valid expression of state power in response to a property crime. Although the death penalty is enacted, it does not provide the narrative closure that signals a return to the normal social order. The subversive potential of a text like *Jack Rann* partially lies in its part of a cycle of telling and retelling of criminal tales, implying that even after the fictional death of Lindridge's version of Jack Rann, the text is always open to further retelling in a different moment of time.

The significance for penny fiction as a whole is not that every penny serial featuring a highwayman has taken the same approach as Lindridge has in his interpretation of John Rann's life. This chapter on *Jack Rann* however helps outline the range of politics available to working-class readers in penny fiction. On the surface Jack's adventures might seem similar to Valentine's: both often rely on misdirection of the senses, Valentine through auditory misdirection, Jack through visual misdirection through his various disguises. Both texts rely on farce, yet the meanings created in their contexts are vastly different.

Chapter Four

Paul Jones by Pierce Egan the Younger

INTRODUCTION

Among the various strands that make up the diverse set of texts that we now call 'penny bloods', a significant number of the corpus contains nautical themes. The earliest nautical penny fiction that can be seen as part of the penny fiction boom of the 1830s and 1840s is *History of the Pirates of All Nations* (1836-7), an anthology-style serial written by Thomas Peckett Prest and jointly distributed by Lloyd and Purkess.[1] Prest again wrote a nautical text in 1841, *Gallant Tom: or, The Perils of a Sailor, Ashore and Afloat*, and wrote various others throughout the decade.[2] The nautical romance proved to be popular, and Lloyd and Purkess supplemented their catalogue by reprinting American texts, such as *The Corsair; the Foundling of the Sea* (1847) by Harry Hazel (the original bearing the subtitle 'An American Romance') and *I'm Afloat, I'm*

---

[1] The original issues seem to be largely lost. Advertisements for the serial can be found in for example *Lives of the Most Notorious Highwaymen, Footpads, and Murderers* (Saturday July 9, 1836, issue 11), another serial attributed to Prest.
[2] These include *The Smuggler King; or, The Foundling of the Wreck* (1844), *The Ocean Child: or, The Lost Vessel* (1846), *Jack Junk: or, the Tar for All Weathers: a Romance of the Deep Blue Sea* (1849), *Ben Bolt: or, The Perils of a Sailor* (1850), *Richard Parker: or, The Mutiny at the Nore: A Romance* (1851), and *My Poll and My Partner Joe: Or, Pretty Poll of Putney: A Nautical Romance* (1851).

Afloat (1847), a reprint of *Roderick the Rover, or The Spirit of the Wave* (1847) by Maturin Murray Ballou (writing as Lieutenant Murray). Aside from overt fiction, (supposedly) non-fictional accounts of the dangers and thrills of nautical life could count on a sizable readership as well: Lindridge edited over eighty issues of a penny serial titled *Tales of Shipwrecks and Adventures at Sea*, a testament to its popularity, collected in a single volume in 1847.[3] Pierce Egan the Younger, who wrote several serialised novels in the 1840s, published his own take on a nautical adventure with *Paul Jones*, a fictionalised account of the historical John Paul Jones. As was common during his lifetime, Egan's stories were initially serialised in a weekly format, before being collected in two volumes in 1842.[4] It was later reprinted in penny numbers, and collected in a single volume as *Paul Jones; the Pirate* in 1850 by Purkess.[5] Egan, the son of author and journalist Pierce Egan (1772-1849), was born in 1814 in London, and died in 1880.[6] He also worked as an illustrator, and created a series of etchings to accompany his father's serial, *The Pilgrims of the Thames, in Search of the National* (1838). Egan's early works focused on the medieval period, including his most popular story *Wat Tyler* (1841) and *Robin Hood and Little John* (1840). The authors of Egan's entry in the *Oxford Dictionary of National Biography* state that 'Egan's early works [...] cannot be said to be realistic or historically accurate.'[7] As will be discussed below, despite borrowing the name of John Paul Jones, Egan's story only draws from Paul Jones's life in the very loosest of terms, in a similar manner to Lindridge in *Jack Rann*. During the 1850s Egan

---

[3] James Lindridge, *Tales of Shipwrecks and Adventures at Sea. Being a Collection of Faithful Narratives of Shipwrecks, Mutinies, Fires, Famines, and Disasters, incidental to a Sea Life; Together with Celebrated Voyages, Amusing Tales, Tough Yarns, and Interesting Anecdotes* (London: William Mark Clark, 1847).
[4] J. W. Ebsworth and Megan A. Stephan, 'Egan, Pierce James (1814–1880), novelist', in *Oxford Dictionary of National Biography* <https://www.oxforddnb.com/> [accessed September 2022].
[5] Pierce Egan the Younger, *Paul Jones; the Pirate* (London: G. Purkess, 1850). This chapter refers to this version throughout.
[6] Ebsworth and Stephan, 'Egan, Pierce James'.
[7] Ebsworth and Stephan, 'Egan, Pierce James'.

contributed several stories to *Reynolds's Miscellany*, before moving his focus to the *London Journal*, where he wrote serials until his death.

Pierce Egan's *Paul Jones* ostensibly tells the story of John Paul Jones, a historical figure of Scottish birth who lived in the eighteenth century (1747-1792) and gained renown as a naval commander for the American Navy during the American Revolutionary War. Before the publication of Egan's take on Paul, John Paul Jones had already been the subject of other fictional texts; finding Scott's *The Pirate* (1822) lacking in a truthful representation of life on board a ship, James Fenimore Cooper published *The Pilot* in 1823, taking the 1779 sea battle between John Paul Jones and Captain Pearson as its subject.[8] *The Pilot* was adapted for the stage three times.[9] Only a couple of years later, Allan Cunningham published *Paul Jones: A Romance* (1826). Initially apprenticed to a merchant ship, the historical Paul steadily climbed through ranks until he became captain of a ship through exceptional circumstances: both the master and first mate of the brigantine *John* died at sea, and out of gratitude for taking over command of the ship and bringing it to port safely, Paul was made master of the *John* and a percentage of its cargo.[10] Paul was a controversial figure; in 1770 was accused of cruelty after a sailor died a couple of weeks after being flogged by Paul.[11] Although he was cleared of these charges, he subsequently was accused of killing a member of his crew, who Paul claimed was mutinous. The exact timing of this event seems to be uncertain; sources put the death of the crew member between 1770 and 1773.[12] After this event he fled to Virginia, and

---

[8] Frederick Burwick and Manushag N. Powell, *British Pirates in Print and Performance* (New York: Palgrave Macmillan, 2015), p. 87.
[9] From Burwick and Powell, *British Pirates*, p. 88: Edward Fitzball, *The Pilot; or, A Tale of the Sea* (Adelphi, 31 October 1825); William Bayle Bernard, *The Pilot: A Tale of the Sea* (Coburg, 17 July 1826); Thomas J. Dibdin, *Paul Jones; or, The Solway Mariner* (Adelphi, 12 February 1827; renamed *The Pirate's Doom; or, The Solway Mariner*, 19 February 1827).
[10] Burwick and Powell, *British Pirates*, p. 91.
[11] Burwick and Powell, *British Pirates*, p. 91.
[12] Burwick and Powell, p. 91, state 1770; 'John Paul Jones', *Britannica* (2022), <https://www.britannica.com/biography/John-Paul-Jones-United-States-naval-officer> [accessed 26 September 2022], states 1772; Joseph Callo, *John Paul Jones:*

changed his name to John Paul Jones.[13] In 1775 he joined the newly formed Continental Navy as first lieutenant.[14] In the following years he commanded several ships, participating in naval battles with the British. After 1787 he joined the Russian Navy, and he died in relative obscurity in Paris in 1792. While Paul Jones is considered a naval hero from an American perspective (especially in retrospect, as Paul Jones was reburied in the Maryland upon Theodore Roosevelt's request in 1905),[15] British perceptions were less unequivocally celebratory. Paul's knowledge of the Irish and British coasts was beneficial in his Continental Navy career, but also caused him to be seen as a traitor by British contemporaries.[16] A 1779 pamphlet notes that (British) society 'justly execrates him as a monster of ingratitude and cruelty.'[17] This pamphlet goes to great lengths to present Paul as a villain, including claiming that as a teenager Paul 'seemed to derive a peculiar satisfaction from putting the domestic animals about the house [to] the most extreme torture' and having 'debauched three young women' in the neighbourhood by age seventeen, leading to two pregnancies.[18] In the surviving biographical information available, there is no evidence that Paul's villainy extended to such lengths, but the pamphlet gives an insight into the rumours that might have circulated around Paul at the latter half of the eighteenth century.

While Egan does draw from some of the biographical information on Paul available at the time, his John Paul Jones is neither a villain nor a straightforward hero. Nor is the nautical plot the sole focus of the text – it also includes a significant domestic plot that sits uneasily alongside the nautical adventures, creating a contrast that reflects on the generic

---

America's First Sea Warrior (Annapolis: Naval Institute Press, 2006), p. 11 states 1773.
[13] Burwick and Powell, *British Pirates*, p. 91. 'John Paul Jones', *Britannica*.
[14] Callo, *John Paul Jones*, p. 23.
[15] Callo, *John Paul Jones*, pp. 182-183.
[16] A 1779 poem for example includes the line 'The pi–pirate, trai–traitor comes, d–n him, Paul Jones.' *Paul Jones: or the Fife Coast Garland. A Heroi-Comical Poem. In Four Parts.* (Edinburgh: [n. pub.], 1779), p. 1.
[17] *Authentic Memoirs of Captain Paul Jones, The American Corsair* (London: A Hogg, [1779?]), p. 7.
[18] *Authentic Memoirs*, p. 11, p. 12.

dimensions of the text. *Paul Jones* draws from themes borrowed from the nautical melodrama that was popular in the first half of the nineteenth century, yet it also complicates them. The following section will place *Paul Jones* within the wider context of British nautical fiction, briefly outlining the literary and dramatic imagination leading up to the publication of *Paul Jones*, providing the foundation for the subsequent section on the juxtaposition between the abundance of domestic melodrama and the adventures of its sailing characters. Not only do these plots clash, creating a fragmented narrative, the text moves between the highly emotional register of the melodramatic to pun-filled speech consisting of nautical metaphors. The text self-consciously reflects on this generic incompatibility through the humorous dialogue of one of the main characters, Gasket, whose sea-faring language clashes with the ideals of domesticity. This chapter traces this humour, first as it reflects on domesticity, and subsequently expanding this understanding of the text's politics regarding the nation state and finally, the empire. The clash between the order represented by the domestic ideal and the destabilising force of a nautical existence finds its expression in Paul Jones's characterisation, the subject of the subsequent section. It reveals how the rigidity of class and status within the text determines his tragic ending, and how this intersects with the text's ideas on freedom and the nation. Finally, not only does the humour of *Paul Jones* refer to its generic uncertainties, it also reveals anxieties relating to race and empire through the laughter *with* and *at* the text's (unnamed) black character. Overall, *Paul Jones* moves away from the successful integration of ideas of familial order and nationhood that can be found in the nautical melodrama from the early nineteenth century, to a reflection on their incompatibility.

PRIVATEERS, BUCCANEERS, AND OTHER PIRATES

The sea as a literary element has a long history – as Egan writes, the sea is 'the theme of the poet, and the writers of prose over the world – the subject of many a pleasant history, and many a terrible one'.[19] As Europeans explored regions unknown to them, in the seventeenth and eighteenth centuries a new transatlantic economy was formed, transporting large quantities of people and goods across the Atlantic.[20] Readers craved narratives concerning these new places and the dangers of long sea voyages such as shipwrecking and piracy. For the English literary imagination the period roughly between 1660 and 1730, sometimes called the 'golden age of piracy,' has had an enduring influence on how sea voyages and their dangers are depicted in prose.[21] During this time, piracy thrived along the Atlantic coastlines, the Indian Ocean, and particularly in the Caribbean Sea.[22] As Antonio Sanna writes, 'The period was renowned for the multiple efforts on the part of the English, French, and Spanish governments to eradicate the actual threat represented' by pirates.[23] Through various means (including mass executions of captured pirates, increased by the incentive of rewards for capture, and naval patrols) piracy in the Caribbean declined strongly in the 1720s, and many of the notorious pirates known to the public had either been killed in combat or executed by the end of the decade.[24] In the late seventeenth century, stories about pirates spread through travel narratives and autobiographical texts, as well as through anthologies of exploits of famous pirates. According to Richard Frohock, readers were fascinated by the Americas and South Pacific, and the sea narratives, and the 'shocking hardship and cruelty' they contained.[25] Collections such as John Esquemelin's Dutch-language *De Americaensche Zee-Roovers* (1678,

---

[19] Egan, *Paul Jones*, p. 4. For a general introduction to nautical fiction, see Margaret Cohen, *The Novel and the Sea* (Princeton: Princeton University Press, 2010).
[20] Peter Linebaugh and Marcus Rediker, *The Many-Headed Hydra. Sailors, Slaves, Commoners, and the Hidden History of the Revolutionary Atlantic* (Boston: Beacon Press, 2000), p. 2.
[21] Antonio Sanna, 'Historical and Fictional Pirates. A Review' in *Pirates in History and Popular Culture*, ed. by Antonio Sanna (Jefferson: McFarland & Company, Inc., Publishers, 2018), pp. 7-24, p. 8.
[22] Sanna, 'Historical and Fictional Pirates', p. 8.
[23] Sanna, 'Historical and Fictional Pirates', p. 8.
[24] Sanna, 'Historical and Fictional Pirates', p. 12.
[25] Richard Frohock, *Buccaneers and Privateers: The Story of the English Sea Rover, 1675-1725* (Newark: University of Delaware Press, 2012), p. 9.

subsequently translated to *The Buccaneers and Marooners of America* in English in 1684)[26] and Captain Charles Johnson's *A General History of the Robberies & Murders of the Most Notorious Pirates* (1724)[27] anthologised stories about various (in)famous pirates, including Captain Avery, Captain Thatch (also known as Blackbeard), and Bartholomew Roberts. *General History* inspired pirate tales into the nineteenth century, with writers such as Scott, Edgar Allan Poe, and Robert Louis Stevenson referring to it as inspiration for their own works.[28] Other pamphlets such as *The King of Pirates* (1720), occasionally attributed to Defoe, focused on the exploits of a single pirate (and their crew); in this case Captain Avery.[29] Perceptions of sea marauders ranged from outright condemnation of the violence they inflicted to glorification of their bravery, and many shades of ambivalence in between. Especially privateers, sailors who waged war against vessels of other nations, legitimised by a 'letter of marque', were polarizing figures, as their violence was supposedly state-sanctioned. The cultural impact of these nautical narratives should not be underestimated; as Frohock writes,

> Widely distributed and read, piracy and privateering narratives contributed significantly to England's imaginative, literary rendering of the Americas in the late seventeenth and early eighteenth centuries, and collectively they provided a venue for public discourse about sea voyages and their position within empire.[30]

In particular, Mackie has argued, pirate stories offered a space in which to explore imperialism. She writes that, '[i]n the eighteenth century, piracy is a concept useful for the definition of the line between legitimate

---

[26] Frohock, *Buccaneers and Privateers*, p. 10.
[27] Sanna, 'Historical and Fictional Pirates', p. 13. Captain Charles Johnson is a pseudonym. It is unclear whether the author was a naval officer or whether they merely styled themselves as one for increased credibility.
[28] Sanna, 'Historical and Fictional Pirates', p. 14.
[29] *The King of Pirates: Being an Account of the Famous Enterprises of Captain Avery, The Mock King of Madagascar* (London: A. Bettesworth, 1720).
[30] Frohock, *Buccaneers and Privateers*, p. 2.

and illegitimate commercial practices.'[31] It was the flexibility of the piratical trope that allowed it to be 'a marker of the very instabilities of those lines that define social and ethical standards.'[32]

In the nineteenth century the interest in pirates had not abated, even though the century witnessed a decline in pirate activity, especially in the Atlantic region.[33] According to Grace Moore, 'the pirate underwent a metamorphosis in the nineteenth-century literary imagination in both British and American literature.' More specifically, '[r]epresentations of the pirate shifted from the dangerous, uncouth cutthroats like the notorious Blackbeard, to the brooding Romanticism of Byron's corsair and the swashbuckling charisma of figures such as Captain Hook and Long John Silver.'[34] Byron published his tale in verse *The Corsair*, featuring a charismatic pirate captain named Conrad in 1814.[35] Rather than an irredeemable villain, Conrad is 'defiant, alienated and misanthropic [...], yet also sensitive, honourable and faithful.'[36] It is his ability for romantic affection that elevates Conrad from the stereotype of the cruel and unfeeling pirate; Byron writes that Conrad is 'Link'd with one virtue, and a thousand crimes.'[37] He also eschews the excesses of pirate life, such as indulging in drink and food. Conrad 'Ne'er seasons he with mirth their jovial mess', and a goblet filled with wine 'passes him untasted still'.[38] It is because he 'shuns the grosser joys of sense' that 'His mind seems nourish'd by that abstinence', increasing his capacity for strategy and bringing success to his crew.[39] Conrad is positioned as an

---

[31] Erin Mackie, *Rakes, Highwaymen, and Pirates: The Making of the Modern Gentleman in the Eighteenth Century* (Baltimore: Johns Hopkins University Press, 2009), p. 126.
[32] Mackie, *Rakes*, p. 126.
[33] Grace Moore, 'Introduction', in *Pirates and Mutineers of the Nineteenth Century. Swashbucklers and Swindlers*, ed. by Grace Moore (London: Routledge, 2016), p. 1.
[34] Moore, 'Introduction', p. 1.
[35] Lord Byron, *The Corsair. A Tale.* (London: John Murray, 1814).
[36] Mel Campbell, 'Pirate Chic: Tracing the Aesthetics of Literary Piracy', in *Pirates and Mutineers of the Nineteenth Century. Swashbucklers and Swindlers*, ed. by Grace Moore (London: Routledge, 2016), pp. 11-22, p. 15.
[37] Byron, *The Corsair*, p. 95.
[38] Byron, *The Corsair*, p. 4.
[39] Byron, *The Corsair*, p. 5.

anti-hero, as different from other pirates and honourable in certain ways. Campbell writes that 'for Byron, pirates were attractive figures because they operated outside the legal and moral constraints of mercantile bourgeois society.'[40] Byron's *Corsair* became a cultural touchstone for later pirate texts, including penny bloods. As we shall see, *The Corsair* was clearly a source of inspiration for Egan as well; he inserts quotations from the work at the start of some of the chapters in *Paul Jones*, and the plot of *Paul Jones* in some ways resembles that of *The Corsair*.

Nautical stories did not only permeate the literary imagination; in the nineteenth century the sea was also brought to the stage with increased frequency. The nautical melodrama reached peak popularity in the 1820s and 1830s.[41] Some early penny serials, such as *Martin's Annals of Crime; or new Newgate Calendar* (1837) or *The History and Lives of the Most Notorious Pirates of All Nations* (serialised 1836-1837), draw inspiration and material from older anthologised works.[42] It is from the nautical melodrama, however, that the penny nautical romance draws most of its inspiration, occasionally going as far as literally lifting passages from nautical melodramas or rewriting them for their reading audiences. The 1829 'tar drama' *Black-Eyed Susan* by Douglas Jerrold was particularly successful, and was 'performed 400 times in different London theatres, reaching Cambridge, Norwich, Exeter, Durham, Liverpool and Dublin,

---

[40] Campbell, 'Pirate Chic', p. 14.
[41] Marvin Carlson, 'He Never Should Bow Down to a Domineering Frown: Class Tensions and Nautical Melodrama' in *Melodrama. The Cultural Emergence of a Genre*, ed. by Michael Hays and Anastasia Nikolopoulou (New York: St. Martin's Press, 1996), pp. 147-166, p. 151.
[42] *Martin's Annals of Crime; or new Newgate Calendar, and general record of tragic events, including Ancient and Modern Modes of Torture, &c.: comprehending a history of the most notorious murderers, traitors, highwaymen, pirates, burglars, pickpockets, adulterers, ravishers, decoyers, incendiaries, poachers, swindlers, and felons and rogues of every description* (London: William Mark Clark, 1837-1838). *The History and Lives of the Most Notorious Pirates of All Nations; narrating a series of gallant sea-fights, dreadful murders, daring attacks, horrid cruelties and barbarities; also their Debauched and Profligate Manner of Living, places of refuge, &c. &c.* (London: E. Lloyd, 1836-1837).

before the end of its first year.'[43] *My Poll and My Partner Joe*, the penny romance by Thomas Peckett Prest, not only takes names and plot points from the nautical drama of the same title by John Thomas Haines, but also transcribes full conversations.[44] As the chapter on Lindridge's *Jack Rann* underlines as well, incorporating stage scripts into penny serials was a common tactic employed by penny writers to either profit from the audience of the play for the sale of their serial, or simply to provide material for their own interpretation. Another nautical melodramas that inspired penny serials include *Jack Junk* (1849; based on *Captain Bertram*, 1836), and *The Mutiny at the Nore* (1830, another play by Jerrold) which was adapted by Prest into *Richard Parker; or, the mutiny at the Nore*, published in a single volume in 1851.

As Marvin Carlson writes, 'The great sea battles and victories of the Napoleonic Wars provided a major new impetus for theatricalization of nautical themes now more closely than ever tied with national pride, patriotism, and civic and social virtue.'[45] Although patriotism was a cornerstone of the nautical drama, this was not a straightforward or uncomplicated part of the narrative; the mutinies at Bounty, Spithead, and Nore were well-publicised, and life as a sailor was oppressive and dangerous.[46] Besides patriotism, influenced by the developing domestic drama, sexual rivalry became a common element of the nautical melodrama, through which class tensions and anxieties were addressed.[47] The common script of the domestic drama features some variation of 'a virtuous but poor young woman, loved by virtuous but poor young man but pursued by a corrupt and ruthless aristocrat, […] who uses his superior power, wealth, social position to advance his own suit.'[48] The plot of *Black-Eyed Susan* illustrates how a domestic plot was

---

[43] Robert Burroughs, 'Sailors and Slaves: The "Poor Enslaved Tar" in Navel Reform and Nautical Melodrama', *Journal of Victorian Culture*, 16:3 (2011), 305-322, p. 309.
[44] John Thomas Haines, Esq., *"My Poll and My Partner Joe.", A Nautical Drama, in Three Acts.* (London: John Cumberland, 1832).
[45] Carlson, 'He Never Should Bow,' p. 151.
[46] Carlson, 'He Never Should Bow,' p. 153.
[47] Carlson, 'He Never Should Bow,' pp. 153-154.
[48] Carlson, 'He Never Should Bow,' pp. 153-154.

integrated with a nautical theme. The story follows a sailor, William, who fought in the Napoleonic Wars, and his wife Susan. Susan is pursued by various male characters, including her landlord, a smuggler, and William's captain. If a superior officer is cast as the pursuer, this leads to complications, as a sailor challenging a captain was considered mutiny, 'and thus threaten[ed] the very military order'.[49] The climax of the story revolves around William striking his commanding officer, an act that could lead to his execution. This complication collapses in the conclusion of the story, as William is revealed to have been discharged before striking the captain. His execution is averted, and his domestic life with Susan is secured. While the nautical melodrama offered the thrills and suspense of life at sea, at the same time it 'packaged accounts of working-class life within a sentimental frame of family values and a conventional social order', which Jeffrey Cox denotes as its 'domestic form'.[50] As will become clear in this chapter, *Paul Jones* draws on nautical melodrama tropes, but where the domestic and nautical plots are integrated into a cohesive whole in *Black-Eyed Susan*, these two aspects have become unstable in *Paul Jones* – an instability that the humour of the text draws attention to and exploits. Egan adapts the sexual rivalry that Carlson describes as the driving force of nautical melodrama for *Paul Jones'* plot, although he refigures this script in subtle ways. The domestic plot will be analysed in more detail below, showing how the humour reveals a rift between the domestic and nautical, and in its extension, the patriarchal hierarchies of state and home.

While a highwayman character like Jack Rann, though a criminal, is a sympathetic hero due to a vaguely nostalgic gloss of nationalism, a pirate's position within penny blood is less positive. The British reprint of Murray Ballou's *Roderick the Rover*, retitled *I'm Afloat, I'm Afloat* for the British audience, bears a preface which illustrates how piracy needed to be justified to make the story more palatable to its readership. Ballou's story features Roderick, a captain and freebooter with a 'singularly brave

---

[49] Carlson, 'He Never Should Bow,' p. 154.
[50] Jeffrey N. Cox, 'The Ideological Tack of Nautical Melodrama', in *Melodrama. The Cultural Emergence of a Genre*, ed. by Michael Hays and Anastasia Nikolopoulou (New York: St. Martin's Press, 1996), pp. 165-189, p. 168.

and chivalrous disposition' and a 'strict rule never to commit violence on any save the Spaniards, unless he was first opposed by them'.[51] Later in the narrative Roderick is revealed to be an aristocrat from the Isle of Man named Lord William Withingham, cementing his identity not only as not like the other pirates ('he was actuated by an entirely different spirit from what animated [other freebooters]'[52]), but also as thoroughly British. Yet despite the lengths the text goes to prove to the reader that Roderick is honourable, the new preface Lloyd added to the British version is almost apologetic in tone:

> The buccaneer of that period must not be confounded with the blood-thirsty, cruel and rapacious pirate. […] Though our Roderick was dauntless in the fight, he was ever ready to stay the effusion of blood, and put a step to unnecessary violence; and when circumstances allowed him one more to tread his native shores, we find him gladly abandoning scenes where little more than infamy was to be gained, to pass the remainder of his days in the domestic and social duties dear to the patriot's heart.[53]

Roderick's reticence towards violence is reminiscent of the limit of play present in Lindridge's *Jack Rann*; Jack too is described as avoiding lethal violence wherever possible. Besides illustrating the stereotype of a pirate ('blood-thirsty', 'cruel', and 'rapacious'), the preface struggles with one of the core paradoxes of the nautical romance: an irresolvable tension between maritime adventures, and the draw of domesticity. The preface suggests that when given the opportunity, Roderick attended to domestic and social duties rather than his courageous adventures at sea; yet at the same time, it is the maritime adventures that provide the hook

---

[51] Lieutenant Murray, *Roderick the Rover: or, The Spirit of the Wave* (Boston: Gleason's Publishing Hall, 1847), p. 10.
[52] Murray, *Roderick the Rover*, p. 22.
[53] *I'm Afloat, I'm Afloat: or, Roderick the Rover. A Romance* (London: E. Lloyd and G. Purkess), preface.

of the story. Notably, the title is 'Roderick the Rover', not 'Roderick the Gentleman'.

One facet of this tension arises from the figure of the pirate itself. According to Erin Mackie, the subjectivity of the pirate is 'at odds with the ideology of heteronormative domesticity.'[54] Like the figure of the rake and the highwayman, the pirate partakes in 'a refusal and/or evasion of modern heteronormativity.'[55] Not only does the pirate live 'outside the boundaries of conventional European society', he is a sexual, economic, and political transgressor;[56] and one aspect of this refusal of heteronormativity might lie in transgressive desire, as is the topic of Hans Turley's influential study *Rum, Sodomy, and the Lash* (1999), a study of homoerotic desire in fictional representations of pirates in the eighteenth century. Unlike the highwayman, Mackie notes, 'the early eighteenth-century pirate is rarely portrayed as "gallant" or gentleman-like in any way.'[57] This observation applies to the pirate in 1840s penny fiction as well – unlike the uncertain class of Jack Rann, the pirate in penny fiction is overwhelmingly presented as a villain. Roderick, one of the rare 'honourable' pirates in penny fiction, is a gentleman by birth, and as the quotation taken from *Afloat*'s preface above shows, the text works hard to try to convince the reader that Roderick's piracy should be excused. Prest's pirates are closely aligned to the figure of the rake, being determined through their voracious and single-minded pursuit of an unwilling female character. It is these associations that surround the figure of the pirate in the penny blood, therefore, and in the following sections it will become clear how *Paul Jones* navigates this tension between domesticity and its potential failure.

---

[54] Mackie, *Rakes*, p. 117.
[55] Mackie, *Rakes*, p. 117.
[56] Hans Turley, *Rum, Sodomy, and the Lash. Piracy, Sexuality, and Masculine Identity* (New York: New York University Press, 1999), p. 14.
[57] Mackie, *Rakes*, p. 115.

A Sailor's Speech

At the start of Egan's story, Paul is twenty years old, and works as a pressed captain of the main top aboard the *Wildfire*. Egan uses some of the biographical information available about Paul, including his birthplace in Kirkcudbright in Scotland, an apprenticeship as a teenager, and visiting his brother in Virginia. Paul's childhood is characterised by his desire to be at sea, as '[a]ll the day it was in my sight or thoughts, and at night it was the constant subject of my dreams.'[58] As with any penny blood worth its salt, *Paul Jones* contains various subplots, coincidences and diversions along the way; within the first volume it quickly becomes clear that Paul's story is merely half of what Egan intends to tell. In the first chapter, Paul immediately has an opportunity to prove his bravery, as a fellow sailor falls into the sea and is attacked by a shark. Paul jumps into the sea; even though the sailor is brought to safety by the first lieutenant of the ship, Paul faces the shark.[59] This heroic battle that ensues is underlined by the vivid description of the shark and 'its many rows of terrible teeth' and the drawn-out ensuing confrontation during which caused the sea to 'become so thickened with blood by the mad and desperate plunges of the monster, that Paul could not use his eyes beneath the water'.[60] It is not immediately resolved whether or not Paul survives the battle with the shark – the chapter ends on a cliffhanger, instead introducing a second plot. The tonal change from the action-packed naval setting of the previous chapter is jarring. Instead, the setting is now a hedge-lined country lane near Grasmere, where a pale maiden 'plucked a flower and gazed upon it,' 'lost in some recollection which would not be other than sorrowful, from the melancholy expression with which it was entertained.'[61] The young woman,

---

[58] Egan, *Paul Jones*, p. 86.
[59] Paul's battle with the shark might have been inspired by an anecdote in *Black-Eyed Susan*, where a seaman 'snatches up a knife, overboard he jumps, dives under Billy, and in a minute the sea was as red as marine.' in: Douglas Jerrold, *Comedies and Dramas* (London: Bradbury and Evans, 1854), p. 274.
[60] Egan, *Paul Jones*, p. 11.
[61] Egan, *Paul Jones*, p. 14.

Florence, is captured by a man carrying a cudgel, Jasper, who gives her a choice: 'either be my wife by your own consent, or my mistress by compulsion.'[62] The chapters alternate between Paul at sea and the woman-in-peril plot featuring Florence, the lover of lieutenant Prior aboard the *Wildfire*, often using a cliffhanger to create suspense when the focus moves between the plots. Nor is Florence the only woman in peril; while she is pursued by the son of her protectors, Alice, a shipwrecked woman picked up by the *Wildfire*, is being kept from her lover (eventually revealed as Paul), by her father. The text is self-aware that vast swathes, especially of the first volume, are only tangentially connect to Paul Jones; after an especially long chapter during which the narrative exclusively focuses on Florence and Jasper, spanning more than eighty pages in the Purkess print, the first line of the next chapter reads:

> The hero of this novel, if it has a hero, which it is possible may be doubted seeing that the incidents are as yet more than equally shared by other characters—however, he that should be the hero of this work, John Paul, has been for a long while left swinging in his hammock in deep slumber. Let us now wake him out of it.[63]

Although the draw of the work's title, *Paul Jones*, would have been Paul's connection to the American navy, Paul does not join the navy until the 55th issue (out of 63 total). The majority of the plot from the first volume well into the second one revolves around the pursuit of Florence; her various escapes and recaptures by Jasper or villains connected to him, leading to her eventual rescue by John Paul on the Isle of Man. This plot is neatly wrapped up by the death of Jasper, his co-conspirer Churleigh, and of Churleigh's daughter Joan (who Jasper seduced, and later killed their illegitimate child to prevent discovery of his actions). Eustace Prior and Florence marry, despite her father's wishes. Although they briefly accompany Paul to his brother's home in Virginia and are involved in the fight with a lecherous French captain and shipwreck on

---

[62] Egan, *Paul Jones*, p. 16
[63] Egan, *Paul Jones*, p. 196.

their way to America, their relevance to the plot largely concludes with their marriage, and they are only occasionally mentioned in the latter half of the second volume. This section focuses on Paul's maritime exploits; his frustrations with England and his eventual joining of the American navy; the battles he is involved with, and the struggles with the 'egalitarian' Americans; and his doomed romance with Alice. While Paul seeks glory as a naval commander for the American navy in order to be worthy of the aristocratic Alice's hand, Alice warns him she will not wed him if he raises arms against England. Despite this warning, Paul persists, and the final moments of the story find him lauded by the French for the defeat of an English vessel, and as he visits Alice's house, learns of her death of a broken heart. He exclaims 'crying in a tone of the bitterest anguish—"For this – for this I fought against my native land!"', and runs away, 'he knew not where.'[64]

Compared to the pranks of Valentine Vaux and humorous adventures of Jack Rann, the humour present in *Paul Jones* is more subtle. As in *The String of Pearls*, the humorous passages are interspersed by other tonal registers, such as that of the heightened emotional language of melodrama mainly associated with Florence's predicament, and the more action-focussed naval battle scenes. In the following, I will first examine the gentle humour of Gasket, a sailor aboard the *Wildfire* and Paul's trusty companion throughout the book. Gasket's eccentric speech is peppered with nautical metaphors, which become particularly pronounced when he speaks of matters related to courting and matrimony. While *Paul Jones* attempts to encapsulate both the nautical and the domestic within its plot, Gasket's speech reveals the ultimate futility of this attempt, and foreshadows the tragic ending for its eponymous hero. Therefore, not only is the perceived incompatibility of nautical and domestic concerns at the root of the humour of the text, it reflects more widely on the generic tension of the text itself.

Gasket's eccentric type of speech is a fictional sea-faring slang, a common trope in nautical fiction. Throughout the story, from his first ominous dialogue ('there is one in this ship doomed – you may laugh,

---

[64] Egan, *Paul Jones*, p. 544.

and shake your head like a top-sail sheet block in a gale'), his speech is peppered with nautical terminology.[65] This is part of a larger phenomenon, as the British interest for nautical stories in the eighteenth and nineteenth centuries extended to nautical language. As Janet Sorenson writes,

> by midcentury, print descriptions of voyages that included maritime jargon were top sellers, poems and novels used and explained nautical terms, and William Falconer's glossary of technical nautical terms, *A Universal Dictionary of the Martine*, appeared – and went through six editions by 1789.[66]

In the nineteenth century, this fascination continued in the nautical melodrama. As Cox notes, 'nautical jargon [...] would mark the "tar" throughout the history of the nautical melodrama.'[67] It is important to note that eighteenth- and nineteenth-century representations of nautical language bore little relationship to the reality of speech on board British ships. Influenced by global travel and the various languages they encountered in foreign ports, spoken on board by passengers, captives, or sailors of various origins, British sailors would pick up words or phrases from other languages, yet these are very rarely included in fictional representations.[68] What is significant, then, is not the presence of nautical slang in itself, but how it is used in the text.

Gasket's nautical language is part of a larger tendency in the British literary imagination where the language of British sailors is depicted as 'limiting, a linguistic confinement that mirrored the sailor's supposedly insular being, trapped in the confines of the ship.'[69] In other words, for a career sailor like Gasket, who has no family or relations on land, his only

---

[65] Egan, *Paul Jones*, p. 5.
[66] Janet Sorenson, *Strange Vernaculars. How Eighteenth-Century Slang, Cant, Provincial Languages, and Nautical Jargon Became English* (Princeton: Princeton University Press, 2017), p. 232.
[67] Cox, 'Nautical Melodrama', p. 175.
[68] Sorenson writes: 'For the most part, the multilingual mix of eighteenth-century seafarers remains unrecorded.' Sorenson, *Strange Vernaculars*, p. 234.
[69] Sorenson, *Strange Vernaculars*, p. 231.

frame of reference is life onboard a ship, and therefore all of his thoughts and experiences are expressed through nautical comparisons. Gasket's speech is similar to how Sorensen argues that using obscure and opaque nautical terms causes 'the mobile figures of seamen and their language seem to be safely enclosed, not cosmopolitan but lodged in place in their ship.'[70] This separation of spheres is pointed out within the text itself, as the sailor Andrew speaks to his sweetheart, Martha, Florence's maid:

> "Can't you talk sensible English, John?" said Martha, rather perplexed – "I don't understand half of what you have said." "Sensible English!" repeated Andrew, with surprise – "Lord ha mercy, how ignorant you are in these inland parts – I have spoken your true lingo, which it's proper for a seafaring man who's all fair and above board and no lubber, to talk, and you don't read the bunting. Well, I s'pose it's all natural and proper, 'long-shore people talk 'long-shore talk, and sea people speak in the fashion of those whose craft is their home, and the deep sea their country.[71]

This quotation shows the distinction between nautical speech and 'sensible' English, or the English of those on land. Nautical speech is considered 'proper' for the sailing characters, but is (comically) unintelligible to those who 'don't read the bunting' – in other words, those who do not sail. This quote therefore not only reveals the separate spheres that language divides, it also points towards how the sailors in *Paul Jones* might consider 'the deep sea their country', which destabilises the idea of the British sailor as quintessentially British and the concept of nationhood. This topic will be further explored below, but first, we will dive deeper into the nautical speech itself.

Gasket's speech constructs his identity as a sailor, and separates him from characters that do have land-based connections such as Paul and lieutenant Prior. Not only is this separation one of class, it also presents the archetype of the sailor as the antithesis to domestic concerns,

---

[70] Sorensen, *Strange Vernaculars*, p. 232.
[71] Egan, *Paul Jones*, p. 250.

particularly marriage. In one of Gasket's long monologues, he acquaints Paul with lieutenant Prior's backstory, in which all matters are expressed through nautical-inspired metaphors. Referring to Prior's social status, he says 'he belongs to a family that carry a high peak in London, but haven't much shot in their locker', meaning that although they are of high birth, the family lacks money.[72] He continues by describing that at a social function, Prior 'fell in with a little schooner—the prettiest bit of craft he ever clapped his eyes on,' comparing Florence to a ship. This overlay of nautical identification continues throughout his monologue, describing how:

> he ranged alongside of her, and. I fancy, in their first engagement with their eyes, she boarded his heart, and carried it in the smoke, so that he hauled down his colours to her, and followed in her wake. Well, you see, as I take it, the cut of his jib being very ship shape, she hauled her wind, hove too, and would have no objection for him to rub her name out and put his own there, but her owners wouldn't consent, because his lockers were low.[73]

In these relentless metaphors Prior and Florence are personified ships, engaging in a form of nautical manoeuvring. Florence's family are referred to as 'owners', and marriage is signified through the changing of one's name on their hull. Later, Gasket describes how a former shipmate of Prior was related to Florence; or, in Gasket's words, 'He happened to be some relation to the lady whose flag Mr. Prior carried at the fore', not only expressing domestic matters through nautical terms, but also combining the ideas of nationhood and romantic allegiance through the metaphor of a flag.[74] The humour of these passages lies in the juxtaposition between the two speech registers which are merged together by Gasket. It reveals an incompatibility which gently mocks the incompatibility of these two elements in the structure of the text as a whole. Before reflecting on the broader generic repercussions of this

---

[72] Egan, *Paul Jones*, p. 6.
[73] Egan, *Paul Jones*, p. 6.
[74] Egan, *Paul Jones*, p. 100.

incompatibility, however, I will first briefly analyse how the humour itself functions.

The comical images of courtship between naval vessels are best understood when seen as an expression of what Bergson termed 'inelasticity': an incongruous experience 'where one would expect to find the wide-awake adaptability and the living pliableness of a human being', one finds rigidity instead.[75] As discussed in the chapters on *The String of Pearls* and *Valentine Vaux*, Bergson sees laughter as a societal corrective, where behaviour outside of a societal norm causes laughter in others. Bergson has a specific type of behaviour in mind, as living in society requires an 'elasticity of body and mind'. In other words, we need to be able to acutely assess and understand what is required of us in social situations. As Bernard Prusak writes in his evaluation of Bergson's work on laughter, 'the mispronounced word, missed allusion, misunderstood joke, abnormality, eccentricity, obliviousness to what is *a la mode* or *de rigueur*' can all be comic flaws.[76] Gasket's inability to speak of domestic matters without the nautical metaphors illustrates an inability to moderate his speech to suit the occasion. According to Bergson, society abhors this rigidity, whether of 'body, mind [or] character' – he states that 'This rigidity is the comic, and laughter is its corrective.'[77] One can think for example of a comedy of manners where social cues are taken literally rather than being able to understand their subtext, or of physical comedy, where characters might move rigidly. Bergson's attribution to laughter's function as corrective has been argued to be too narrow; Prusak provides the example that if we for example laugh at an animal, it is unlikely that laughter is seeking to correct that animal's behaviour.[78] Gasket's eccentric speech provides an interesting case in point: while intended to be humorous, there is little in terms of a corrective response. Paul appreciates Gasket as his 'light-

---

[75] Bergson, *Laughter*, p. 10.
[76] Prusak, 'Rereading Bergson', p. 378.
[77] Bergson, *Laughter*, p. 21.
[78] Prusak, 'Rereading Bergson', p. 384. I would counter this argument with the observation that Bergson only intends to describe laughter at other *humans*, not animals.

hearted, gay messmate'.[79] This is not true for all laughter in *Paul Jones*, however. When it is revealed that Gasket mistook the appearance of Florence at Prior's sickbed as a ghost, 'Paul smiled at Gasket's mistake'.[80] Later in the same passage, Gasket compares Florence to an angel, to which 'she raised her finger at him with a reproving smile and turned away.'[81] This interaction shows that laughter (or in this case, a smile) can and does serve as a social corrective within the text. Florence's response clearly signals to Gasket that comparing her to a spiritual being transgresses a social norm, expressed through the qualifier 'reproving', as well as the physical movements that accompany it, such as turning away from him. Smiling or laughter, are not understood as essentially corrective in *Paul Jones* – laughter has different functions in different contexts, which *include* correcting certain behaviours.

Bergson's idea of inelasticity provides more insight into the humorous underpinnings of the nautical speech throughout *Paul Jones*. Gasket's inability to move beyond the nautical sphere is particularly visible when Gasket relays a journey to the British mainland. Intending to visit Prior at Cambridge, he 'soon found a craft on four wheels that made the voyage every day, [...] and found it just ready to run out of port.'[82] This comic section is likely to have been inspired by a similar comic interlude in Fitzball's theatrical adaptation of Cooper's *The Pilot*, in which a seaman named Long Tom Coffin, born at sea like Gasket, left the sight of the sea only once, as 'outside passenger of a craft the landsfolk named a coach' between Liverpool and Plymouth.[83] In Egan's version of this comic setup, Gasket realises there was 'room for one cabin passenger', but 'I knew my duty better than to stow myself there' – showing an acute sense of class awareness, as a seat inside a stagecoach was more expensive and associated with middle-class passengers.[84]

---

[79] Egan, *Paul Jones*, p. 485.
[80] Egan, *Paul Jones*, p. 354.
[81] Egan, *Paul Jones*, p. 354.
[82] Egan, *Paul Jones*, p. 102.
[83] Edward Fitz-Ball, *The Pilot: A Nautical Burletta, in Three Acts* (London: John Cumberland, [1825?]), p. 12.
[84] Egan, *Paul Jones*, p. 102.

Gasket chooses instead to sit on the roof, where he will be more exposed to the elements. However, before he has made himself comfortable, or as he puts it, 'made my anchorage good', conflict arises. He tells Paul: 'a fellow claps on to my leg to haul me down, but I gave him a lurch with my starboard pin, and down he tumbled into the mud.'[85] Not only does this passage create a comically alienating effect in which a commonplace mode of transportation is transformed into an incongruous one, even Gasket's own body becomes comically subsumed into the nautical language when he refers to his right leg as a 'starboard pin'. This distancing between the objects of reality – a coach, one's leg – creates space for the violence of the interaction between Gasket and his fellow passenger, both physical as well as verbal as he threatens to 'keel-haul whoever laid a grappling iron upon me', to be softened. As we have seen in previous chapters, for violence to be seen as humorous it needs to be delineated in some way. Every text creates its own boundaries for what is playful violence and what is not, which in turn reveals information on the politics that underpin the text.[86] Comparably to *Jack Rann*, the limits of play in *Paul Jones* are defined by consequence; like Jack, Paul baulks at lethal violence. Later in Gasket's recounting of his adventures with Prior in England, he reports punching a man between the eyes ('I sent [my arm] bang between his toplights') and 'paid him over the head and eyes until I clapped a stopper on his jaw' until he 'dropped down like a log.'[87] Paul responds:

> "Good God! Gasket, you didn't kill the man?" cried Paul, hastily.
> "No," he replied, with a short chuckle; "no, but I flattened his gib sheet in handsomely; [...][88]

The dialogue assures that the limits of play have not been exceeded; that despite the violence of the encounter, Gasket is a sympathetic character. The return of the humorous language in Gasket's response

---

[85] Egan, *Paul Jones*, p. 102.
[86] See Davis, *Farce*, p. 85.
[87] Egan, *Paul Jones*, p. 106.
[88] Egan, *Paul Jones*, p. 106.

cements the comic intent of the scene, while at the same time reducing the emotional validity of the violence by using metaphor to describe the injury. Ultimately, Gasket's violence bears no consequences, neither leading to complications in the plot nor emotionally, being limited to a comic aside. The lack of consequences of Gasket's violence is intertwined with his symbolic confinement to the ship's sphere of influence – while Gasket can set foot on land, he is excluded from the emotionally laden domestic melodrama that characterises the land-based plots of the text. This scene underlines that even when he does escape the physical confines of a ship, Gasket cannot escape the linguistic limits of his sphere. His speech not only excludes him from participation within the domestic plot, it also sets him apart in class terms. Gasket's use of nautical language acts as a foil to Paul, who is able to self-consciously regulate his speech depending on his situation. Responding to his captain, Paul says, 'In the forecastle, Sir, I speak the lingo of my messmates, [...] in the cabin I fit my speech to the station of those in whose presence I stand.'[89] While Gasket can only translate domestic principles through nautical metaphor, Paul is capable of communicating in various registers, linguistically freeing him from the confines of the ship. This juxtaposition between the nautical and the domestic is the subject of the following section.

DOMESTIC MATTERS AND THE NATION

The thematic linking of the domestic plot and the nautical themes are signalled from the first sentence of *Paul Jones*:

> The sea, whose bosom hath borne such vast fleets such huge specimens of man's handicraft, and such humble ones—who hath borne so many to their destination safely, and swallowed others so remorselessly; who hath in its slumber smiled, and seemed so gentle and placid to those whom a few short hours subsequently it has filled with horror at his wrath, lashed in its fury and engulped unsparingly, so that they may never more

---

[89] Egan, *Paul Jones*, p. 87.

glad with their presence the eyes of those who hold them treasured in their memories, and who, with hearts that deferred hope makes sick, are waiting anxiously for their arrival at home.[90]

This quotation not only emphasises the capriciousness of the sea, and its forceful unpredictability that routinely led to the death of sailors, foreshadowing peril and thrilling adventures, it also frames these dangers through the prism of the loved one waiting for the sailor's return at home. The nautical adventures not only gain emotional potency by the presence of a (usually female) character connected to the sailors, these adventures gain meaning through the contrast between the two environments. In *Paul Jones*, this dynamic not only plays out between Paul and his sweetheart Alice, but is replicated across the proliferation of heterosexual pairs in the story. Many of the named characters are in some form of romantic relationship, including Eustace Prior, a lieutenant on the *Wildfire*, and Florence Ranklyn; even Martha, Florence's maid, is matched with John Andrew, the sailor who is shipwrecked with Alice. The romantic pairs of *Paul Jones* are constantly torn apart through circumstance; both Paul and Prior are prevented from marrying their lovers by the woman's family. I argue that this grouping together of the nautical and the domestic in *Paul Jones* reveals underlying anxieties surrounding domestic, nautical, and national identity. It is the distance between the domestic and the nautical that creates a humorous effect as discussed above, and this antithesis is never fully resolved throughout the text.

While the heroes of the story aim to protect their romantic partners, the villainous characters, on the other hand, are marked by disrupted or transgressive sexual relationships. The villain of the land-based plot, Jasper Chough, means to force Florence to be his wife or mistress, and had an extramarital child with Joan Churleigh, who he never married and abandoned. Jack Churleigh, Joan's father, aids Jasper to kidnap Florence; and he too is marked as having experienced a tragic love:

---

[90] Egan, *Paul Jones*, pp. 3-4.

"You never knew what it was to love passionately, heart and existence being mere trash with her your soul is set upon," cried Jasper.

"How do you know?" cried Churleigh, in a rough voice, which sounded strangely agitated; "how do you know? How should you know? Speak for yourself man, not for me; and don't allude to any subject of the sort again, that's all!" he added, fiercely.[91]

Even taking into account the generic preoccupations of the nautical melodrama, Egan's *Paul Jones* seems to create an encompassing theme of domesticity, in which all major characters figure through their relationship to domesticity – the presence (or absence) of romantic relationships, whether deemed acceptable or transgressive.

The emphasis on domesticity is an inheritance of the nautical melodramas of the 1820s and 1830s. Cox explains the ideological work done by nautical melodramas as a partial response to the troubling experiences during the Napoleonic war. He writes,

> At some level, these nautical melodramas want to assert that all the dislocations of years of war, of internal political strife, of deep social and cultural questioning ultimately leave the order of the family, the military, the state, and providence in place.[92]

Egan's *Paul Jones* complicates this legacy of the nautical melodrama. *Paul Jones* takes this domestic preoccupation from the nautical melodrama, and melds it with humour expressed through metaphoric language. It expresses anxiety over the compatibility of these ideals of order and the primacy of the family with seafaring culture, which as we have seen above, functions not only linguistically but also metaphysically as its own society separate from land-based hierarchies. Tension between the nautical and the domestic is central to the nautical melodrama *Black-Eyed Susan*, briefly discussed above. William, the play's hero, is on trial for

---

[91] Egan, *Paul Jones*, p. 134.
[92] Cox, 'Nautical Melodrama', p. 179.

striking his captain with a cutlass to defend his wife, when he appeals to the Court Martial: 'That your honours, whilst it is your duty to condemn the sailor, may, as having wives you honour and children you love, respect the husband.'[93] While William (ostensibly) transgressed proper hierarchy as a sailor, he fulfilled his role as a husband by defending the honour of his wife. Where this tension is dissolved and values are realigned by the conclusion of the play, in *Paul Jones* the gap between the nautical and the domestic opens further. This shift is reflected in the text's treatment of its sailor characters.

Within the nautical melodrama, a new archetype of the sailor as 'figure of sexual propriety, righteous action, and domestic virtue' is created.[94] This newly reformed tar stood in contrast to previous stereotypes of sailors, characterised by Valerie Burton as a Jack Tar being 'footloose, careless and fancy-free', who 'roams the world without constraint of home and family, half hero and half reprobate', connected with being 'rude, crude and feckless' and promiscuity.[95] It is the former archetype of the sailor that can be found for example in the preface to Prest's first nautical romance, *Gallant Tom* from 1841, where he writes to have 'endeavoured to adhere as closely to nature in his sketch of the honest and hardy sailor – brimful of loyalty, love, and liberality – as possible'.[96] In *Paul Jones*, both the honourable and the careless sailor stereotypes are present; while many of the named sailor characters like Gasket are described as hearty, honest, and hardworking, there are also occasional references to this other stereotype, when for example many sailors from the Wildfire spend all their money immediately when reaching English shore 'making their money fly like the name of their vessel'. Similarly, the text refers to the 'thoughtless acts of seaman in general.'[97] Yet at its core, the anxiety of *Paul Jones* revolves around what

---

[93] Jerrold, *Comedies and Dramas*, p. 282.
[94] Cox, 'Nautical Melodrama', p. 178.
[95] Valerie Burton, 'The Myth of Bachelor Jack: Masculinity, Patriarchy and Seafearing Labour', in *Jack Tar in History. Essays in the History of Maritime Life and Labour*, ed. by Colin Howell and Richard J. Twomey (Fredericton: Acadiensis Press, 1991), pp. 179-198, pp. 179-180.
[96] Thomas Peckett Prest, *Gallant Tom; or, The Perils of a Sailor Ashore and Afloat* (London: Edward Lloyd, 1841).
[97] Egan, *Paul Jones*, p. 230, 238.

had made the 'careless' sailor so dangerous – his disregard of home and hearth as the foundation of order in society. The definition of what Cox considers the quintessential Jack Tar illustrates this danger. He argues that the ideological construct of the nationalist British sailor upholds domestic and national values:

> the tar has gone out into the world, confronted the enemy, perhaps been shipwrecked [...] He has lived in proximity to the Other, and yet all he wants is a return to the same, thus validating, in a way that Jon Bull cannot, the British status quo.[98]

Throughout the above analysis, Paul remains somewhat of an enigma. Paul is initially introduced in contrast to Gasket. The first issue opens to Paul and his friend conversing as their ship, the *Wildfire*, lays becalmed. Gasket, the older of the pair, is described as an archetypical honest sailor. He 'bore evidence of many years' exposure to the air, and hard work', 'his features were open and frank', 'his skin almost the colour of copper', and with an 'honest, ingenuous look about him', his 'heart was of the true material'.[99] His physique underlines the physicality of work on a ship, as 'his shoulders were broad, his figure sturdy, and his hands large, and, with his labour, as hard as iron'. Paul shares similarities with the sailor, yet also stands apart: he 'was quite as tall, almost as brown, and nearly as robust, save that in all his limbs there was a character of the higher order than those of the elder'. The description continues:

> His feature were regular and manly, decidedly handsome, and not the less so for the quick glances of a brilliant black eye, or the impatient curl of his upper lip; his hands and feet were small for his statue, and his bearing altogether, albeit he reclined so carelessly, was that of one who was more fitted to command than be commanded.[100]

---

[98] Cox, 'Nautical Melodrama', p. 178.
[99] Egan, *Paul Jones*, p. 5. Following quotations also from this section.
[100] Egan, *Paul Jones*, p. 5.

The quotation not only shows how personality is embedded in physical attributes (such as impatience), but also how class is embodied. Although Paul performs physical labour just like Gasket, the text suggests that this is not his natural state. He is '*almost* as brown' and '*nearly* as robust' (emphasis mine); drawing attention to the bodily discrepancies between the two characters. The size of Paul's hands and feet, too, underline that Paul is not someone who is 'fitted' to physical labour – he is more suited 'to command than be commanded'. In the dialogue between the two, Paul foreshadows his own status as the hero of the story. He claims 'I have a strange impression that before very long I shall make one among the men of whom the world speak loudly'.[101] He labels this desire as ambition, describing it as 'the desire to have your name spoken of with wonder and praise—to have your fame in men's mouths after your death, and be held up to future generations as a model of bravery, of honour, and worth'.[102] The speech introduces one of the central themes of the plot: Paul's desire for glory above all else that will eventually lead to his downfall. While Paul is a sympathetic character, honourable, courageous, and loyal to his sweetheart, he is best understood as a tragic Byronic hero, whose characterization constantly needs to mitigate and negotiate the reading public's expectations of what it means to be a pirate.

Both Paul and Gasket are defined by their fraught relationship with domesticity and nationhood, and therefore complicate the ideological construct of the British sailor that Cox describes. Paul is driven by an ambition for glory, which proves to be incompatible to his domestic desires: although Alice loves him, she refuses to marry him if he takes up arms against Britain. His potential domestic happiness, therefore, is intimately entangled in notions of loyalty to the nation. Paul's wishes for glory are expressed not for their own sake, but as their instrumentality to achieve domesticity:

---

[101] Egan, *Paul Jones*, p. 7.
[102] Egan, *Paul Jones*, p. 8.

he knew that his name would be blazoned along the coast – that it would prove a terror to those who had wronged him, and a harbinger of joy to one whom he knew would recognise in his actions the undying desire to win *her* hand, which reigned supreme in his bosom.[103]

As Paul betrays this value by joining the American navy, both him and Alice are excluded from the 'happy ending' of domesticity through her death. Equally, Gasket is more closely aligned to the values of the British Tar (honest, hardworking), yet he considers the ship his home.[104] He is in love with Florence, Prior's sweetheart, an uneven match that is not taken seriously by his friends.[105] On his deathbed, he notes how he 'thought she'd take it ill, that one so rough as I, who had no kin, should be so howdashus [sic] as to love her.'[106] His lack of national identity is directly connected to his frustrated domestic desires, stating that no suitable wife will pay him any attention: 'Why should I e'er expect any lass with plenty of relations to case a kind eye on one who don't know who he belongs to, or where his family came from.'[107] Later, he adds: 'Matrimony is a port I shall never enter.'[108] It is therefore not surprising that when Alice rejects Paul, she invokes the nation:

> "It is enough," exclaimed Alice, mournfully. "We must part, Paul for ever."
> "No, no; oh say not so, Alice," cried Paul, bitterly. "Be just to me."

---

[103] Egan, *Paul Jones*, p. 444.
[104] Regarding his relationship to England, he says: 'England had always behaved well to me, and when I turned against her it went against my conscience sorely, but then I loved you better than England, and I wouldn't have fought against you for any pay or flag in the world.' Egan, *Paul Jones*, p. 534.
[105] See Egan, *Paul Jones*, p. 405: '"Steady," cried Eustace, joining in the laugh; "I can't suffer you to make love to my wife, Gasket. I think you had better join Paul in his trip."'
[106] Egan, *Paul Jones*, p. 536.
[107] Egan, *Paul Jones*, p. 405.
[108] Egan, *Paul Jones*, p. 406.

"I am, Paul," she replied, a little proudly. "and to my country too, even at the expense of my own happiness – but let that pass. You have taught me that a public trust should rise superior to private feelings; my country places a trust in me as in all her children. I will not betray it."[109]

Referring to herself as the 'child' of the nation, the structure of the family is directly imposed upon the nation as a whole. Alice embodies the ideal subject: one who puts aside any personal desires to follow her duty to her country.

Lieutenant Prior and Florence, on the other hand, act as a foil to the double tragedy of Paul and Gasket. Prior's desires are within his own social status, and he achieves the domestic goals that Paul and Gasket cannot. After their marriage, the Priors' domestic bliss excludes them from the remainder of the plot. Now Florence takes her place as illustrated by the Victorian ideal of domesticity, summarised by Kimberly Reynolds and Nicola Humble as the 'virtuous wife-mother, centre of hearth and home, repository of the conscience of the bourgeois industrialist state, devoted to the domestic crafts, entirely without sexual impulses'. [110] This role is incompatible with the sexual danger represented by Jasper or the French captain Langais, who pursue her. The domestic role provides a woman with safety and care; in *Paul Jones*, a fortune teller predicts that Florence will have a 'better and quieter fate' than Jasper, and states that 'The eagle is often struck with the hunter's shaft, while the dove is made a household thing to love and cherish.'[111] The message is clear: independence will only lead to tragedy, while being kept within the house, becoming so closely associated with it as to almost becoming one with the other household 'things', provides a woman with love and respect. It is therefore unsurprising that the newlywed Priors no longer are of any importance to the plot after their marriage: the maritime adventures are incompatible with domestic

---

[109] Egan, *Paul Jones*, p. 483.
[110] Kimberly Reynolds and Nicola Humble, *Victorian Heroines. Representations of Femininity in Nineteenth-century Literature and Art* (New York: Harvester Wheatshelf, 1993), p. 11.
[111] Egan, *Paul Jones*, p. 171.

safety. It is notable that after their marriage, Prior joins the navy, signalling a return to the social order not only at home, but also on a national level. Even Paul's status as a hero is intimately connected with the pursuit of domestic bliss. Discussing his initial meeting with Prior, Paul states:

> When I was pressed and brought on board [Prior] saw me and recognised me as the person he had seen in his dream, and from that moment he has had a strong conviction that in some way I shall be able to do him a great service in his love affair.[112]

Aiding Prior in saving Florence and securing their domestic safety underlines Paul's status as the text's hero. Yet at the same time, Paul's status as an outlaw prohibits him from achieving the same.

It is exactly this frustrated domesticity that Gasket's humour exploits. Domesticity is only possible for those whose desires do not transgress class boundaries. The sailor Andrew, for example, finds happiness with a maid, illustrating that it is not class (or occupation) itself that determines whether idealised domesticity is possible. Gasket's comical speech therefore gently mocks the core theme of the text. It provides a comic foil to the tragedy that unfolds throughout the story, lightening what otherwise might have been a straightforward tragedy, retaining a playful quality to the text until the tragedy unfolds in the final parts of the story. As Paul attempts to gain the glory and the girl that lie beyond his station in life, so does Gasket's speech reach towards a possibility of merging the transgressiveness of a sailor with no loyalty to any flag with the domestic life that only exists within the patriarchal hierarchy of nation and home. Underneath the domestic preoccupation therefore, lies the theme of reaching beyond conventional constraint, which, according to *Paul Jones*, is always doomed to collapse. As Gasket's language seeks to bridge the gap between his station in life and the domesticity he desires, the results of this can only be comic. This desire for *more*, for freedom beyond the bounds of the rigid social structure that *Paul Jones* posits, is the subject of the remainder of this section.

---

[112] Egan, *Paul Jones*, p. 111.

As pointed out earlier, the public sentiment towards the historical John Paul Jones was ambiguous at best. While some might appreciate his skill as a naval commander, his major achievements were at the expense of the British navy. Considering the preface that Lloyd added to *Roderick*, it is likely that piracy was largely incompatible with heroism for the 1840s reading public, and it is therefore not surprising that Egan decided to establish Paul as a hero before he joins the American cause. Paul is at the centre of the question of what it means to live a life at sea when there is a societal expectation to be the head of a family. In particular, he is torn between a desire to elevate himself to be Alice's class equal, yet at the same time the only avenue available to him goes against Alice's wishes. The tragedy lies in the impossibility of going against his word, causing dishonour:

> Here was the prize he had looked forward to as the summit of his wishes, of his ambition, ready to be his, if he would but utter one word, and abjure America; [...] On the one hand, he was bound in honour to be true to the service he had accepted; on the other, his happiness, while he lived, depended upon his union with Alice; [...] Either course was fraught with anguish to him, and he groaned aloud as the struggle between love and duty raged in his bosom.[113]

Paul's desire for glory is best understood as part of Egan's modelling of him as a Byronic hero; a nineteenth century interpretation of the hero who 'provides his audience with a satisfying vicarious experience of power *and* empowerment, autonomy, mastery, and defiance of oppressive authority.'[114] Egan occasionally adds quotes from Byron at the beginning of chapters, and Paul and Alice's ultimately tragic ending is inspired by Byron's *The Corsair*, as signalled by a section taken from Byron's poem heading the final chapter in which Paul discovers Alice's

---

[113] Egan, *Paul Jones*, p. 481-2.
[114] Atara Stein, *The Byronic Hero in Film, Fiction, and Television* (Carbondale: Southern Illinois University Press, 2004), pp. 1-2.

death.[115] Paul stands apart from the other characters; he is determined by his prowess as a sailor and a captain. Yet like the Byronic hero, he is excluded from the life with Alice he seeks. As D. Michael Jones writes,

> The Byronic hero is thus defined by an internal classlessness that is deepened by his exile from any recognizable domestic life. [...] The Byronic hero's inability to find wholeness and redemption in domesticity – in what will become by midcentury the ideal for men – leaves him to roam, forever outside of stable class and domestic constructions.[116]

This classlessness is expressed in *Paul Jones* by the instability between Paul's potential and his class reality. In the passage above, Paul is portrayed as nobler than Gasket, and he is able to speak to his superiors as might a peer. Mr Manners, Alice's father, tells Paul how he had hoped to elevate him:

> I thought of a thousand ways to remove you from the station in which fate had placed you, and instal [sic] you in a higher one, in which your natural capabilities, would have found a wide and honourable field for displaying themselves, and raise you to the height it was my opinion you deserved.[117]

Yet despite these intentions and Paul's own desire for glory, he is ultimately doomed to roam restlessly, as in Jones' description of the Byronic hero.

Redemption in domesticity is not available to Paul, and he does not represent a meaningful disruption of the hierarchies of nation and home. Just like how authority is reinstated through the creation of chaos in

---

[115] In *The Corsair*, Conrad returns to his home to discover his wife, Medora, has died of grief – though unlike in *Paul Jones*, her grief was caused by assuming him dead.
[116] D. Michael Jones, *The Byronic Hero and the Rhetoric of Masculinity in the 19th Century British Novel* (Jefferson: McFarland & Company, Inc., Publishers, 2017), p. 10.
[117] Egan, *Paul Jones*, p. 501.

Valentine Vaux, so does *Paul Jones* present the rupture of Paul with the British nation only to reinforce Britain as a cohesive principle and its hierarchy as just. In *Paul Jones*, the lack of freedom and absolute discipline required by the captain is justified throughout the text. In one case, the topic is addressed directly, when the captain of the Wildfire is described as

> a stern man in his station, and preserved that immeasurable distance between the captain and the common man when in the exercise of his duties, which elevated him almost to a deity, while the sailor was lowered to the humblest slave; but as this is necessary to preserve strict discipline, it is not regarded as a hardship.[118]

Comparisons between sailors and slaves, where the extreme obedience in all matters required from sailors was compared to the loss of freedom of enslaved people, were in the first half of the nineteenth century used to push for naval reform. As Burroughs states, 'slaves and sailors were entwined in the collective imagination by characteristics assigned to both groups in popular discourses', which included fecklessness, innocence, joviality, as well as intemperateness or uncouthness.[119] Burroughs writes that 'Naval ships depended upon a social order that was hierarchical, regimented and disciplined.'[120] *Paul Jones* implies that once this strict hierarchy is levelled, a ship's crew will become ineffective and even cowardly. These ideas are expressed through Paul's interactions with various American sailors.

Although ostensibly Paul supports the American cause of independence from England, the American characters are consistently portrayed in a negative light. Paul struggles in particular with their notion of equality, which undermines the absolute hierarchy that is the norm aboard British ships; as Egan writes, 'no position in life, where command is in the hands of one person, is power so absolute as that of a

---

[118] Egan, *Paul Jones*, p. 88.
[119] Burroughs, 'Sailors and Slaves', p. 313.
[120] Burroughs, 'Sailors and Slaves', p. 315.

naval commander'.[121] The Americans, on the other hand, 'were too ridiculously influenced by some absurd notions of etiquette also, which completely set discipline and obedience at defiance.'[122] Paul struggles with this difference in ideology: 'His crew were a source of much trouble to him; [...] each man considering that he had rather a right to be requested than commanded, and it was only by persuasion, and, in some cases, violent coercion, that he got them into anything like subordination.'[123] Paul's frustration with the equality the American sailors require goes beyond a cultural misunderstanding. When Paul tries to motivate them through appealing to fight 'for the honour of their country, for their honour as men', this leaves the Americans cold.[124] The text states that 'they did not like the risk; here was too much of a personal feeling involved to take in much of the honour of their country.'[125] *Paul Jones*'s particular flavour of nationalism intersects with the idea of hierarchy as a necessary part of naval life. In *Paul Jones*, the Americans prefer to retreat rather than fight, while the English, used to following every command, do so even at the risk of their own life. In the battle between Paul's ship, the *Ranger*, and the English *Drake*,

> [The Englishmen] returned to their duty with all the energy which they might have been expected to have shown if their own individual interest had been concerned in gaining the victory; they had no thoughts of disobeying their captain, and certainly no thoughts of retreating, and fought with a steadiness and courage which ought to have made them successful. Paul, on the other hand, directed the efforts of an unwilling crew; men, who it would be wrong to say were not brave, but whose mistaken notions of equality – where strict

---

[121] Egan, *Paul Jones*, p. 455. It should be noted that in *Paul Jones* England and Britain are used interchangeably. Additionally, on p. 479 Alice states: 'England and Scotland are one, Paul, [...] one king governs us, the same laws rule us, we act in concert, we are as one nation; you must consider us as one.'
[122] Egan, *Paul Jones*, p. 455.
[123] Egan, *Paul Jones*, p. 444.
[124] Egan, *Paul Jones*, pp. 454-455.
[125] Egan, *Paul Jones*, p. 455.

obedience to one, if he be a competent man, is so necessary for success – rendered them as difficult to manage as if they had been cowards.[126]

The text suggests not only that a certain degree of deference is necessary in a crisis situation, where every second can make the difference between life and death – it states that the Americans function under a *mistaken* notion of equality. In *Paul Jones*, not all are made equally, and this chapter has already shown that those who attempt to step outside of their station meet a tragic end. Despite Paul's displeasure with England for not giving him a post in its navy, the Americans are portrayed as overly individualist and cowardly. During the battle, the English crew of the *Drake* 'had no thoughts of disobeying their captain, and certainly no thoughts of retreating, and fought with a steadiness and courage'.[127] *Paul Jones* reiterates the justness of hierarchy and its connection to the nation even at a time when that hierarchy is potentially threatened by Paul's destabilising effect. After the victory, Paul gives a speech to the defeated English, praising them for 'the devotion which the English had paid to the honour of their country' and the 'admirable discipline, the order and obedience which the crew had evinced'.[128] Their strength lies in their investment and trust in social hierarchy; as Paul states, 'It is only this implicit confidence of the seamen in their captain, and ready obedience to their commands, which makes the English, as a people, invincible.'[129] Therefore, while Paul might rebel against his class, neither he as a character nor the text itself moves beyond the concept of class and hierarchy itself. While the text presents a character like Paul, who is unfairly kept from reaching his full potential within his own society, it ultimately presents a pessimistic interpretation of transgression. While English society might have its problems – as Paul is not able to thrive within its confines – it at the same time suggests that any levelling of hierarchy would undermine the social order, as represented by the Americans.

---

[126] Egan, *Paul Jones*, p. 459.
[127] Egan, *Paul Jones*, p. 459.
[128] Egan, *Paul Jones*, p. 467.
[129] Egan, *Paul Jones*, p. 467.

Ultimately, despite the movements towards subversion, *Paul Jones* does not succeed in breaking free from its own thematic occupation of hierarchy. It never truly merges the disparate spheres of the nautical and the domestic. The repercussions of this rigid approach to class and status carries beyond the confines of the ship. Van Kooy and Cox have argued that nautical melodrama 'reassured audiences that, regardless of any momentary disruptions, the patriarchal order of God, king, father, and overseer remained secure.'[130] In *Paul Jones*, the patriarchal order is affirmed throughout, yet at the same time it displays an undercurrent of dissatisfaction with this status quo. Social hierarchy is further complicated by the treatment of the text's only black character, the topic of the final section of this chapter.

LAUGHTER, RACE, AND EMPIRE

Aside from the nautical humour outlined above, a different kind of laughter can be found in *Paul Jones*: one in which the laughter is created by or at the expense of a black character. While Gasket's benign nautico-domestic speech provides a gentle laughter that resonates with the text's broader themes of accepting one's place in life, the laughter surrounding *Paul Jones*'s sole black character strikes a different chord. The dynamics expressed in the two humorous scenes have broader repercussions for *Paul Jones*'s engagement with slavery and empire. It bears emphasising that, as in the preceding, the labelling of a scene as 'humorous' merely implies that there is textual evidence that the scene is intended to be so – it carries no value judgement from the author of this thesis that the scene *is* humorous. As we will see in this section, the two scenes featuring the *Wildfire*'s black cook initially expresses ambivalence, which later evolves into a scene in which the whipping of the black character (who remains nameless during the encounter) is used for comedic effect.

After Paul has survived his battle with the shark, described above, he goes to his berth to change into dry clothes, while his shipmates engage in fanciful conjecture about whether Paul was swallowed by the shark

---

[130] Dana Van Kooy and Jeffrey N. Cox, 'Melodramatic Slaves', *Modern Drama*, 55:4 (2012), 459-475, p. 462.

and cut his way out. In the ensuing scene a sailor nicknamed 'Stretch-out Dick' becomes the target of communal ribbing by his fellow sailors. The ship's black cook is an important character in the scene, as he repeatedly heckles Stretch-out Dick, to the delight of the crowd present. This scene shows not only how laughter works as a correctional force, it also points towards the text's stance towards race, class, and religion. Stretch-out Dick, named 'from his propensity to get the weather gage of possibility in a yarn', suggests the possibility of Paul's cutting himself from the belly of the shark, which 'was instantly greeted with a loud shout of laughter from all around.'[131] This communal, faceless laughter causes Dick to be defensive, responding:

> "Ah!" cried Stretch-out Dick, when the laugh subsides, "you needn't open your ports and grin like a lot of niggers over a rum keg; the thing ain't unpossible [sic], seeing we have scripter to tell us of one who did a trick which leaves what Johnny Paul's done a long way to leeward."
> "What's that?" asked Gasket [...]
> "What's that!" repeated Dick, with great contempt. "Upon what water have you been sailing, that you don't know that? Did you ever read the scripter?"
> "I can read bunting, but not books," replied Gasket, coolly [...].[132]

Dick's response to the laughter melds the humorous nautical lingo ('ports' as substitutes for mouths) with a racist metaphor, foreshadowing the role race will play in the continuation of the scene. By comparing the faceless laughter with a specifically racialised *black* laughter, Dick attempts to invalidate the correctional force of the laughter, in particular by using derogatory language such as 'niggers over a rum keg'. Dick's attempt at minimization of the laughter of the crowd he faces through racial comparison is unsuccessful, however, as it is the black cook who subsequently heckles Dick repeatedly, to the mirth of the surrounding

---

[131] Egan, *Paul Jones*, p. 24.
[132] Egan, *Paul Jones*, p. 24.

sailors. Dick is positioned as unsympathetic – his bad temper when faced with laughter and pretension singles him out as a comic victim, comparable to dynamics we have identified in *Valentine Vaux* and *Jack Rann*. He perceives himself superior due to his familiarity with scripture, while this superiority is immediately undermined by his mispronunciation as 'scripter'. Gasket, though illiterate, counters that he is literate in other ways, being able to 'read bunting' and 'hand, reef and steer'. Humble Gasket admits to not know much of religious matters, creating a foil to the comedy of Dick's pretension. Gasket's speech induces a 'murmur of applause from the listeners', signalling their approval.[133] As Dick continues his retelling of the Old Testament story of Jonah and the large fish (in this case, a whale),[134] the black cook interjects:

> "[Jonah] snored so loud, that he was heard above the roaring of the wind and rattling blocks […]"
> "What, him snore make dat noise?" rather incredulously asked a black, who was cook, and who, with extended eyes and mouth, was listening to Stretch-out Dick's tale.
> "To be sure," replied Dick, "do you think some men can't snore as if they had a speaking trumpet to their nose?"
> "No, but him tink dis Jonah hab dam large nose, dat all," and he showed his white teeth, in a satisfied grin at his own wit; a roar of laughter from the men accompanied his sally, which Dick seemed by no means to enjoy.[135]

Where Gasket was a sympathetic foil of the honest, straightforward sailor, the black cook is a cruder foil to Dick, the comic victim of the scene. While early sixteenth- and seventeenth-century representations of black characters in British fiction (and particularly theatre) portrayed them as threatening, violent, or aggressive, in the eighteenth- and nineteenth centuries slavery became the lens through which black

---

[133] Egan, *Paul Jones*, p. 24.
[134] Dick's retelling roughly coincides with the first two chapters of the Book of Jonah.
[135] Egan, *Paul Jones*, p. 25.

characters were understood.[136] For the comic black character, the popularity of Jim Crow performances in Britain during 1836-1839 was a pivotal period, during which a black comic grotesque archetype was created which portrayed 'black people as dim-witted, oddly-framed and fundamentally comical.'[137] Crow performances, popularised by Thomas D. Rice, typically featured a white performer in blackface in the role as Jim Crow, a slave, singing songs and dancing in a peculiar manner. As Hazel Waters writes in her study on race and British theatre that Crow performances were the beginning of a new development in British attitudes to race. The 'vengeful African of yesteryear' evolved into 'a comic black American slave, grotesque in appearance, manners and language'.[138] She notes that 'the grotesquerie proved the authenticity; the less recognisably human, the more valid the portrayal.'[139] The comedy of the performances lay in the perceived distance between individuals in British society and enslaved people, expressed through the idiosyncratic dance which incorporated complex jumping manoeuvres, as well as specific language. According to Waters, Crow was typified by 'his misuse of language and insistence on calling himself a 'gemman', at odds with his [...] grotesque appearance; his faithfulness to a good master; [and] his mixture of (generally good-hearted) cunning and stupidity.'[140]

Egan's black cook figures in this same comic tradition. He is less of a character, and more of a trope come to life; his speech heavily relies on black stereotypes, and in the subsequent scene he displays a similar disposition to Waters's description of the Jim Crow character. He expresses a certain amount of good-natured cunning, as he counters Stretch-out Dick's protestations. Dick's expresses anger at the laughter at his expense, calling the cook a 'black lump of a monkey' and claiming that he has heard of a man 'whose nose was so long that he was obliged

---

[136] Hazel Waters, *Racism on the Victorian Stage. Representation of Slavery and the Black Character* (Cambridge: Cambridge University Press, 2007), p. 11.
[137] Tom Scriven, 'The Jim Crow Craze in London's Press and Streets, 1836-1839', *Journal of Victorian Culture*, 19:1 (2014), 93-109, p. 94.
[138] Waters, *Racism*, p. 89.
[139] Waters, *Racism*, p. 102.
[140] Waters, *Racism*, p. 109.

to keep a man to brush off the flies, that were fond of settling on the tip of it.'[141] The cook retorts, 'Ah, 'em berry long noses, and berry long yarns were you come from, Masser Dick,' leading to 'another laugh at Dick's expense from the bystanders'.[142] The cook seems unruffled by Dick's racial abuse, instead continuing to undermine his story through mockery and repetition, supported by the laughing crowd. The scene shows a certain ambivalence to race; on one hand, the cook is never named, but merely referred to as 'the black', or when other characters are angry with him, he faces demeaning slurs. The cook is not even given a comic nickname such as Stretch-out Dick, or any of the other characters that only make a brief appearance in the text. The cook is referred to as '*the black*' (emphasis mine), which gives an impression of generalization – that this character stands for the entirety of all black people, and therefore does not require a name. It represents an elision of identity into a nameless, communal identity where one member stands for the whole. Yet on the other hand, it is the cook's mocking of Dick that leads to a communal approving laughter. While there is an undeniable flatness to the cook's character, the confrontation between Dick and the cook subtly refigures the power dynamics between laughter and the black comic character. The laughter in this scene is not quite at the black character's expense – despite his racist depiction, the laughter from the others is the laughter of approval, not derision.

> "That was in old ancient times," said Gasket, with a laugh.
> "I told you so just now," replied Dick.
> "Em berry odd it nebber do dat now," ejaculated the nigger with a grin, in which the hearers joined.[143]

The scene displays a complicated relationship to race, one which both draws on existing racist tropes as well as pushing these tropes beyond their boundaries. As Sarah Meer writes about nineteenth-century melodrama, this scene too both 'complicate[s] racial thinking, even if it

---

[141] Egan, *Paul Jones*, pp. 25-26.
[142] Egan, *Paul Jones*, p. 26.
[143] Egan, *Paul Jones*, p. 26.

also reproduced it.'[144] The cook is not a menacing character, and Dick's impotent anger at the cook's harmless comments are part of the power dynamics displayed in the scene. Dick first attempts to intimidate the cook through verbal abuse, before attempting to attack the cook physically. The text revels in displaying the verbal abuse:

> "You black-muzzled, bow-shanked, jury-rigged, binnacle-eyed, shahk-heeled nigger, I'll make your inky mug as scarlet as the figure-head of the Red Lion sloop of war [...]"
> Gasket stept [sic] between him and the negro, who rolled his white-looking eye-balls round, half in glee, half in fright, for fear Dick should keep his promise.[145]

The insults, all hyphenated for a rhythmic effect, focus on physical characteristics. They combine references to dark skin ('inky', 'black') to the animalistic ('muzzled') as well as nautical terms ('bow-shanked', 'jury-rigged', 'binnacle-eyed'). The stylistic choice of presentation as well as the incongruous images suggest this tirade is intended to be humorous. At the same time Dick's threat of violence is sufficiently valid for Gasket to place himself between Dick and the cook to protect him. As the cook continues to heckle Dick, particularly by repeating variations of 'tings different in ol' anshun times', signalling his disbelief at the scripture Dick tries to explain, Dick eventually has had enough:

> Dick's patience was exhausted at the laugh that resounded once more, and he sprung at the negro to give him a thrashing, but the black was too nimble for him, and escaped to the waist, while Dick's messmates interfered to prevent him following, and restored him speedily to good humour.[146]

---

[144] Sarah Meer, 'Melodrama and Race', in *The Cambridge Companion to Melodrama* ed. by Carolyn Williams (Cambridge: Cambridge University Press, 2018), pp. 192-205, p. 202.
[145] Egan, *Paul Jones*, pp. 27-28.
[146] Egan, *Paul Jones*, p. 29.

This conclusion underlines the dynamics described thus far: while cook's mockery gains the crowd's approval, and Dick's swearing is deemed acceptable (at no point do any of the characters, including Gasket, voice disapproval), an escalation to physical violence would ruin the joke. The cook does not deserve a 'punishment' in the shape of a beating by Dick for his communally sanctioned mocking. The return to balance once the humorous confrontation has run its course, which we also discussed in the context of Valentine's raucous crowds, therefore involves the other sailors protecting the cook from harm by distracting Dick. The return to balance thus signals a narrative closure to the humorous interlude.

Through the quotations concerning the cook, physical descriptions are reiterated throughout, particularly relating to his facial expressions. From his 'extended eyes and mouth', 'white teeth, in a satisfied grin' and 'his white-looking eye-balls' (all taken from above quotations), these all signal a preoccupation with the cook's body. By referring to the whiteness of his teeth and eyeballs, Egan draws on an unspoken contrast – they appear whiter due to the cook's dark skin. Beyond the superficial preoccupation with difference between white and black phenotypes, *Paul Jones* connects the black cook with a physicality that transforms the cook's body into a site of carnivalesque pleasures. This becomes particularly clear in a later scene, in which the cook is whipped to the amusement of the other sailors. In this section of the story, the cook aids John Paul in his quest to speak to his lover Alice, after she has been saved from a shipwreck by the *Wildfire*. The captain, however, had forbidden the two lovers to speak, and seeks to find out how they managed to communicate aboard his ship. The cook had fastened a rope to a rail of the ship allowing Paul to use it to climb to the window of the room where Alice had been confined. The cook is presented as dependable: he was someone 'whom Paul knew to be one he could trust.'[147] Gasket and John Andrews are questioned, but they reveal nothing. Even when threatened with physical violence, 'neither showed the smallest indication of alarm, or care for the punishment they were likely to undergo.'[148] When

---

[147] Egan, *Paul Jones*, p. 210.
[148] Egan, *Paul Jones*, p. 210.

subsequently the cook is questioned, however, he is initially grinning, but quickly presents a 'trembling aspect' and is described as 'shrinking as if he expected the blow to arrive every instant'.[149] Though terrified, he is not keen to give up Paul, following the racial stereotype as discussed by Waters popularised by Crow performances of the black character as faithful to a good master.[150] This faithfulness transgresses the hierarchy of the ship, however, as the cook lies to the captain to cover for Paul. For this, he receives a whipping.

During this scene, the whipping is presented as comical. As the quartermaster aims a blow at the cook, the cook 'dexterously darted from him, dodged him round the captain, screaming and jabbering like a monkey' and 'twisted about like an eel'.[151] Describing a black person in animalistic terms is part of a stereotype that developed throughout the 1830s and 1840s, assigning 'a certain animal quality' to black characters.[152] This dehumanisation serves as a comical distancing technique, relegating the physical pain experienced by the cook as less psychologically valid. At the same time, he speaks about himself in third person: 'He speak a trute; he wish he may be cussed for ebber, but he speak a trute.'[153] Again, this falls in line with nineteenth-century black stereotypes.[154] In this scene, this type of speech underlines the cook's lack of subjectivity: just as he is described as *the* black, equally he is incapable of speaking as an individual 'I'. It is a further dehumanisation that reduces the cook to his body. Through this dehumanisation his body becomes a site of carnivalesque pleasure; particularly his buttocks. Egan writes:

> The quartermaster, a smart seaman, who was delighted with the fun, caught him with the bight of the rope over the part of the frame which sailors denominate the stern, and which polite

---

[149] Egan, *Paul Jones*, p. 211.
[150] Waters, *Racism*, p. 109.
[151] Egan, *Paul Jones*, p. 212.
[152] Waters, *Racism*, p. 104.
[153] Egan, *Paul Jones*, p. 212.
[154] Waters, *Racism*, p. 93.

landsmen designate the seat of honour. Nature had been bountiful to the negro in quantity, but had been sparing in the thickness of skin, and the effects of the blow, given with a strong arm, was to make him leap three or four feet in the air [...]¹⁵⁵

It is no coincidence that the cook's comical leaping closely resembles descriptions of Jim Crow's dance. The euphemisms mark the transgressive pleasure of the whipping, which are shared in a communal setting. The cook runs along the ship's deck,

all the while accompanied by the laughter and jeers of the people, who all enjoyed the discipline of the negro with the most exquisite delight, each wishing they had the starting of him.[156]

This scene therefore reverses the comic situation of the heckling of Stretch-out Dick. In that scene, the crew laughs *with* the cook, while the whipping scene reduces the cook to the laughing stock. Beyond the stereotypical representation of race as has been noted throughout, the humorous scenes reveals an instability in the cook's status – his ribbing of a white sailor is sanctioned by the crowd, yet he himself receives a racially charged punishment when transgressing the hierarchy of command on the ship. His depiction is undeniably racist, yet he is depicted as both part of and separate to the laughing community on the ship at the same time, a precarious social position that is in line with *Paul Jones'* broader engagement with the history of slavery and empire.

By the 1840s, it had been roughly a decade after the formal abolition of slavery in most of the British Empire (in practice, forced labour was allowed in the West Indies but was renamed 'apprenticeship').[157] According to Burroughs, 'Much Victorian writing about slavery is

---

[155] Egan, *Paul Jones*, p. 212.
[156] Egan, *Paul Jones*, p. 213.
[157] Richard Huzzey, *Freedom Burning. Anti-Slavery and Empire in Victorian Britain* (Ithaca: Cornell University Press, 2012), p. 10.

complacently patriotic and self-congratulating'.[158] As Richard Huzzey shows in his extensive study of anti-slavery sentiment in Victorian Britain, *Freedom Burning* (2012), there was broad societal support for anti-slavery in the lead up to the Emancipation Act (1833). While anti-slavery was 'a coherent ideology insofar as it saw the social norm of slavery as inimical to the national good (be that good defined by prosperity, godliness, or honor)', *how* abolition should be achieved was less clear, and 'there could be disagreements over the racial equality or inequality of Africans to Europeans, the use of tariff barriers to promote free labor, or the morality of compensating slaveholders for emancipation'.[159] In the debates leading up to the Emancipation Act, the discussions concerned how and when abolition should happen, as '[e]ven those who opposed an act for immediate emancipation had grudgingly adopted the language of anti-slavery.'[160] After passing the Emancipation Act, however, the momentum for racial equality deflated:

> Beyond self-satisfaction, neither the parliamentary leaders of the emancipation struggle nor the British public at large had any great sense of what an anti-slavery nation should do next; the Anti-Slavery Society had no plan to rally support for abolitionist movements in Europe or the Americas.[161]

Paul Jones is a part of this cultural moment. The story displays a sense of satisfaction at having formally abandoned slavery:

> "I fancied but now I was in England, in one of her choicest spots," he said, giving a half glance at the beautiful view beneath him; " but to hear your words would make me swear I was in some despotic land, where slavery was at its highest

---

[158] Burroughs, 'Sailors and Slaves', p. 307.
[159] Huzzey, *Freedom Burning*,
[160] Huzzey, *Freedom Burning*, p. 9.
[161] Huzzey, *Freedom Burning*, p. 9. See also Waters, *Racism*, p. 107.

point; however, I do not think I am your slave—I do not think I am likely to be."[162]

In this quotation the picturesqueness of the English countryside is contrasted with a hypothetical 'despotic land', a place where slavery is still practiced – however, *Paul Jones* is ostensibly set around 1775-1779.[163] It predates even the 1807 act outlawing the trade of enslaved people, yet this piece of dialogue seems to suggest that England has, at the very least, passed the peak of its engagement with slavery. As Marty Gould writes, melodrama 'tended to be more ideological than informational in its broader aims and cultural function.'[164] *Paul Jones* engages in a sanitization of Britain's past, where the public sentiment from the 1840s is projected backwards into the late 1770s, giving the impression that despotism and its associated slavery had always been Other to Britain. It is therefore unsurprising that *Paul Egan* does not feature a single enslaved character, speaking or otherwise. Slavery is only occasionally referenced as a practice that induces disgust. While Paul discloses his life's history to his captain, he displays grief when he shares the death of a beloved fellow sailor: he 'hastily brushed his eyelid, as if to disturb a tear which memory had brought there', yet when he continues his story 'in a clear voice', the emotional register while discussing his time aboard two different slavers is muted.[165] About his first stint about a West Indies slaver, all he discloses is that 'it was a trade I found did not suit me'.[166] He subsequently becomes engaged as 'first mate of a beautifully built vessel, which also was engaged in the slave trade', and 'while at Porto Rico, I determined in disgust to quit and come home in another vessel.'[167] In Paul's recount of these experiences, only the word 'disgust' signals any moral or emotional response to the transatlantic slave trade. When

---

[162] Egan, *Paul Jones*, p. 64.
[163] Though the text does not mention specific years, some events roughly coincide with events from John Paul Jones's life.
[164] Marty Gould, 'Melodrama and Empire', in *The Cambridge Companion to English Melodrama*, ed. by Carolyn Williams (Cambridge: Cambridge University Press, 2018), pp. 176-191, p. 178.
[165] Egan, *Paul Jones*, p. 87.
[166] Egan, *Paul Jones*, p. 87.
[167] Egan, *Paul Jones*, p. 87.

read in the broader context of the remarks, it is striking how the death of one (white) sailor causes Paul to wipe away a tear, whereas the grotesque suffering propagated aboard the slave ships only creates a dispassionate 'disgust'.

Paul Jones reveals an unwillingness to engage with Britain's history – a sordid past that does not suit the nationalist narrative of a triumph over the horrors of slavery. Yet at the same time, its treatment of its sole black character expresses anxieties over racial equality and a black person's place in the microcosm of society at a naval ship. On one hand the cook is part of the crew, protected by them when engaging in socially corrective laughter. On the other, the cook is caught in an impossible position where he either betrays Paul or his captain, and only comical physical violence resolves this instability. *Paul Jones* engages with the history of slavery and empire through 1840s ideology, not interested in accurately representing this past, but rather distancing itself from this past and creating a national identity on the basis of liberty through hierarchy. As Gould writes, 'Melodrama was a powerful – and popular – vehicle for transmitting the jingoistic ideologies, as well as the images of the national character, that formed the bedrock of popular imperialism.'[168] *Paul Jones* promotes an adherence to state and patriarchy, distancing itself from slavery. Yet its only black character does not neatly fit into these categories, creating comic disturbances that both reiterate as well as push against stereotypes that were prevalent at the time.

CONCLUSION

> My line is nearly all run out, John – there is not half-a fathom to unreeve. I don't want to slip my wind in this narrow hammock – let me be going free when I spring my luff for the long voyage; lay me upon deck, John, that when my soul goes aloft, if it pleases the Almighty, it should go up like bunting up the pen'ant halyards – that my eyes may look their last upon the blue water, as they did their first.[169]

---

[168] Gould, 'Melodrama and Empire', p. 176.
[169] Egan, *Paul Jones*, p. 532.

Loyal Gasket is mortally wounded in a naval battle with the English, yet even in his dying speech his nautical metaphors persist. As has been discussed above, the humour of the rigidity of Gasket's worldview mirrors *Paul Jones'* view of the inflexibility of social hierarchy. At the same time as the ideological primacy of state and home are constructed, *Paul Jones* alternatingly laughs and laments at the tragic consequences of such a constrained society. As Gould writes, 'there was little – if any – room for emancipation in melodrama's commitment to normative hierarchical structures of order.'[170] In *Paul Jones* small transgressions lead to laughter: Stretch-out Dick's pretension, or Gasket's romantic desire for someone above his social class. As in the case of the whipping of the black cook, a comic punishment is sufficient to restore equilibrium after a transgression. Other attempts at transgression, most notably Paul's desire for glory that undermines both the nation as well as domestic happiness, lead to melodramatic tragedy. *Paul Jones* reinforces hierarchy – between its characters, aboard the naval ships, and in its disparagement of the misplaced American ideals of equality. At the same time, it reaches out beyond conventional restraints – even though this movement is doomed to collapse in on itself. Paul receives the accolades he craved, yet Alice has died due to his actions. *Paul Jones* is a text in turmoil, where change collapses back into generic hierarchy. Yet, through its gentle laughter, it pushes against these concepts, presenting a text that never fully resolves its core anxieties.

---

[170] Gould, 'Melodrama and Empire', p. 179.

Conclusion

This thesis has explored the generic dimensions of four early penny bloods by different authors. It has done so by analysing the humour present in these texts, which reveal the power relationships between various characters and how they relate to broader societal structures such as class and race. Emphasis is placed on how the penny blood relates to other fictional genres, both within literature as well as popular theatre. In the first chapter on Rymer's *The String of Pearls*, I discussed the current scholarship on the text and subsequently diverged from current Marxist interpretations to incorporate carnivalesque humour. It also explores how *The String of Pearls* engages with melodrama and romance, two generic inheritances it combines in its emotional repertoire. The second chapter on Prest's *Valentine Vaux* focused on understanding the episodic plot structure, reminiscent of the picaresque, showing how the repetition of a certain comic script reinforces conservative social structures. Lindridge's *Jack Rann*, the subject of the third chapter, draws on a long tradition of highwayman stories. Its humour is expressed through disguises, which unsettle class boundaries and underpin the transgressive nature of the text. Egan's *Paul Jones*, finally, draws from the nautical tradition – nautical melodrama in particular – and melds it with humour to express anxieties around domesticity, national identity, and empire.

Returning to the question posed in the introduction of whether there is a generic coherence in the penny blood in terms of theme and trope, I posit that the genericity of the penny blood lies within its capacity to absorb and reconfigure other generic forms like nautical melodrama, criminal biographies, Newgate calendars, and Gothic romance within itself. It is this amalgam that creates its popular appeal at the time: it combines familiarity with novelty. The penny blood is a particularly porous genre in the sense that any source, whether it be a newspaper article, a play, a song, or simply a popular novel, can spark a successful penny serialisation.[1] Its hodgepodge of tone is part of its appeal. At the same time, they display a certain propensity for humour and laughter; a resistance to a fully serious tone. The incorporation of humour can range from an overwhelmingly comic text such as *Valentine Vaux*, with only few moments of seriousness, to including humour only occasionally as a foil to its more melodramatic components, such as in *Paul Jones*. First and foremost, the penny blood seeks to *entertain*, not to inform or educate. This is reflected in the politics of the penny blood, which are internally contradictory and span a range from transgressive (*Jack Rann*) to reaffirming law and order (*Valentine Vaux*). While the penny blood might borrow themes from radical literature, as argued by Breton, it rarely refers directly to contemporary political discourses.[2] The heroes of the penny blood are usually of humble birth, of a working or middle-class background, and their direct family plays little to no role in the story. In *Jack Rann* Jack's family is briefly introduced, but the narrative moves on swiftly to his highway exploits, and his parents play no role in the remainder of the story. The female main characters, however, are sometimes more embedded within a family structure, such as Johanna in *The String of Pearls* and to a lesser extent, Alice and Florence in *Paul Jones*. This reflects the association of the woman with the home and family life, which fuels the various domestic plots that have been discussed throughout this thesis.

As has become clear, it would be reductive to typify the penny blood solely by its violent content. Violence and gore are not present in every issue, as one would expect if this was its sole selling point to its readership. Instead, significant sections involve the heightened emotions of melodrama, or humorous interludes that might or might not contain any violence, or feature adventures or chase scenes that rely on thrilling their readers through tension rather than gore. The violence that *is* present is complex and multifaceted; it is used to invoke horror, but also laughter. Throughout this thesis, the variations and nuances of comic

---

[1] The origins of Prest's *My Poll and My Partner Joe: Or, Pretty Poll of Putney: A Nautical Romance* (1851) can be traced back to a song from Charles Dibdin Pitt called 'The Waterman'. See *The London Complete Songster; or, Musical Boquet* (London: William Lane, [1775?]), pp. 87-88.
[2] Breton, *Penny Politics*, p. 88.

violence have been scrutinised, showing how comic violence intersects with ideas of social hierarchy. Through the carnivalesque, it has shown how comic violence is not necessarily a destructive force – it can also be generative. As such, this thesis has provided a clear contribution to the current scholarship on the penny blood by reinterpreting the centring of violence within the genre as a whole. This thesis represents a new approach to penny bloods, assembling its meaning through its various disparate elements. Not only is it the first work that takes stock of the humour that permeates the genre, it also moves past the few authors that have been recognised in current scholarship by reading Prest and Rymer alongside relative unknowns Lindridge and Egan.

In the introduction to this thesis I questioned whether the term 'penny blood' is a suitable label for the genre as a whole. While its ubiquitous usage is not a problem in itself, the term deserves a critical reframing whenever it is used rather than perpetuating stereotypical representations of the texts it refers to that stem from late-nineteenth-century moralistic exhortations. 'Domestic romance' stands as a suitable alternative, particularly as this thesis has shown that a preoccupation with the home and the nation is part of the texts' foundations. Although a fair amount of penny bloods were subtitled 'A Domestic Romance' or similar, others were advertised simply as 'novels'. This suggests that although domestic romance is a label that would be closer to the expectations of the nineteenth-century reader, it still might not fully encapsulate the diversity of texts. I briefly considered the somewhat ominous combination of 'domestic blood', combining both the focus on the penny fiction hero's journey towards (or away from) domesticity with its more violent propensities. Ultimately, more research is needed in the nuances between penny bloods advertised under different generic labels. As such, 'penny blood' and the broader term 'penny fiction' will suffice for now to facilitate scholarly communication – provided that usage of the term is examined critically and reflectively.

Although this thesis provides a deeper understanding of the generic underpinnings of the genre, there are still many aspects of the penny blood that remain underexplored. In this section I will highlight three areas of further research that I consider to be particularly fruitful to expand penny blood studies beyond its current scope. While the circular relationship between penny magazines, penny theatre, and criminal broadsides have been critically explored in previous scholarship, the complicated reciprocal relationship between the penny blood and penny theatre remains opaque.³ Within the texts studied in this thesis, *A String of Pearls* was adapted into a play, while Lindridge plagiarised several sections from a play while writing *Jack Rann*. This connection deserves further research, as it is one of the foundations of penny fiction as a whole. Secondly, many penny bloods contain an illustration for every issue; of the texts discussed in this thesis, the collected editions of *Valentine Vaux*, *Jack Rann*, and *Paul Jones* all contain illustrations. This thesis focuses on the textual level as is suitable for its aims, but much remains to be explored in the visual aspects of the penny blood.⁴ Finally, penny magazines not only contained serialised fiction, but also shorter fiction pieces that might be concluded within the issue. I have not yet come across any study that solely focuses on these short stories, which deserve to be read within the penny blood framework as well. Contrasting the content and tone of these pieces with the longer works could provide more insight into the reading experience of the nineteenth-century penny periodical reader.

Beyond these specific topics, there is of course still much to be gained from continuing along the lines of existing research. Approaches with a Gothic bent will find much still to analyse within the lesser known texts of the penny blood – Prest's *The Death Ship* (1846) for example features an interesting refiguring of eighteenth-century Gothic romance with a nautical twist. The production aspect of the penny press has been a fruitful avenue of research so far, and will yield further insights as the intricacies of the interplay between the various actors within the publishing landscape are unravelled. Despite the prevalence of authors like Prest and Rymer in penny fiction research, due to the size of their bodies of work, many of their stories remain unexamined in any depth. My hope is that my research will be the starting point for other scholars interested in aspects of early nineteenth-century penny fiction that

---

³ Jacobs, 'Blood in the Street', p. 322.
⁴ One study that successfully applies this perspective is Laura Daniel Buchholz, 'Illustrations and Text: Storyworld Space and the Multimodality of Serialized Narrative', *Style*, 48:4 (2014), 593-611.

stretch beyond the Gothic or its violent content. Penny fiction studies brings together scholars from many different backgrounds and disciplines, and that combined and intersectional knowledge will be necessary to fully understand the significance of penny bloods to early Victorian society. If anything, I hope I have done the penny blood justice and presented the penny blood holistically. While I do not disagree with assessments that penny fiction can be repetitive and frustrating, I have aimed to also draw attention to its joys: its capacity for engaging adventures and diverse tropes, its dedication to humour and capriciousness. Reading penny bloods has been a genuine pleasure, and I hope that many others will discover this fascinating period of Britain's literary history in the future.

Bibliography

Acton, Eugenia de, *The Nuns of the Desert; or, The Woodland Witches*, Vol. II, (London: Minerva Press, 1805)

Adcock, John, 'James Lindridge', *Yesterday's Papers Archive* <http://yesterdayspapersarchive.blogspot.com/2009/02/james-lindridge.html> [accessed 26 September 2022]

Adcock, John, 'The Purkess Family of Dean Street', *John Adcock* <http://johnadcock.blogspot.com/2014/04/the-purkess-family-of-dean-street.html> [accessed 26 September 2022]

Andrews, Malcolm, *Dickensian Laughter. Essays on Dickens and Humour* (Oxford: Oxford University Press, 2013)

Anthony Mandal, 'Gothic Fiction, from Shilling Shockers to Penny Bloods', in *The Cambridge History of the Gothic*, ed. by Dale Townshend and Angela Wright (Cambridge: University of Cambridge Press, 2020), pp. 139-161

Arnold, Dana, *Re-presenting the Metropolis. Architecture, urban experience and social life in London 1800-1840* (Aldershot: Ashgate Publishing Limited, 2000)

Authentic Memoirs of Captain Paul Jones, The American Corsair (London: A Hogg, [1779?])

Bailey, Peter, 'Breaking the Sound Barrier: A Historian Listens to Noise', *Body and Society*, 2:2 (1996), 49-66

Bakhtin, Mikhail, *Rabelais and His World*, trans. by Hélène Iswolsky, (Bloomington: Indiana University Press, 1964)

Baldick, Chris, and Robert Mighall, 'Gothic Criticism', in *A New Companion to the Gothic*, ed. by David Punter (Chichester: Blackwell Publishing, 2012), pp. 267-287

Barzilai, Shuli, 'The Bluebeard Barometer: Charles Dickens and Captain Murderer', *Victorian Literature and Culture*, 32:2 (2004), 505-524

Bassil-Morozow, Helena, *The Trickster in Contemporary Film* (London: Routledge, 2012)

Beattie, James, 'On Fable and Romance' in *Dissertations Moral and Critical* (London: W. Strahan & T. Cadell, 1783), pp. 505-574

Bell, Ian A., 'Eighteenth-century crime writing', in *The Cambridge Companion to Crime Writing*, ed. by Martin Priestman (Cambridge: Cambridge University Press, 2003), pp 7-18

Bergson, Henri, *Laughter. An Essay on the Meaning of the Comic*, trans. by Cloudesly Brereton and Fred Rothwell (London: Macmillan and Co., 1911)

Botting, Fred, *Gothic* (London: Routledge, 2014)

Bratton, Jacky, 'Romantic Melodrama', in *The Cambridge Companion to British Theatre, 1730-1830*, ed. by Jane Moody and Daniel O'Quinn (Cambridge : Cambridge University Press, 2007), pp. 115-127

Breton, Rob, *The Penny Politics of Victorian Popular Fiction* (Manchester: Manchester University Press, 2021)

Brooks, Peter, *The Melodramatic Imagination* (New Haven: Yale University Press, 1995)

Brown, Charles Brockden, *Wieland; or The Transformation, and Memoirs of Carwin, the Biloquist* (Oxford: Oxford University Press, 2009)

Buchholz, Laura Daniel, 'Illustrations and Text: Storyworld Space and the Multimodality of Serialized Narrative', *Style*, 48:4 (2014), 593-611

Burroughs, Robert, 'Sailors and Slaves: The "Poor Enslaved Tar" in Navel Reform and Nautical Melodrama', *Journal of Victorian Culture*, 16:3 (2011), 305-322

Burton, Valerie, 'The Myth of Bachelor Jack: Masculinity, Patriarchy and Seafaring Labour', in *Jack Tar in History. Essays in the History of Maritime Life and Labour*, ed. by Colin Howell and Richard J. Twomey (Fredericton: Acadiensis Press, 1991), pp. 179-198

Burwick, Frederick, and Manushag N. Powell, *British Pirates in Print and Performance* (New York: Palgrave Macmillan, 2015)

Byron, Lord, *The Corsair. A Tale.* (London: John Murray, 1814)

Byron, Michael, *Punch and Judy. Its origin and evolution* (Aberdeen: DaSilva Puppet Books, 1972)

Callo, Joseph, *John Paul Jones: America's First Sea Warrior* (Annapolis: Naval Institute Press, 2006)

Campbell, Mel, 'Pirate Chic: Tracing the Aesthetics of Literary Piracy', in *Pirates and Mutineers of the Nineteenth Century. Swashbucklers and Swindlers*, ed. by Grace Moore (London: Routledge, 2016), pp. 11-22

Carey, John, *The Violent Effigy: A Study of Dickens' Imagination* (London: Faber and Faber, 2008)

Carlson, Marvin, 'He Never Should Bow Down to a Domineering Frown: Class Tensions and Nautical Melodrama' in *Melodrama. The Cultural Emergence of a Genre*, ed. by Michael Hays and Anastasia Nikolopoulou (New York: St. Martin's Press, 1996), pp. 147-166

Carrell, Amy, 'Historical views of humor', in *The Primer of Humor Research* ed. By Victor Raskin (Berlin: Mouton de Gruyter, 2008), pp. 303-332

Carroll, Noël, *Humour: A Very Short Introduction* (Oxford: Oxford University Press, 2014)

Castle, Terry, *Masquerade and Civilization. The Carnivalesque in Eighteenth-Century English Culture and Fiction* (Stanford: Stanford University Press, 1986)

Chrisman, Laura, *Rereading the Imperial Romance* (Oxford: Clarendon Press, 2000)

Christoff, Maria, and Barry Dauphin, 'Freud's Theory of Humor', in *Encyclopedia of Personality and Individual Differences*, ed. by Virgil Zeigler-Hill and Todd K. Shackelford (New York: Springer, 2017)

Churchill, David, *Crime Control and Everyday Life in the Victorian City. The Police and the Public* (Oxford: Oxford University Press, 2017)

Clavell, John, *A Recantation of an ill led Life. Or A discouverie of the High-way Law.* (London: Richard Meighen, 1628)

Cockton, Henry, *The Life and Adventures of Valentine Vox, the Ventriloquist* (London: W. Nicholson & Sons, [1890?]),

Cohen, Margaret, *The Novel and the Sea* (Princeton: Princeton University Press, 2010).

Connor, Steven, *Dumbstruck. A Cultural History of Ventriloquism* (Oxford: Oxford University Press, 2004)

Coutinho, Maria Antónia, and Florencia Miranda, 'To Describe Genres: Problems and Strategies' in *Genre in a Changing World*, ed. by Charles Bazerman, Adair Bonini and Débora Figueiredo (West Lafayette: Parlor Press, 2009), pp. 35-56

Cox, Jeffrey N., 'The Ideological Tack of Nautical Melodrama', in *Melodrama. The Cultural Emergence of a Genre*, ed. by Michael Hays and Anastasia Nikolopoulou (New York: St. Martin's Press, 1996), pp. 165-189

Cozzi, Annette, 'Men and Menus: Dickens and the Rise of the "Ordinary" English Gentleman,' in *The Discourses of Food in Nineteenth-Century British Fiction* (Basingstoke: Palgrave, 2010), pp. 39-69

Danow, David K., *The Spirit of Carnival. Magical Realism and the Grotesque* (Lexington, Kentucky: The University Press of Kentucky, 1995)

Davies, Helen, *Gender and Ventriloquism in Victorian and Neo-Victorian Fiction. Passionate Puppets* (Basingstoke: Palgrave Macmillan, 2012)

Davis, Jessica Milner, *Farce* (London: Methuen & Co Ltd, 1978)

'December 1774 (o17741207-1)' in *Old Bailey Proceedings Online* <www.oldbaileyonline.org> [accessed 26 September 2022]

[Defoe, Daniel?], 'An Effectual Scheme For the Immediate Preventing of Street Robberies', (London: J. Wilford, 1731)

'Demoralizing Publications', *The People's Newsletter*, 20 June 1847

Derrida, Jacques, 'The Law of Genre', trans. by Avital Ronell, *Critical Inquiry*, 7:1 (1980), 55-81

Dickens, Charles, 'Nurse's Stories', in *The Uncommercial Traveller* (London: Chapman & Hall Ld., 1868), pp. 174-186

Dickens, Charles, 'The Lost Arctic Voyagers', *Household Words*, 2 December 1854, pp. 361-365

Dickens, Charles, *Oliver Twist, or, The Parish Boy's Progress* (London: Penguin Books, 2003)

Dickens, Charles, *The Life and Adventures of Nicholas Nickleby* (London: Chapman and Hall, 1839)

Duff, David, 'Introduction', in *Modern Genre Theory* (London: Routledge, 2014), pp. 1-24

Duncan, Edward, 'John Rann, d. 1774', *London Lives* <https://www.londonlives.org/static/RannJohnExecuted1774.jsp> [accessed 26 September 2022]

Duncan, Ian, *Modern Romance and Transformations of the Novel. The Gothic, Scott, and Dickens* (Cambridge: Cambridge University Press, 1992)

Eagleton, Terry, *Humour* (New Haven: Yale University Press)

Ebsworth, J. W., and Megan A. Stephan, 'Egan, Pierce James (1814–1880), novelist', in *Oxford Dictionary of National Biography* <https://www.oxforddnb.com/> [accessed September 2022]

Edward Lloyd and His World. Popular Fiction, Politics and the Press in Victorian Britain, ed. By Sarah Louise Lill and Rohan McWilliam (New York: Routledge, 2019)

Egan the Younger, Pierce, *Paul Jones; the Pirate* (London: G. Purkess, 1850)

Elferen, Isabella van, *Gothic Music. The Sounds of the Uncanny* (Cardiff: University of Wales Press, 2012)

Ellis, Kate Ferguson, 'Can You Forgive Her? The Gothic Heroine and Her Critics', in *A New Companion to the Gothic* ed. by David Punter (Chichester: Wiley-Blackwell, 2012), pp. 457-468

Encyclopaedia Britannica: or, a Dictionary (Edinburgh: Archibald Constable and Company, 1823)

Fahnestock, Jeanne, 'The Heroine of Irregular Features: Physiognomy and Conventions of Heroine Description', *Victorian Studies*, 24:3 (1981), 325-350

Falke, Cassandra, 'On the Morality of Immoral Fiction: Reading Newgate Novels, 1830-1848', *Nineteenth-Century Contexts*, 38:3 (2016), 183-193

Faller, Lincoln B., *Turned to Account. The forms and functions of criminal biography in late seventeeth- and early eighteenth-century England* (Cambridge: Cambridge University Press, 2008)

Figueroa-Dorrego, Jorge, and Cristina Larkin-Galiñanes, *A Source Book of Literary and Philosophical Writings about Humour and Laughter* (London: Sage, 2005)

Fitz-Ball, Edward, *The Pilot: A Nautical Burletta, in Three Acts* (London: John Cumberland, [1825?])

Foucault, Michel, *Discipline and Punish. The Birth of the Prison*, trans. by Alan Sheridan (New York: Vintage Books, 1995)

Frohock, Richard, *Buccaneers and Privateers: The Story of the English Sea Rover, 1675-1725* (Newark: University of Delaware Press, 2012)

Frost, Thomas, *Reminiscences of a Country Journalist* (London: Ward and Downey, 1886)

Frow, John, *Genre* (London: Routledge, 2006)

Frye, Northrop, *Anatomy of Criticism. Four essays* (Princeton: Princeton University Press, 2000 [1957])

Fuchs, Barbara, *Romance* (New York: Routledge, 2004)

Fudge, Erica, 'Why it's easy being a vegetarian', *Textual Practice*, 24:1 (2010) 149-166

'A full and particular Account of the Life and extraordinary Transactions of John Rann, otherwise Sixteen-Strings Jack, who was hanged for a Robbery on the Highway,' in *The Malefactor's Register; or, New Newgate and Tyburn Calendar* Vol. V (London: Alex Hogg, 1779), pp. 138-146

Gasperini, Anna, *Nineteenth Century Popular Fiction, Medicine and Anatomy. The Victorian Penny Blood and the 1832 Anatomy Act* (Basingstoke: Palgrave Macmillan, 2019).

Gatrell, V.A.C., *The Hanging Tree. Execution and the English People 1770-1868* (Oxford: Oxford University Press: Oxford, 1994)

Gay, John, *The Beggar's Opera and Polly*, ed. by Hal Gladfelder (Cambridge: Cambridge University Press, 2013)

A Genuine Account of the Life of John Rann, Alias Sixteen-string Jack (London: Bailey, [1774?])

Gladfelder, Hal, 'Introduction', in John Gay, *The Beggar's Opera and Polly*, ed. by Hal Gladfelder (Cambridge: Cambridge University Press, 2013)

Godwin, William, 'Of History and Romance' (1797), <http://www.english.upenn.edu/~mgamer/Etexts/godwin.history.html> [accessed 26 September 2022]

Goldblatt, David, *Art and Ventriloquism* (London: Routledge, 2006)

Gould, Marty, 'Melodrama and Empire', in *The Cambridge Companion to English Melodrama*, ed. by Carolyn Williams (Cambridge: Cambridge University Press, 2018), pp. 176-191

Haines, Esq., John Thomas, *"My Poll and My Partner Joe.", A Nautical Drama, in Three Acts.* (London: John Cumberland, 1832)

Haining, Peter, *Sweeney Todd: The Real Story of the Demon Barber of Fleet Street* (London: Anova Books, 2007)

Halliday, Robert, 'New Light on Henry Cockton', *Notes and Queries*, 41:3 (1994), 349-351

Harrison, Mark, *Crowds and History. Mass Phenomena in English Towns, 1790-1835* (Cambridge: Cambridge University Press, 1988)

Haywood, Ian, *The Revolution in Popular Literature. Print, Politics and the People, 1790-1860* (Cambridge: Cambridge University Press, 2004)

Hazlitt, William, *Lectures on the English Comic Writers*, ed. by William Hazlitt [the son] (London: John Templeman, 1841)

Hennelly, Jr, Mark M., 'Victorian Carnivalesque', *Victorian Literature and Culture*, 30:1 (2002) 365-381

Hill, Leslie, *The Cambridge Introduction to Derrida* (Cambridge: Cambridge University Press, 2007)

Hobbes, Thomas, *Leviathan*, ed. by G.A.J. Rogers and Karl Schuhmann, Vol. I (London: Continuum, 2005)

Hobsbawm, E. J., *Bandits. Revised Edition* (New York: Pantheon Books, 1981)

Hobson, Robert W., 'Voices of Carwin and Other Mysteries in Charles Brockden Brown's "Wieland".' *Early American Literature*, 10:3 (1975), 307-309

Horner, Avril, and Sue Zlosnik, *Gothic and the Comic Turn* (Basingstoke: Palgrave Macmillan, 2005)

Houston, Gail Turley, 'Broadsides at the Board: Collations of *Pickwick Papers* and *Oliver Twist*', *Studies in English Literature, 1500-1900*, 31:4 (1991), 735-755

Hultzsch, Anne, 'The Crowd and the Building: Flux in the Early *Illustrated London News*', *Architecture and Culture*, 6:3 (2018), 371-386

Hurd, Richard, *Letters on Chivalry and Romance* (London: A. Millar, 1762)

Huzzey, Richard, *Freedom Burning. Anti-Slavery and Empire in Victorian Britain* (Ithaca: Cornell University Press, 2012)

I'm Afloat, I'm Afloat: or, Roderick the Rover. A Romance (London: E. Lloyd and G. Purkess)

Ibitson, Avid A., '"A book in his hand, - but it couldn't be a prayer-book": The Self-Awareness of William Harrison Ainsworth's Newgate Novels', *Journal of Victorian Culture*, 23:3 (2018), 332-349

Iser, Wolfgang, *The Act of Reading: A Theory of Aesthetic Response* (Baltimore: Johns Hopkins University Press, 1978)

Jackson, Esq., William, *The New and Complete Newgate Calendar; or, Villany Displayed in All its Branches*, Vol. V (London: Alex Hogg, 1795)

Jacobs, Edward, 'Blood in the Street: London Street Culture, "Industrial Literacy," and the Emergence of Mass Culture in Victorian London', *Nineteenth-Century Contexts*, 18 (1995), 321-347

James, Louis, 'The Trouble with Betsy', in *The Victorian Periodical Press: Samplings and Soundings*, ed. by Joanne Shattock and Michael Wolff (Leicester: Leicester University Press, 1982), pp. 349-366

James, Louis, *Fiction for the Working Man. 1830-1850* (Harmondsworth: Penguin, 1974)

Jameson, Fredric, 'Magical Narratives: Romance as Genre', *New Literary History*, 7:1 (1975), 135-163

Jerrold, Douglas, *Comedies and Dramas* (London: Bradbury and Evans, 1854)

John A. Hodgson, 'An Other Voice: Ventriloquism in the Romantic Period', *Romanticism on the Net*, 16, (1999)

'John Paul Jones', *Britannica* (2022), <https://www.britannica.com/biography/John-Paul-Jones-United-States-naval-officer> [accessed 26 September 2022]

Jones, D. Michael, *The Byronic Hero and the Rhetoric of Masculinity in the 19th Century British Novel* (Jefferson: McFarland & Company, Inc., Publishers, 2017)

Jones, Timothy, *The Gothic and the Carnivalesque in American Culture* (University of Wales Press, 2015),

Killeen, Jarlath, 'Victorian Gothic Pulp Fiction', in *The Victorian Gothic. An Edinburgh Companion*, ed. by Andrew Smith and William Hughes (Edinburgh: Edinburgh University Press, 2012), pp. 43-56

King, Andrew, '"Literature of the Kitchen": Cheap Serial Fiction of the 1840s and 1850s', in *A Companion to Sensation Fiction*, ed. by Pamela K. Gilbert (Chichester: Wiley-Blackwell, 2011), pp. 38-53

Knight, Stephen, 'Introduction' in *Robin Hood in Greenwood Stood. Alterity and Context in the English Outlaw Tradition*, ed. by Stephen Knight (Turnhout: Brepols Publishers, 2011)

Kulka, Tomáš, 'The Incongruity of Incongruity Theories of Humor', *Organon*, 14:3 (2007), 320-333

Laqueur, Thomas W., 'Crowds, carnival and the state in English executions, 1604-1868' in *The First Modern Society. Essays in English History in Honour of Lawrence Stone*, ed. by A.L. Beier, David Cannadine and James M. Rosenheim (Cambridge: Cambridge University Press, 1989) pp. 305-356

Larkin-Galiñanes, Cristina, 'An overview of Humor Theory', in *The Routledge Handbook of Language and Humor*, ed. By Salvatore Attardo (New York: Routledge, 2017), pp. 4-16

Léger-St-Jean, Marie, 'George Purkess' in *Price One Penny* <http://www.priceonepenny.info/database/show_publisher.php?publisher_id=72> [accessed 26 September 2022]

Léger-St-Jean, Marie, 'Luke Somerton', in *Price One Penny* <http://www.priceonepenny.info/database/show_title.php?work_id=126> [accessed 26 September 2022]

Léger-St-Jean, Marie, 'Thomas Peckett Prest and the Denvils' in *Edward Lloyd and His World. Popular Fiction, Politics and the Press in Victorian Britain*, ed. by Sarah Louise Lill and Rohan McWilliam (New York: Routledge, 2019), pp. 114-131

Lill, Sarah Louise, 'In for a Penny: The Business of Mass-Market Publishing 1832-90', in *Edward Lloyd and His World. Popular Fiction, Politics and the Press in Victorian Britain*, ed. by Sarah Louise Lill and Rohan McWilliam (New York: Routledge, 2019)

Lill, Sarah Louise, and Rohan McWilliam, 'Introduction. Edward Lloyd, Eminent Victorian' in *Edward Lloys and His World. Popular Fiction, Politics and the Press in Victorian Britain* ed. by Sarah Louise Lill and Rohan McWilliam (New York: Routledge, 2019)

Lindridge, James, *Jack Rann. Alias Sixteen-String Jack* (London: G. Purkess, 1840)

Lindridge, James, *Tales of Shipwrecks and Adventures at Sea. Being a Collection of Faithful Narratives of Shipwrecks, Mutinies, Fires, Famines, and Disasters, incidental to a Sea Life; Together with Celebrated Voyages, Amusing Tales, Tough Yarns, and Interesting Anecdotes* (London: William Mark Clark, 1847)

Linebaugh, Peter, and Marcus Rediker, *The Many-Headed Hydra. Sailors, Slaves, Commoners, and the Hidden History of the Revolutionary Atlantic* (Boston: Beacon Press, 2000)

Lintott, Sheila, 'Superiority in Humor Theory', *The Journal of Aesthetics and Art Criticism* 74:4 (2016), 347-358

'Literary Notices', *Age*, 10 November 1839

Lloyd's Weekly London Newspaper, 17 May 1846

Mack, Robert L., *The Wonderful and Surprising History of Sweeney Todd* (London: Continuum, 2007)

Mackay, Charles, *Extraordinary Popular Delusions and the Madness of Crowds* (London: Wordsworth, 1995)

Mackie, Erin, *Rakes, Highwaymen, and Pirates: The Making of the Modern Gentleman in the Eighteenth Century* (Baltimore: Johns Hopkins University Press, 2009)

Martin's Annals of Crime; or new Newgate Calendar, and general record of tragic events, including Ancient and Modern Modes of Torture, &c.: comprehending a history of the most notorious murderers, traitors, highwaymen, pirates, burglars, pickpockets, adulterers, ravishers, decoyers, incendiaries, poachers, swindlers, and felons and rogues of every description (London: William Mark Clark, 1837-1838).

McClelland, J.S., *The Crowd and the Mob. From Plato to Canetti* (Abingdon: Routledge, 1989)

McKay, Sinclair, *The Lady in the Cellar: Murder, Scandal and Insanity in Victorian Bloomsbury* (London: White Lion Publishing, 2018)

McKenzie, Andrea, 'The Real Macheath: Social Satire, Appropriation, and Eighteenth-Century Criminal Biography', *The Huntington Library Quarterly*, 69:4 (2006), 581-605

Meer, Sarah, 'Melodrama and Race', in *The Cambridge Companion to Melodrama* ed. by Carolyn Williams (Cambridge: Cambridge University Press, 2018), pp. 192-205

Meredith, George, *An Essay on Comedy and the Uses of the Comic Spirit* (London: A. Constable, 1905 [1877]),

Miles, Robert, *Ann Radcliffe. The Great Enchantress* (Manchester: Manchester University Press, 1995)

Miller, Carolyn R., 'Genre as Social Action' *Quarterly Journal of Speech* 70 (1984), 151-167

Miller, Dean A., *The Epic Hero* (Baltimore: The Johns Hopkins University Press, 2000)

Moore, Grace, 'Introduction', in *Pirates and Mutineers of the Nineteenth Century. Swashbucklers and Swindlers*, ed. by Grace Moore (London: Routledge, 2016)

More, Thomas, *Utopia*, ed. by George M. Logan and Robert M. Adams (Cambridge: Cambridge University Press, 2002)

Morgan, Jamie, 'Portrayals of Protest: G.W.M. Reynolds and the Industrious Classes' (doctoral thesis, University of Sheffield, 2017)

Mountague Esq., James, *The Old Bailey Chronicle; Containing a Circumstantial Account of the Lives, Trials, and Confessions, of The Most Notorious Offenders, Who Have Suffered Death, and Other Exemplary Punishments*, Vol. IV (London: S. Smith, 1788)

'The Murderous Barber; Or, Terrific Story of the Rue de la Harpe at Paris', in *The Wonders of the Universe; or Curiosities of Nature and Art.* (Exeter: J. & B. Williams, 1836), pp. 1-3

Murray, Lieutenant, *Roderick the Rover: or, The Spirit of the Wave* (Boston: Gleason's Publishing Hall, 1847)

Nesvet, Rebecca, 'Blood Relations: Sweeney Todd and the Rymers of London', *Notes and Queries*, 64:1 (2017), 112-116

Nilsen, Alleen and Don, 'Literature and humor', in *The Primer of Humor Research*, ed. by Victor Raskin (Berlin: Mouton de Gruyter, 2008), pp. 243-280

'October 1774 (s17741019-1)' in *Old Bailey Proceedings Online* <www.oldbaileyonline.org> [accessed 26 September 2022]

Owen, Robert, *Lectures on the Marriages of the Priesthood of the Old Immoral World, Delivered in the Year 1835, Before the Passing of the New Marriage Act* (Leeds: J. Hobson, 1840)

Paul Jones: or the Fife Coast Garland. A Heroi-Comical Poem. In Four Parts. (Edinburg: [n. pub.], 1779)

Penny Dreadfuls and the Gothic: Investigations of Pernicious Tales of Terror, ed. By Nicole C. Dittmer and Sophie Raine (Cardiff: University of Wales Press, 2023 [forthcoming])

Pitt, Charles Dibdin, 'The Waterman', in *The London Complete Songster; or, Musical Boquet* (London: William Lane, [1775?]), pp. 87-88

Pitt, George Dibdin, *Sweeney Todd, The Barber of Fleet Street; or, The String or Pearls. A Legendary Drama in Two Acts* (London: John Dicks, 1883)

Pollard, A. J., *Imagining Robin Hood. The Late-Medieval Stories in Historical Context* (Abingdon: Routledge, 2004)

Portwine, Timothy, [Thomas Peckett Prest], *The Adventure of Valentine Vaux; or, The Tricks of a ventriloquist* (London: E. Lloyd, 1840)

Powell, Sarah, 'Black Markets and Cadaverous Pies: The Corpse, Urban Trade and Industrial Consumption in the Penny Blood', in *Victorian Crime, Madness and Sensation*, ed. by A. Maunder & G. Moore (Hampshire: Ashgate, 2004)

Prest, Thomas Peckett, *Gallant Tom; or, The Perils of a Sailor Ashore and Afloat* (London: Edward Lloyd, 1841)

Prest, Thomas Peckett, *Luke Somerton; or, The English Renegade* (London: Edward Lloyd, 1845)

Prest, Thomas Peckett, *The Smuggler King; or, The Foundling of the Wreck* (London: Edward Lloyd, 1844)

Prior, Paul, 'From Speech Genres to Mediated Multimodal Genre Systems: Bakhtin, Voloshinov, and the Question of Writing' in *Genre in a Changing World* ed. by Charles Bazerman, Adair Bonini and Débora Figueiredo (West Lafayette: Parlor Press, 2009), pp. 17-34

Prusak, Bernard G., 'Le rire à nouveau: Rereading Bergson', *The Journal of Aesthetics and Art Criticism*, 64:4 (2004), 377-388

Punter, David, 'Scottish and Irish Gothic' in *The Cambridge Companion to Gothic Fiction*, ed. by Jerrold E. Hogle (Cambridge: Cambridge University Press, 2002), pp. 105-125

Punter, David, *The Literature of Terror. A History of Gothic Fictions from 1765 to the present* (Harlow: Longman, 1996)

Pykett, Lyn, 'The Newgate novel and sensation fiction, 1830-1868', in *The Cambridge Companion to Crime Fiction*, ed. by Martin Priestman (Cambridge: Cambridge University Press, 2003), pp. 19-39

Rawlings, Philip, *Drunks, Whores, and Idle Apprentices: Criminal Biographies of the Eighteenth Century* (Cambridge: Cambridge University Press, 1992)

Reeve, Clara, *The Progress of Romance*, Vol. I (Colchester: W. Keymer, 1785)

Reynolds, Kimberly, and Nicola Humble, *Victorian Heroines. Representations of Femininity in Nineteenth-century Literature and Art* (New York: Harvester Wheatshelf, 1993)

Riley, Brian Patrick, '"It's Man Devouring Man, My Dear": Adapting Sweeney Todd for the Screen', *Literature/Film Quarterly*, 38:3 (2010), 205-216

Robinson, Alistair, 'Vagrant, Convict, Cannibal Chief: Abel Magwitch and the Culture of Cannibalism in *Great Expectations*', *Journal of Victorian Culture*, 22:4, (2017), 450-464

Rosalind Crone, *Violent Victorians. Popular entertainment in nineteenth-century London* (Manchester: Manchester University Press, 2012)

Rose, Jonathan, *The Intellectual Life of the British Working Classes* (New Haven 2002)

Russel, Deborah, 'Gothic Romance' in: *Romantic Gothic*, ed. by Angela Wright and Dale Townshend (Edinburgh: Edinburgh University Press, 2016), pp. 55-72

Rymer, James Malcolm, *Sweeney Todd. The String of Pearls*, ed. by Dick Collins (Ware: Wordsworth Editions, 2010)

Rymer, James Malcolm, *The String of Pearls; or, The Barber of Fleet Street. A Domestic Romance* (London: E. Lloyd, 1850)

Sanday, Peggy Reeves, *Divine Hunger: Cannibalism as a Cultural System* (Cambridge: Cambridge University Press, 1986)

Sanders, Andrew, 'Victorian Romance: Romance and Mystery' in *A Companion to Romance from Classical to Contemporary*, ed. by Corinne Saunders (Oxford: Blackwell, 2004), pp. 375-388

Sanna, Antonio, 'Historical and Fictional Pirates. A Review' in *Pirates in History and Popular Culture*, ed. by Antonio Sanna (Jefferson: McFarland & Company, Inc., Publishers, 2018)

Schmid, Susanne, 'Eighteenth-Century Travellers and the Country Inn' in *Drink in the Eighteenth and Nineteenth Centuries*, ed. by Susanne Schmid and Barbara Schmidt-Haberkamp (London: Pickering & Chatto, 2014), pp. 59-70

Schmidt, Leigh Eric, 'From Demon Possession to Magic Show: Ventriloquism, Religion, and the Enlightenment', *Church History*, 67:2 (1998), 274-304

Schneider, Ralf, 'The Invisible Center: Conceptions of Masculinity in Victorian Fiction – Realist, Crime, Detective, and Gothic', in *Constructions of Masculinity in*

British Literature from the Middle Ages to the Present, ed. by Stefan Horlacher (New York: Palgrave Macmillan, 2011), pp. 147-168

Schöberlein, Stefan, 'Speaking in Tongues, Speaking without Tongues: Transplanted Voices in Charles Brockden Brown's Wieland', *Journal of American Studies*, 51:2 (2017), 535-552.

Scott, Reginald, *The Discoverie of Witchcraft*, ed. by Brinsley Nicholson (London: Elliot Stock, 1886 [1584])

Scott, Walter, 'Impromptu. To Monsieur Alexandre', in *The Poetical Works of Sir Walter Scott, with A Sketch of His Life*, ed. by J.W. Lake (Philadelphia: J. Crissy, 1838)

Scott, Walter, *The Prose Works of Sir Walter Scott, Bart*, Vol. IV (Edinburgh: Robert Cadell, 1834)

Scriven, Tom, 'The Jim Crow Craze in London's Press and Streets, 1836-1839', *Journal of Victorian Culture*, 19:1 (2014), 93-109

Shaw, Joshua, 'Philosophy of Humor', *Philosophy Compass*, 5:2 (2010), 112-126

Shoemaker, Robert B., 'The Street Robber and the Gentleman Highwayman: Changing Representations and Perceptions of Robbery in London, 1690-1800', *Cultural and Social History*, 3 (2006), 381-405

Shoemaker, Robert B., 'The Street Robber and the Gentleman Highwayman: Changing Representations and Perceptions of Robbery in London, 1690-1800', *Cultural and Social History*, 3 (2006), 381-405

Sieber, Harry, *The Picaresque* (Abingdon: Routledge, 2018)

Smith, Andrew, *Gothic Death 1740-1914. A Literary History* (Manchester: Manchester University Press, 2016)

Smith, Helen R., 'Introduction' in: *Penny Dreadfuls and Boys' Adventures. The Barry Ono Collection of Victorian Popular Literature in the British Library* by Elizabeth James and Helen R. Smith (London: The British Library, 1998)

Smith, Helen, *New Light on Sweeney Todd, Thomas Peckett Prest, James Malcolm Rymer and Elizabeth Caroline Grey* (London: Jarndyce, 2002)

Sorensen, Janet, *Strange Vernaculars. How Eighteenth-Century Slang, Cant, Provincial Languages, and Nautical Jargon Became English* (Princeton: Princeton University Press, 2017)

Spencer, Herbert, *Essays: Scientific, Political, & Speculative*, Vol. II (London: Williams and Norgate, 1891)

Spooner, Catherine, *Post-Millennial Gothic. Comedy, Romance and the Rise of Happy Gothic* (London: Bloomsbury, 2017)

Spraggs, Gillian, *Outlaws & Highwaymen. The Cult of the Robber in England from the Middle Ages to the Nineteenth Century* (London: Pimlico, 2001)

Springhall, John, '"A Life Story for the People"? Edwin J. Brett and the London "Low-Life" Penny Dreadfuls of the 1860s', *Victorian Studies*, 33:2 (1990), 223-246

Stein, Atara, *The Byronic Hero in Film, Fiction, and Television* (Carbondale: Southern Illinois University Press, 2004)

Swales, John M., 'Worlds of Genre - Metaphors of Genre' in *Genre in a Changing World* ed. by Charles Bazerman, Adair Bonini and Débora Figueiredo (West Lafayette: Parlor Press, 2009), pp. 3-16

Taylor, Antony, *Lords of Misrule. Hostility to Aristocracy in Late Nineteenth- and Early Twentieth-Century Britain* (Basinstoke: Palgrave Macmillan, 2004)

The History and Lives of the Most Notorious Pirates of All Nations; narrating a series of gallant sea-fights, dreadful murders, daring attacks, horrid cruelties and barbarities; also their Debauched and Profligate Manner of Living, places of refuge, &c. &c. (London: E. Lloyd, 1836-1837)

The King of Pirates: Being an Account of the Famous Enterprises of Captain Avery, The Mock King of Madagascar (London: A. Bettesworth, 1720).

The New Newgate Calendar, ed. by Lord Birkett (London: The Folio Society, 1960)

The Premier, Vol. I (London: Henry Colburn and Richard Bentley, 1831)

Todorov, Tsvetan, *The Fantastic. A Structural Approach to a Literary Genre*, trans. by Richard Howard (Cleveland: The Press of Case Western Reserve University, 1973)

'Tragedy in the Rue de la Harpe, Paris,' ed. by Harold Furness, *Famous Crimes*, 44 (1890[?]), pp. 115-118

Trodd, Colin, Paul Barlow and David Amigoni, 'Introduction: Uncovering the grotesque in Victorian culture', in *Victorian Culture and the Idea of the Grotesque* ed. by Colin Trodd, Paul Barlow and David Amigoni (Aldershot: Ashgate, 1999), pp. 1-20

Turley, Hans, *Rum, Sodomy, and the Lash. Piracy, Sexuality, and Masculine Identity* (New York: New York University Press, 1999)

Van Kooy, Dana, and Jeffrey N. Cox, 'Melodramatic Slaves', *Modern Drama*, 55:4 (2012), 459-475

Vaninskaya, Anna, 'The Late-Victorian Romance Revival: A Generic Excursus', *English Literature in Transition, 1880-1920*, 51:1 (2008), 57-79

Vox, Valentine, *I Can See Your Lips Moving. The History and Art of Ventriloquism* (Kingswood: Kaye & Ward Ltd, 1981)

Wahrman, Dror, *The Making of the Modern Self. Identity and Culture in Eighteenth-Century England* (New Haven: Yale University Press, 2006)

Walpole, Horace, *The Castle of Otranto and Hieroglyphic Tales*, ed. by Robert L. Mack (London: Everyman, 1993)

Waters, Hazel, *Racism on the Victorian Stage. Representation of Slavery and the Black Character* (Cambridge: Cambridge University Press, 2007)

White, Jerry, *London in the 19th Century. A Human Awful Wonder of God* (London: Vintage Books, 2008)

White, Matthew, '"Rogues of the Meaner Sort"? Old Bailey Executions and the Crowd in the Early Nineteenth Century', *The London Journal*, 33:2 (2008), 135-153

Wicks, Ulrich, 'The Nature of Picaresque Narrative: A Modal Approach', *PMLA*, 89:2 (1974), 240-249

Wollstonecraft, Mary, *An Historical and Moral View of the Origin and Progress of the French Revolution; and the Effect it Has Produced in Europe* (London: J. Johnson, 1794)

Wordsworth, William, *The Prelude; or, Growth of a Poet's Mind* (New York: D. Appleton & Company 1850)

Ingram Content Group UK Ltd.
Milton Keynes UK
UKHW021955220323
418981UK00012B/381